iBATIS in Action

iBATIS in Action

CLINTON BEGIN
BRANDON GOODIN
LARRY MEADORS

MANNING
Greenwich
(74° w. long.)

For online information and ordering of this and other Manning books, please go to www.manning.com. The publisher offers discounts on this book when ordered in quantity. For more information, please contact:

Special Sales Department
Manning Publications Co.
Cherokee Station
PO Box 20386 Fax: (609) 877-8256
New York, NY 10021 email:manning@manning.com

Manning Publications Co.
Cherokee Station
PO Box 20386
New York, NY 10021

Copyeditor: Liz Welch
Typesetter: Gordan Salinovic
Cover designer: Leslie Haimes

ISBN 1-932394-82-6
Printed in the United States of America
1 2 3 4 5 6 7 8 9 10 – MAL – 11 10 09 08 07

To our families

brief contents

contents

preface

In my career as a software developer, I have worked in many diverse environments. Within a single company, software will often be developed in many different ways. When you consider the various challenges, people, and tools that make up a developer's day-to-day world, you quickly realize just how diverse that world is. I never know what surprising challenges the next consulting project will bring, so I always keep a variety of tools in my toolbox. For a few years, iBATIS was just a little chunk of code that saved me some time when I would normally be handcoding JDBC.

So how did iBATIS go from being a tool in my toolbox to an Apache project used by thousands? I had never intended to make iBATIS a full-blown open source project. The source was out there, but I hadn't marketed it or actively shared it with anyone. Enter JPetStore.

On July 1, 2002, I posted my response to the Pet Store story that was traveling the Internet. A large software company in Redmond was claiming that the C# language and the .NET platform were vastly more productive than Java, by several orders of magnitude. I'm a technology agnostic, and even though C# and .NET are pretty decent, I just couldn't accept a claim like that. So I spent my evenings for a couple of weeks writing JPetStore in the shadow of the "monstrosities" that had been fashioned by the enterprise software vendors. JPetStore created much discussion in the Java community. The hottest issue was its lack of an Enterprise JavaBeans (EJB) persistence layer—replaced instead by a tiny little framework called iBATIS.

I'm often asked, "Why didn't you use other open source tools?" At the time there were no other tools like iBATIS. There were plenty of code generators, but I'll spare you my soapbox rant on development-time and build-time code generation. I'll just say that anything that can be generated can also be generalized into a framework. And that's what iBATIS essentially is: a generalized framework for quicker JDBC coding.

The next question often asked is, "Why not use an object/relational mapping tool?" An O/RM tool can be used in the right environment. It works very well when you have full control over your database and the object model: you can easily achieve ideal mappings and avoid nightmarish tweaking and jumping through hoops due to a mismatch between the two. However, no one would dream of mapping an object model to the kinds of databases that I usually work with. With a decent O/RM tool, like Hibernate or TopLink, you probably *could*. The question is, *should* you map it?

Someone once told me a story about a guy with a hammer who saw everything as a nail...you know the one. O/RM tools are frameworks. Frameworks are built on constraints and assumptions. Those constraints and assumptions are ideal in certain environments, but not in all environments...not everything is a nail. Our job as software developers is to match ideal solutions to the problems at hand—not to use the only solution we know or the most popular solution or the hottest solution on the Net—but the one that best solves the problem we are facing. For different environments, we need different tools—iBATIS is one of them.

Today iBATIS has been implemented in three languages: Java, C#, and Ruby. It is maintained by a team of more than a dozen developers and it has a community of thousands of developers. You can read about it in books and articles and blogs on the Web. While iBATIS isn't the top dog of persistence, and it likely never will be, it is a success story. I realized that the day I stopped answering questions on the mailing list: the community had taken over.

A self-sustaining community is the true mark of success of an open source project. If you've read this far, I assume you're part of that community. So let me join you in celebrating the success of our little framework.

CLINTON BEGIN

acknowledgments

Writing books is harder than writing software. Having been through both, we, the three authors of this book, can easily agree on that. And when you notice the number of people who were involved in our book, we're sure you'll agree as well.

The talented and committed people at Manning Publications deserve a lot of the credit. Special thanks to publisher Marjan Bace, production director Mary Piergies, and our development editor, Jackie Carter. Without Jackie, the book would have never been started—or completed. She made the call, she cracked the whip, and she put up with the three of us without prescribing any drugs to deal with our severe attention deficit disorder. Thanks, Jackie, for going above and beyond to make this book happen at both ends.

Next, we would like to thank our reviewers, who had the tough job of reading our book and commenting on more than just technical errors—something software developers are good at. They also had to tell us what was good and what was bad about the book. They helped us to change the feel of the book, front to back; their input was essential. A big thanks to Sven Boden, Nathan Maves, Rick Reumann, Jeff Cunningham, Suresh Kumar, Scott Sauyet, Dick Zetterberg, Anjan Bacchu, Benjamin Gorlick, Oliver Zeigermann, Doug Warren, Matt Raible, Yoav Shapira, Cos DiFazio, Nick Heudecker, Ryan Breidenbach, and Patrick Peak. Special thanks to Sven Boden who proofread the manuscript for technical accuracy before it went to press.

Without the iBATIS team, we would have neither the software nor the book. As of this writing, the team includes the three authors: Clinton Begin, Brandon Goodin, and Larry Meadors. Two of our reviewers are also on the iBATIS team: Sven Boden and Nathan Maves, who are joined by Jeff Butler and Brice Ruth to form the rest of the iBATIS for Java team. iBATIS also has a .NET implementation, originally created by Gilles Bayon, who has since assembled a highly skilled team of .NET developers, including Ron Grabowski and Roberto Rabe. We've learned a lot from the iBATIS.NET team and they're likely to take the .NET world by storm. More recently, we were joined by Jon Tirsen who implemented iBATIS in Ruby and affectionately named it RBatis. It's the newest member of the family and we have high hopes for its continued success alongside Rails and ActiveRecord.

There's one more member of our team who deserves a special thanks. Ted Husted has truly brought iBATIS from "a tool in Clinton's toolbox" to the Apache project that it is today. He helped build the vision for the .NET version as well as the Apache project as a whole. He showed us the way. Thanks, Ted.

Finally, there's the community. iBATIS would be nowhere without all of the users, contributors, bug finders, documenters, translators, reviewers, authors, bloggers, fellow framework developers—and those of us who are just generally loud and can spread the word. Among these I'd like to name a few people, including Bruce Tate, Rod Johnson, and Matt Raible. We'd also like to thank the staff and communities of a few sites, including IBM Developerworks, JavaLobby.org, DZone.com, InfoQ.com, and TheServerSide.com.

CLINTON BEGIN

Open source software developers are crazy. We spend our days at work for money and our evenings at our keyboards writing open source software (or books) for fame and glory. We fight for the right to earn the respect of those who would just as soon forget us. All the while, every minute we've spent at our keyboards we've spent away from the very people who would give us love and respect for free. No books, no code, no keyboard necessary. For fame and glory we need only to step away from that keyboard, walk upstairs, and look into the eyes of our family. They are ready to offer their full support for our wild and crazy adventures. But with age and maturity we begin to realize that *their loss of our time* is not what we should worry about, but *our loss of their time.*

First, I'd like to thank my wife, Jennifer. She started as the girl behind the bookstore counter, then became my college sweetheart, and eventually I talked her into saying "yes" by bribing her with fine jewelry. Her selflessness, strength, and support have made all of this possible. She's also at least fifty percent responsible for our absolutely precious sons, Cameron and Myles.

I'd also like to thank my parents, Donna and Reginald, for their love and encouragement. In the '80s few parents knew what a computer was, and even if they did, they could not afford one. Somehow my parents managed to find room in the family budget to buy me a Vic-20. They had no idea what I wanted to do with my life, but they trusted me and believed in me enough to let me do it. They led by example with courage and unwavering optimism to show me that success is possible against even the most unrealistic odds.

Finally, I'd like to thank my Aunt Catherine for being the owner of the first x86 computer I ever used and eventually owned—and for trusting a 16-year-old kid enough to lend him $1,600 in 1993 to replace that old 8088.

BRANDON GOODIN

I'm sure that many of us hardcore geeks share the same story. We have fond memories of our first computer and the trusting parents who knew somehow their investment in these confounding machines would reap some benefit. As we grow older, we find ourselves with spouses and children who continue to hope that our endeavors will be lucrative. I'm not sure the payoff has happened yet. But I'm still having a great time!

I wouldn't have been able to pursue my passion for software development without support and encouragement from my family and friends. There have been many who gave me the room to dream, play, work, and fume. To these people I owe a debt of gratitude for giving me the opportunity to do what I love…chuck code!

First, I thank God for the opportunity to write code. There have been many opportunities that have come along in my career that I can only ascribe to providence. To write code and be able to provide for my family is a true blessing.

To my wife, Candas, and children, Felicity, Kailey, and Amery, who have lovingly given me tons of room to spend countless hours noodling at my keyboard, I say thank you. You are the reason I stay motivated.

I'd also like to say thanks to my mom and dad, Gerald and Linda Goodin. When you brought home that first Atari 400 with a BASIC cartridge, I was hooked. The two of you gave me my first taste.

To my friend, Sean Dillon, thanks for all your mentorship and for giving me a huge chance to break into the world of software development.

Finally, but not least, thanks, Clinton, for the golden opportunity to be a part of the iBATIS team.

LARRY MEADORS

After reading the other guys' notes, I feel like I am an echo, but we were all heading in the same direction at the same time, just from different places, with different people. When I received my first computer in 1983, I am sure my parents didn't know what to expect, but it was a powerful addiction, and turned into a great learning tool, too.

There have been so many people who helped me learn technology, and it would be impossible to thank all of them, so I won't even try. I'll just mention the ones who made the biggest impact.

First, I want to thank God for putting me in a place where I have so many supportive friends, and for giving me such a great family who puts up with dad having his notebook on his lap for so many hours every day.

Second, I want to thank my wife, Darla, and my two kiddos, Brandon and Micah, for being so understanding (writing a book takes forever!) and for all the encouragement they offered. They have spent many hours without dad and haven't complained (well, not too much anyway—and not nearly as much as they deserved to).

Last, I want to thank Brandon for introducing me to this iBATIS thing, and Clinton for being the guy who made it work, gave it away, and then invited me to be a part of the team. Thanks, dudes!

about this book

iBATIS is all about simplicity. There was a time when I said, "If I ever need to write a book about iBATIS, I'm doing something wrong." And here I am, writing a book about iBATIS. It turns out that no matter how simple something is, a book is sometimes the best way to learn about it. There's a lot of speculation these days that books might be replaced by e-books or by a jack in the back of our head that uploads information in a matter of seconds. Neither of those sounds terribly comfortable. I like books because they're portable and flexible. I can write on them, bend the pages, crack the spine. Nothing would make me happier than to see a well-worn copy of *iBATIS in Action* littering the floor of a busy developer's office. Success.

CLINTON BEGIN

What you should know

We hope that this book will keep the theme of iBATIS simplicity, but sometimes abstract concepts require more words. Certain chapters may be long and drawn out if you're not concerned with theory. Other chapters will be quick and to the point as if to say, "Here's how it works, and here's an example—now get to it."

The book assumes some knowledge. We expect you to know Java. We won't pull any punches here. This should not be the first or second Java book you've read. You should have felt the pain of using JDBC and possibly even experienced some of the pitfalls of O/RM.

We also expect you to know SQL. iBATIS is a SQL-centric framework. We don't attempt to hide the SQL; it's not generated and you're in full control of it. So you should have some SQL development experience under your belt.

Finally, you should be familiar with XML. As much as we wish there were a better solution, XML just makes sense for iBATIS development. It supports authoring of large blocks of text (i.e., SQL) much better than Java (which has no multiline string support), and it supports rich markup, allowing for the creation of a custom configuration syntax. Future versions of iBATIS may have other means of configuration and development, but for now, it's XML and you need to be familiar with it.

Who should read this book?

The developer community is our primary target audience. We fully expect that you will skip this section, skim through most of the early chapters on higher-level abstract topics, and move on to the first section where you see code. We expect you to read through the book while coding something completely unrelated with *South Park* on the television in the background.

Recovering O/RM users will enjoy iBATIS and this book. O/RM has a history of being a silver bullet solution that simply does not deliver. A lot of projects have started with O/RM but were finished with SQL. iBATIS focuses on solving existing problems without introducing new ones. We're not against using O/RM, but chances are good that you've hit a snag or two when trying to use an O/RM solution where a different approach would have been more efficient.

Architects will enjoy the higher-level section, which discusses the unique approach that iBATIS takes. There is a lot of hype about O/RM, and architects need to be informed that O/RM is not the only way. They need to learn to draw a new box with new lines to that old box that sits beside the O/RM box and connects it with a line to some other box—all the while ensuring that the Law of Demeter is never broken, of course!

Data modelers will probably not want to read this book, but we hope that someone will encourage them to. iBATIS was a product partially created in frustration with the database designs that came from people who refused to follow the rules of proper database normalization (and judicious denormalization). Data modelers will be familiar with the challenges of most legacy and ERP systems that have been built by some of the largest software companies in the world.

Others who should read this book include managers/executives, database administrators, quality assurance/testers, and analysts. Of course, anyone is more than welcome to buy it, if only for the cool cover.

Roadmap

Part 1 of this book offers a high-level introduction of iBATIS. It includes chapters 1 and 2, which describe the iBATIS philosophy and what iBATIS is. These chapters provide background for people interested in the foundations of iBATIS. If you're looking for the more practical application of iBATIS and want to get right down to work, skip to part 2.

Chapters 3 through 7 comprise part 2 of the book, which takes you through the basic applications of iBATIS. These chapters are essential reading if you intend to develop with iBATIS. Chapter 3 walks you through installation of the framework. Chapters 4, 5, and 6 teach you how to work with various kinds of statements. Chapter 7 wraps up part 2 with a detailed discussion of transaction support in iBATIS, which will help ensure that transactions are used properly in your application.

Part 3 begins our discussion of advanced iBATIS topics. Chapter 8 examines Dynamic SQL, which is one of the key innovations of iBATIS and essential for introducing complex query capabilities into your application. Chapter 9 continues the advanced topics with a discussion of caching data. As it turns out, caching is one of the more complex challenges with a SQL mapping framework, and you'll want to read this chapter to ensure that you understand how it's implemented. iBATIS is actually two frameworks in one: the SQL Mapper and the DAO framework. The DAO framework is completely independent, but it's always been part of iBATIS, so it's important to discuss it here. Chapters 10 and 11 discuss the DAO framework in detail. iBATIS is also a flexible framework. Wherever possible, pluggable interfaces have been used so you can include your own custom behavior into the framework. Chapter 12 investigates how you can extend iBATIS to do just that.

Part 4 places iBATIS in the real world. Chapter 13 examines a number of best practices for working with iBATIS. We wrap up the book in chapter 14 with a comprehensive web application called JGameStore. The full source of the JGameStore application is available from the iBATIS homepage and Manning's website. Like all of the source code in this book, JGameStore is licensed under the Apache License 2.0, so you're free to download it and use it as you like.

Source code conventions and downloads

Source code in listings or code terms in text appear in a `fixed-width font like this`. Code annotations accompany many of the listings, highlighting important concepts. In some cases, numbered cueballs link to additional explanations that follow the listing.

You can download the source code for all of the examples in the book and for the JGameStore application from the publisher's website at www.manning.com/begin.

Author Online

Purchase of *iBATIS in Action* includes free access to a private web forum run by Manning Publications where you can make comments about the book, ask technical questions, and receive help from the authors and from other users. To access the forum and subscribe to it, point your web browser to www.manning.com/begin. This page provides information on how to get on the forum once you are registered, what kind of help is available, and the rules of conduct on the forum. It also provides links to the source code for the examples in the book, errata, and other downloads.

Manning's commitment to our readers is to provide a venue where a meaningful dialog between individual readers and between readers and the authors can take place. It is not a commitment to any specific amount of participation on the part of the authors, whose contribution to the AO remains voluntary (and unpaid). We suggest you try asking the authors some challenging questions lest their interest stray!

The Author Online forum and the archives of previous discussions will be accessible from the publisher's website as long as the book is in print.

about the authors

CLINTON BEGIN is a Senior Developer and Agile Mentor for ThoughtWorks Canada. He has been building enterprise applications for nine years based on platforms such as Java and .NET. Clinton has extensive experience with agile methodologies, persistence frameworks, and relational databases. He is the original creator of the iBATIS persistence framework, which he designed in response to the challenges faced by object-oriented developers dealing with enterprise relational databases. Clinton is an experienced speaker, having delivered formal presentations, tutorials, and training sessions from San Francisco to New York City.

BRANDON GOODIN is an independent consultant who has been developing enterprise applications for over seven years, utilizing a varied set of languages and technologies. His industry experience spans manufacturing, health care, e-commerce, real estate, and recreation. He has been contributing to the iBATIS project since 2003.

LARRY MEADORS is an independent consultant offering development, support, and training services. He has been building enterprise web applications with multiple databases and multiple languages since the late '90s, and became involved with the iBATIS project back in the 1.*x* days.

about the title

By combining introductions, overviews, and how-to examples, Manning's *In Action* books are designed to help learning and remembering. According to research in cognitive science, the things people remember are things they discover during self-motivated exploration.

Although no one at Manning is a cognitive scientist, we are convinced that for learning to become permanent, it must pass through stages of exploration, play, and, interestingly, retelling of what is being learned. People understand and remember new things, which is to say they master them, only after actively exploring them. Humans learn in action. An essential part of an *In Action* guide is that it is example-driven. It encourages the reader to try things out, play with new code, and explore new ideas.

There is another, more mundane, reason for the title of this book: our readers are busy. They use books to do a job or solve a problem. They need books that allow them to jump in and jump out easily and learn just what they want, just when they want it. They need books that aid them in action. The books in this series are designed for such readers.

about the cover illustration

The figure on the cover of *iBATIS in Action* is a "Geisiques," an inhabitant of the Har-Geisa region in the Horn of Africa, in what is today the country of Somalia. The illustration is taken from a Spanish compendium of regional dress customs first published in Madrid in 1799. The book's title page states:

> *Coleccion general de los Trages que usan actualmente todas las Nacionas del Mundo desubierto, dibujados y grabados con la mayor exactitud por R.M.V.A.R. Obra muy util y en special para los que tienen la del viajero universal*

which we translate, as literally as possible, thus:

> *General collection of costumes currently used in the nations of the known world, designed and printed with great exactitude by R.M.V.A.R. This work is very useful especially for those who hold themselves to be universal travelers*

Although nothing is known of the designers, engravers, and workers who colored this illustration by hand, the "exactitude" of their execution is evident in this drawing. The "Geisiques" is just one of many figures in this colorful collection. Their diversity speaks vividly of the uniqueness and individuality of the world's towns and regions just 200 years ago. This was a time when the dress codes of two regions separated by a few dozen miles identified people uniquely as belonging to one or the other. The collection brings to life a sense of isolation and distance of that period—and of every other historic period except our own hyperkinetic present.

Dress codes have changed since then and the diversity by region, so rich at the time, has faded away. It is now often hard to tell the inhabitant of one continent from another. Perhaps, trying to view it optimistically, we have traded a cultural and visual diversity for a more varied personal life. Or a more varied and interesting intellectual and technical life.

We at Manning celebrate the inventiveness, the initiative, and, yes, the fun of the computer business with book covers based on the rich diversity of regional life of two centuries ago, brought back to life by the pictures from this collection.

Part 1

Introduction

We begin this book with a high-level introduction to iBATIS. The two chapters that follow will describe the iBATIS philosophy and distinguish it from other persistence solutions. A lot of persistence options are available for Java, and it can be a challenge to know which one to use and when. After reading the chapters in this part, you should understand the principles and values that iBATIS was built on and where you can apply them.

1 The iBATIS philosophy

This chapter covers

- iBATIS history
- Understanding iBATIS
- Database types

Structured Query Language (SQL) has been around for a long time. It's been over 35 years since Edgar F. Codd first suggested the idea that data could be normalized into sets of related tables. Since then, corporate IT has invested billions of dollars into relational database management systems (RDBMSs). Few software technologies can claim to have stood the test of time as well as the relational database and SQL. Indeed, after all this time, there is still a great deal of momentum behind relational technology and it is a cornerstone offering of the largest software companies in the world. All indicators suggest that SQL will be around for another 30 years.

iBATIS is based on the idea that there is value in relational databases and SQL, and that it is a good idea to embrace the industrywide investment in SQL. We have experiences whereby the database and even the SQL itself have outlived the application source code, and even multiple versions of the source code. In some cases we have seen that an application was rewritten in a different language, but the SQL and database remained largely unchanged.

It is for such reasons that iBATIS does not attempt to hide SQL or avoid SQL. It is a persistence layer framework that instead embraces SQL by making it easier to work with and easier to integrate into modern object-oriented software. These days, there are rumors that databases and SQL threaten our object models, but that does not have to be the case. iBATIS can help to ensure that it is not.

In this chapter, we will look at the history and rationale for iBATIS, and discuss the forces that influenced its creation.

1.1 A hybrid solution: combining the best of the best

In the modern world, hybrid solutions can be found everywhere. Taking two seemingly opposing ideas and merging them in the middle has proven to be an effective means to filling a niche, which in some cases has resulted in the creation of entire industries. This is certainly true of the automotive industry, as most of the innovation in vehicle designs has come from mixing various ideas. Mix a car with a cargo van and you have the ultimate family minivan. Marry a truck with an all-terrain vehicle, and you have an urban status symbol known as a sport utility vehicle. Cross a hotrod and a station wagon and you have a family car that Dad isn't embarrassed to drive. Set a gasoline engine side by side with an electric motor, and you have the answer for a great deal of the North American pollution problem.

Hybrid solutions have proven effective in the IT industry too. iBATIS is one such hybrid solution for the persistence layer of your application. Over time, various methods have been developed to enable applications to execute SQL against a database. iBATIS is a unique solution that borrows concepts from several other approaches. Let's start by taking a quick look at these approaches.

1.1.1 Exploring the roots of iBATIS

iBATIS takes the best attributes and ideas from the most popular means of accessing a relational database, and finds synergy among them. Figure 1.1 shows how the iBATIS framework takes what was learned through years of development using different approaches to database integration, and combines the best of those lessons to create a hybrid solution.

The following sections discuss these various approaches to interacting with the database and describe the parts of each that iBATIS leverages.

Structured Query Language

At the heart of iBATIS is SQL. By definition, all relational databases support SQL as the primary means of interacting with the database. SQL is a simple, nonprocedural language for working with the database, and is really two languages in one.

The first is Data Definition Language (DDL), which includes statements like `CREATE`, `DROP`, and `ALTER`. These statements are used to define the structure and design of the database, including the tables, columns, indexes, constraints, procedures, and foreign key relationships. DDL is not something that iBATIS supports directly. Although many people have successfully executed DDL using iBATIS, DDL is usually owned and controlled by a database administration group and is often beyond the reach of developers.

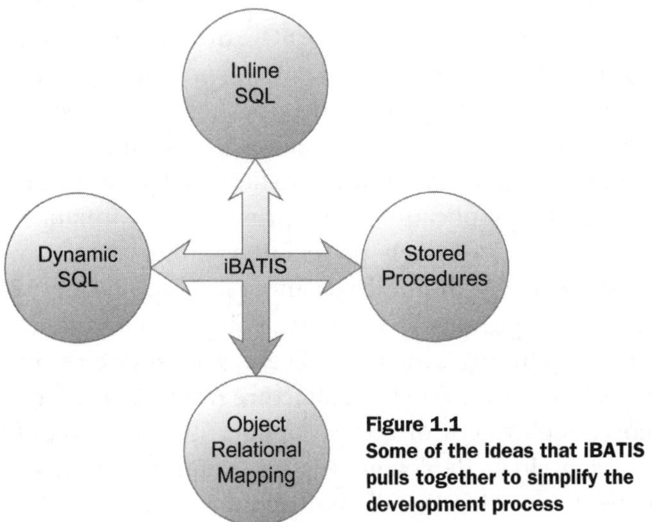

Figure 1.1
Some of the ideas that iBATIS pulls together to simplify the development process

The second part of SQL is the Data Manipulation Language (DML). It includes statements such as `SELECT`, `INSERT`, `UPDATE`, and `DELETE`. DML is used to manipulate the data directly. Originally SQL was designed to be a language simple enough for end users to use. It was designed so that there should be no need for a rich user interface or even an application at all. Of course, this was back in the day of green-screen terminals, a time when we had more hope for our end users!

These days, databases are much too complex to allow SQL to be run directly against the database by end users. Can you imagine handing a bunch of SQL statements to your accounting department as if to say, "Here you go, you'll find the information you're looking for in the BSHEET table." Indeed.

SQL alone is no longer an effective interface for end users, but it is an extremely powerful tool for developers. SQL is the only complete means of accessing the database; everything else is a subset of the complete set of capabilities of SQL. For this reason, iBATIS fully embraces SQL as the primary means of accessing the relational database. At the same time, iBATIS provides many of the benefits of the other approaches discussed in this chapter, including stored procedures and object/relational mapping tools.

Old-school stored procedures

Stored procedures may be the oldest means of application programming with a relational database. Many legacy applications used what is now known as a *two-tier design*. A two-tier design involved a rich client interface that directly called stored procedures in the database. The stored procedures would contain the SQL that was to be run against the database. In addition to the SQL, the stored procedures could (and often would) contain business logic. Unlike SQL, these stored procedure languages were procedural and had flow control such as conditionals and iteration. Indeed, one could write an entire application using nothing but stored procedures. Many software vendors developed rich client tools, such as Oracle Forms, PowerBuilder, and Visual Basic, for developing two-tier database applications.

The problems with two-tier applications were primarily performance and scalability. Although databases are extremely powerful machines, they aren't necessarily the best choice for dealing with hundreds, thousands, or possibly millions of users. With modern web applications, these scalability requirements are not uncommon. Limitations, including concurrent licenses, hardware resources, and even network sockets, would prevent such architecture from succeeding on a massive scale. Furthermore, deployment of two-tier applications was a nightmare. In addition to the usual rich client deployment issues, complex runtime database engines often had to be deployed to the client machine as well.

Modern stored procedures

In some circles stored procedures are still considered best practice for three-tier and N-tier applications, such as web applications. Stored procedures are now treated more like remote procedure calls from the middle tier, and many of the performance constraints are solved by pooling connections and managing database resources. Stored procedures are still a valid design choice for implementing the entire data access layer in a modern object-oriented application. Stored procedures have the benefit of performance on their side, as they can often manipulate data in the database faster than any other solution. However, there are other concerns beyond simply performance.

Putting business logic in stored procedures is widely accepted as being a bad practice. The primary reason is that stored procedures are more difficult to develop in line with modern application architectures. They are harder to write, test, and deploy. To make things worse, databases are often owned by other teams and are protected by tight change controls. They may not be able to change as fast as they need to to keep up with modern software development methodologies. Furthermore, stored procedures are more limited in their capability to implement the business logic completely. If the business logic involves other systems, resources, or user interfaces, the stored procedure will not likely be able to handle all of the logic. Modern applications are very complex and require a more generic language than a stored procedure that is optimized to manipulate data. To deal with this, some vendors are embedding more powerful languages like Java in their database engines to allow for more robust stored procedures. This really doesn't improve the situation at all. It only serves to further confuse the boundaries of the application and the database and puts a new burden on the database administrators: now they have to worry about Java and C# in their database. It's simply the wrong tool for the job.

A common theme in software development is *overcorrection.* When one problem is found, the first solution attempted is often the exact opposite approach. Instead of solving the problem, the result is an equal number of completely different problems. This brings us to the discussion of inline SQL.

Inline SQL

An approach to dealing with the limitations of stored procedures was to embed SQL into more generic languages. Instead of moving the logic into the database, the SQL was moved from the database to the application code. This allowed SQL statements to interact with the language directly. In a sense, SQL became a feature of the language. This has been done with a number of languages, including COBOL, C, and even Java. The following is an example of SQLJ in Java:

```
String name;
Date hiredate;

#sql {
       SELECT emp_name, hire_date
       INTO :name, :hiredate
       FROM employee
       WHERE emp_num = 28959
};
```

Inline SQL is quite elegant in that it integrates tightly with the language. Native language variables can be passed directly to the SQL as parameters, and results can be selected directly into similar variables. In a sense, the SQL becomes a feature of the language.

Unfortunately, inline SQL is not widely adopted and has some significant issues keeping it from gaining any ground. First, SQL is not a standard. There are many extensions to SQL and each only works with one particular database. This fragmentation of the SQL language makes it difficult to implement an inline SQL parser that is both complete and portable across database platforms. The second problem with inline SQL is that it is often not implemented as a true language feature. Instead, a precompiler is used to first translate the inline SQL into proper code for the given language. This creates problems for tools like integrated development environments (IDEs) that might have to interpret the code to enable advanced features like syntax highlighting and code completion. Code that contains inline SQL may not even be able to compile without the precompiler, a dependency that creates concerns around the future maintainability of the code.

One solution to the pains of inline SQL is to remove the SQL from the language level, and instead represent it as a data structure (i.e., a string) in the application. This approach is commonly known as Dynamic SQL.

Dynamic SQL

Dynamic SQL deals with some of the problems of inline SQL by avoiding the precompiler. Instead, SQL is represented as a string type that can be manipulated just like any other character data in a modern language. Because the SQL is represented as a string type, it cannot interact with the language directly like inline SQL can. Therefore, Dynamic SQL implementations require a robust API for setting SQL parameters and retrieving the resulting data.

Dynamic SQL has the advantage of flexibility. The SQL can be manipulated at runtime based on different parameters or dynamic application functions. For example, a query-by-example web form might allow the user to select the fields to search upon and what data to search for. This would require a dynamic change to the `WHERE` clause of the SQL statement, which can be easily done with Dynamic SQL.

Dynamic SQL is currently the most popular means of accessing relational databases from modern languages. Most such languages include a standard API for database access. Java developers and .NET developers will be familiar with the standard APIs in those languages: JDBC and ADO.NET, respectively. These standard SQL APIs are generally very robust and offer a great deal of flexibility to the developer. The following is a simple example of Dynamic SQL in Java:

```
String name;
Date hiredate;
String sql = "SELECT emp_name, hire_date"
       + " FROM employee WHERE emp_num = ? ";
Connection conn = dataSource.getConnection();
PreparedStatement ps = conn.prepareStatement (sql);
ps.setInt (1, 28959);
ResultSet rs = ps.executeQuery();
while (rs.next) {
name = rs.getString("emp_name");
hiredate = rs.getDate("hire_date");
}
rs.close();
conn.close();
```

Should be in try-catch block

Without a doubt, Dynamic SQL is not as elegant as inline SQL, or even stored procedures (and we even left out the exception handling). The APIs are often complex and very verbose, just like the previous example. Using these frameworks generally results in a lot of code, which is often very repetitive. In addition, the SQL itself is often too long to be on a single line. This means that the string has to be broken up into multiple strings that are concatenated. Concatenation results in unreadable SQL code that is difficult to maintain and work with.

So if the SQL isn't best placed in the database as a stored procedure, or in the language as inline SQL, or in the application as a data structure, what do we do with it? We avoid it. In modern object-oriented applications, one of the most compelling solutions to interacting with a relational database is through the use of an object/relational mapping tool.

Object/relational mapping

Object/relational mapping (O/RM) was designed to simplify persistence of objects by eliminating SQL from the developer's responsibility altogether. Instead, the SQL is generated. Some tools generate the SQL statically at build or compile time, while others generate it dynamically at runtime. The SQL is generated based on mappings made between application classes and relational database tables. In addition to eliminating the SQL, the API for working with an O/RM tool is usually a lot simpler than the typical SQL APIs. Object/relational mapping is not a new concept and is almost as old as object-oriented programming languages. There have been a lot of advances in recent years that make object/relational mapping a compelling approach to persistence.

Modern object/relational mapping tools do more than simply generate SQL. They offer a complete persistence architecture that benefits the entire application. Any good object/relational mapping tool will provide transaction management. This includes simple APIs for dealing with both local and distributed transactions. O/RM tools also usually offer multiple caching strategies for dealing with different kinds of data to avoid needless access of the database. Another way that an O/RM tool can reduce database hits is by lazy loading of data. Lazy loading delays the retrieval of data until absolutely necessary, right at the point where the data is used.

Despite these features, object/relational mapping tools are not a silver-bullet solution and do not work in all situations. O/RM tools are based on assumptions and rules. The most common assumption is that the database will be properly normalized. As we will discuss in section 1.4, the largest and most valuable databases are rarely normalized perfectly. This can complicate the mappings and may require workarounds or create inefficiencies in the design. No object relational solution will ever be able to provide support for every feature, capability, and design flaw of every single database available. As stated earlier, SQL is not a reliable standard. For this reason, every O/RM tool will always be a subset of the full capabilities of any particular database.

Enter the hybrid.

1.1.2 *Understanding the iBATIS advantage*

iBATIS is a hybrid solution. It takes the best ideas from each of these solutions and creates synergy between them. Table 1.1 summarizes some of the ideas from each of the approaches discussed earlier that are incorporated into iBATIS.

Table 1.1 Advantages provided by iBATIS, which are the same as those provided by other solutions

Approach	Similar benefit	Solved problems
Stored procedures	iBATIS encapsulates and externalizes SQL such that it is outside of your application code. It describes an API similar to that of a stored procedure, but the iBATIS API is object oriented. iBATIS also fully supports calling stored procedures directly.	Business logic is kept out of the database, and the application is easier to deploy and test, and is more portable.
Inline SQL	iBATIS allows SQL to be written the way it was intended to be written. There's no string concatenation, "setting" of parameters, or "getting" of results.	iBATIS doesn't impose on your application code. No precompiler is needed, and you have full access to all of the features of SQL—not a subset.
Dynamic SQL	iBATIS provides features for dynamically building queries based on parameters. No "query-builder" APIs are required.	iBATIS doesn't force SQL to be written in blocks of concatenated strings interlaced with application code.
Object/relational mapping	iBATIS supports many of the same features as an O/RM tool, such as lazy loading, join fetching, caching, runtime code generation, and inheritance.	iBATIS will work with any combination of data model and object model. There are nearly no restrictions or rules to how either is designed.

Now that you understand the roots of iBATIS, the following sections discuss two of the most important qualities of the iBATIS persistence layer: externalization and encapsulation of the SQL. Together, these concepts provide much of the value and enable many of the advanced features that the framework achieves.

Externalized SQL

One of the wisdoms learned in the last decade of software development has been to design one's systems to correspond to different users of the subsystem. You want to separate out the things that are dealt with by different programming roles such as user interface design, application programming, and database administration. Even if only a single person is playing all of these roles, it helps to have a nicely layered design that allows you to focus on a particular part of the system. If you embed your SQL within Java source code, it will not generally be useful to a database administrator or perhaps a .NET developer who might be working with the same database. Externalization separates the SQL from the application source code, thus keeping both cleaner. Doing so ensures that the SQL is relatively independent of any particular language or platform. Most modern development languages represent SQL as a string type, which introduces concatenation for long SQL statements. Consider the following simple SQL statement:

```
SELECT
  PRODUCTID,
  NAME,
  DESCRIPTION,
  CATEGORY
FROM PRODUCT
WHERE CATEGORY = ?
```

When embedded in a String data type in a modern programming language such as Java, this gentle SQL statement becomes a mess of multiple language characteristics and unmanageable code:

```
String s = "SELECT"
  + " PRODUCTID,"
  + " NAME,"
  + " DESCRIPTION,"
  + " CATEGORY"
  + " FROM PRODUCT"
  + " WHERE CATEGORY = ?";
```

Simply forgetting to lead the `FROM` clause with a space will cause a SQL error to occur. You can easily imagine the trouble a complex SQL statement could cause.

Therein lies one of the key advantages of iBATIS: the ability to write SQL the way it was meant to be written. The following gives you a sense of what an iBATIS mapped SQL statement looks like:

```
SELECT
  PRODUCTID,
  NAME,
  DESCRIPTION,
  CATEGORY
FROM PRODUCT
WHERE CATEGORY = #categoryId#
```

Notice how the SQL does not change in terms of structure or simplicity. The biggest difference in the SQL is the format of the parameter `#categoryId#`, which is normally a language-specific detail. iBATIS makes it portable and more readable.

Now that we have our SQL out of the source code and into a place where we can work with it more naturally, we need to link it back to the software so that it can be executed in a way that is useful.

Encapsulated SQL

One of the oldest concepts in computer programming is the idea of modularization. In a procedural application, code may be separated into files, functions, and procedures. In an object-oriented application, code is often organized into classes and methods. *Encapsulation* is a form of modularization that not only organizes the code into cohesive modules, but also hides the implementation details while exposing only the interface to the calling code.

This concept can be extended into our persistence layer. We can encapsulate SQL by defining its inputs and outputs (i.e., its interface), but otherwise hide the SQL code from the rest of the application. If you're an object-oriented software developer, you can think of this encapsulation in the same way that you think of separating an interface from its implementation. If you're a SQL developer, you can think of this encapsulation much like you'd think of hiding a SQL statement inside a stored procedure.

iBATIS uses Extensible Markup Language (XML) to encapsulate SQL. XML was chosen because of its general portability across platforms, its industrywide adoption, and the fact that it's more likely to live as long as SQL than any other language and any file format. Using XML, iBATIS maps the inputs and outputs of the statement. Most SQL statements have one or more parameters and produce some sort of tabulated results. That is, results are organized into a series of columns and rows. iBATIS allows you to easily map both parameters and results to properties of objects. Consider the next example:

```
<select id="categoryById"
  parameterClass="string" resultClass="category">
      SELECT CATEGORYID, NAME, DESCRIPTION
      FROM CATEGORY
      WHERE CATEGORYID = #categoryId#
</select>
```

Notice the XML element surrounding the SQL. This is the encapsulation of the SQL. The simple `<select>` element defines the name of the statement, the parameter input type, and the resulting output type. To an object-oriented software developer, this is much like a method signature.

Both simplicity and consistency are achieved through externalizing and encapsulating the SQL. More details of the exact usage of the API and mapping syntax will follow in chapter 2. Before we get to that, it's important to understand where iBATIS fits in your application architecture.

1.2 Where iBATIS fits

Nearly any well-written piece of software uses a layered design. A layered design separates the technical responsibilities of an application into cohesive parts that isolate the implementation details of a particular technology or interface. A layered design can be achieved in any robust (3GL/4GL) programming language. Figure 1.2 shows a high-level view of a typical layering strategy that is useful for many business applications.

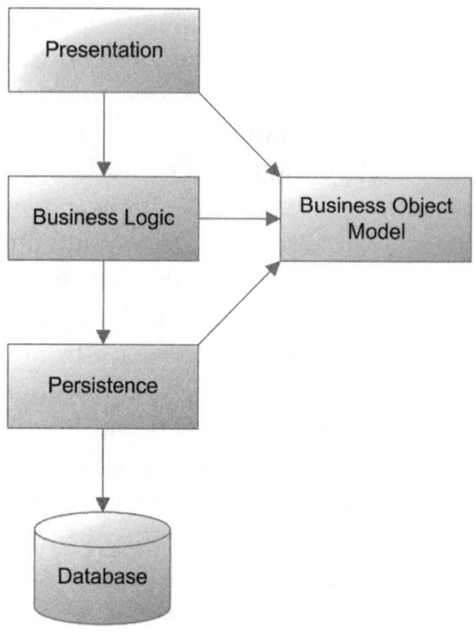

Figure 1.2 A typical layering strategy following the Law of Demeter

You can read the arrows in figure 1.2 as "depends on" or "uses." This layering approach is inspired by the Law of Demeter, which in one form states, "Each layer should have only limited knowledge about other layers: only layers closely related to the current layer."

The idea is that each layer will only talk to the layer directly below it. This ensures that the dependency flows only in one direction and avoids the typical "spaghetti code" that is common of applications designed without layers.

iBATIS is a persistence layer framework. The persistence layer sits between the business logic layer of the application and the database. This separation is important to ensuring that your persistence strategy is not mixed with your business logic code, or vice versa. The benefit of this separation is that your code can be more easily maintained, as it will allow your object model to evolve independently of your database design.

Although iBATIS is heavily focused on the persistence layer, it is important to understand all of the layers of application architecture. Although you separate your concerns so that there are minimal (or no) dependencies on any particular implementation, it would be naive to think that you can be blind to the interaction among these layers. Regardless of how well you design your application, there will be indirect behavioral associations between the layers that you must be aware of. The following sections describe the layers and describe how iBATIS relates to them.

1.2.1 The business object model

The business object serves as the foundation for the rest of the application. It is the object-oriented representation of the problem domain, and therefore the classes that make up the business object model are sometimes called *domain classes.* All other layers use the business object model to represent data and perform certain business logic functions.

Application designers usually start with the design of the business object model before anything else. Even if at a very high level, the classes are identified by deriving them from the nouns in the system. For example, in a bookstore application, the business object model might include a class called `Genre` with instances like `Science Fiction`, `Mystery`, and `Children's`. It might also have a class called `Book` with instances such as `The Long Walk`, `The Firm`, and `Curious George`. As the application grows more advanced, classes represent more abstract concepts, like `InvoiceLineItem`.

Business object model classes may contain some logic as well, but they should never contain any code that accesses any other layer, especially the presentation and persistence layers. Furthermore, the business object model should never depend on any other layer. Other layers use the business object model—it's never the other way around.

A persistence layer like iBATIS will generally use the business object model for representing data that is stored in the database. The domain classes of the business object model will become the parameters and return values of the persistence methods. It is for this reason that these classes are sometimes referred to as *data transfer objects (DTOs)*. Although data transfer is not their only purpose, it is a fair name from the perspective of a persistence framework.

1.2.2 The presentation layer

The presentation layer is responsible for displaying application controls and data to the end user. It is responsible for the layout and formatting of all information. The most popular presentation approach in business applications today are web front ends that use HTML and JavaScript to provide a look and feel to the user via a web browser.

Web applications have the advantage of cross-platform compatibility, ease of deployment, and scalability. Amazon.com is a perfect example of a web application that allows you to buy books online. This is a good use of a web application, as it would be impractical to have everyone download an application just to buy books.

Web applications generally break down when advanced user controls or complex data manipulation are a requirement. In such cases, rich clients that use native operating system widgets like tabs, tables, tree views, and embedded objects are preferred. Rich clients allow for a much more powerful user interface, but are somewhat more difficult to deploy and require more care to achieve the level of performance and security a web application can offer. Examples of rich client technologies include Swing in Java and WinForms in .NET.

Recently the two concepts have been mixed into hybrid clients to attempt to achieve the benefits of both web applications and rich clients. Very small rich clients with advanced controls can be downloaded to the users' desktop, perhaps transparently via the web browser. This hybrid-rich client does not contain any business logic and it may not even have the layout of its user interface built in. Instead, the application look and feel and the available business functionality are configured via a web service, or a web application that uses XML as an interface between the rich client and the server. The only disadvantage is that more software is required to both develop and deploy such applications. For example, both Adobe Flex and Laszlo from Laszlo Systems are based on Macromedia's Flash browser plug-in.

Then of course there is the epitome of all hybrid presentation layers, Ajax. Ajax, a term coined by Jesse James Garrett, used to be an acronym for Asynchronous JavaScript and XML, until everyone realized that it need not be asynchronous, or XML. So now Ajax has simply come to mean "a really rich web-based user interface driven by a lot of really funky JavaScript." Ajax is a new approach to using old technology to build very rich and interactive user interfaces. Google demonstrates some of the best examples of Ajax, putting it to good use with its Gmail, Google Maps, and Google Calendar applications.

iBATIS can be used for both web applications, rich client applications and hybrids. Although the presentation layer does not generally talk directly to the persistence framework, certain decisions about the user interface will impact the requirements for your persistence layer. For example, consider a web application that deals with a large list of 5,000 items. We wouldn't want to show all 5,000 at the same time, nor would it be ideal to load 5,000 items from the database all at once if we weren't going to use them right away. A better approach would be to load and display 10 items at a time. Therefore, our persistence layer should allow for some flexibility in the amount of data returned and possibly even offer us the ability to select and retrieve the exact 10 items that we want. This would improve performance by avoiding needless object creation and data retrieval, and by reducing network traffic and memory requirements for our application. iBATIS can help achieve these goals using features that allow querying for specific ranges of data.

1.2.3 The business logic layer

The business logic layer of the application describes the coarse-grained services that the application provides. For this reason they are sometimes called *service* classes. At a high level, anyone should be able to look at the classes and methods in the business logic layer and understand what the system does. For example, in a banking application, the business logic layer might have a class called `TellerService`, with methods like `openAccount()`, `deposit()`, `withdrawal()`, and `getBalance()`. These are very large functions that involve complex interactions with databases and possibly other systems. They are much too heavy to place into a domain class, as the code would quickly become incohesive, coupled, and generally unmanageable. The solution is to separate the coarse-grained business functions from their related business object model. This separation of object model classes from logic classes is sometimes called *noun-verb separation.*

Object-oriented purists might claim that this design is *less object oriented* than having such methods directly on the related domain class. Regardless of what is *more or less object oriented*, it is a better design choice to separate these concerns. The primary reason is that business functions are often very complex. They usually involve more than one class and deal with a number of infrastructural components, including databases, message queues, and other systems. Furthermore, there are often a number of domain classes involved in a business function, which would make it hard to decide which class the method should belong to. It is for these reasons that coarse-grained business functions are best implemented as separate methods on a class that is part of the business logic layer.

Don't be afraid to put finer-grained business logic directly on related domain classes. The coarse-grained service methods in the business logic layer are free to call the finer-grained pure logic methods built into domain classes.

In our layered architecture, the business logic layer is the consumer of the persistence layer services. It makes calls to the persistence layer to fetch and change data. The business logic layer also makes an excellent place to demarcate transactions, because it defines the coarse-grained business functions that can be consumed by a number of different user interfaces or possibly other interfaces, such as a web service. There are other schools of thought regarding transaction demarcation, but we'll discuss the topic more in chapter 8.

1.2.4 The persistence layer

The persistence layer is where iBATIS fits and is therefore the focus of this book. In an object-oriented system, the primary concern of the persistence layer is the storage and retrieval of objects, or more specifically the data stored in those objects. In enterprise applications persistence layers usually interact with relational database systems for storing data, although in some cases other durable data structures and mediums might be used. Some systems may use simple comma-delimited flat files or XML files. Because of the disparate nature of persistence strategies in enterprise applications, a secondary concern of the persistence layer is abstraction. The persistence layer should hide all details of *how* the data is being stored and how it is retrieved. Such details should never be exposed to the other layers of the application.

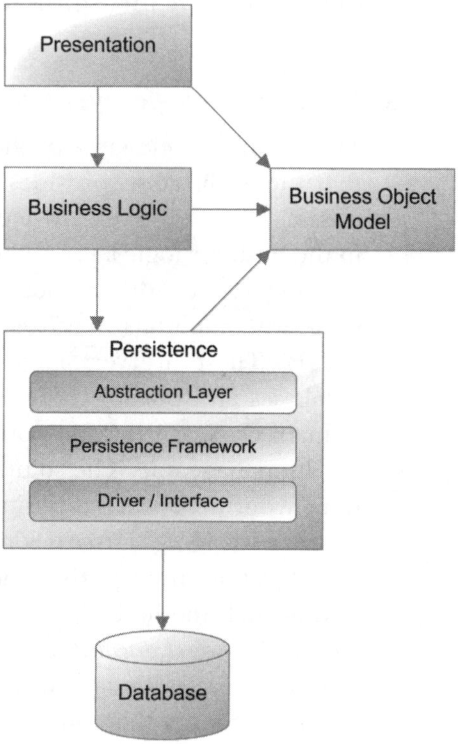

Figure 1.3 Persistence layer zoomed to show internal layered design

To better understand these concerns and how they're managed, it helps to separate the persistence layer into three basic parts: the abstraction layer, the persistence framework, and the driver or interface, as shown in the lower part of figure 1.3.

Let's take a closer look at each of these three parts.

The abstraction layer

The role of the abstraction layer is to provide a consistent and meaningful interface to the persistence layer. It is a set of classes and methods that act as a façade to the persistence implementation details. Methods in the abstraction layer should never require any implementation-specific parameters, nor should it return any values or throw any exceptions that are exclusive to the persistence implementation. With a proper abstraction layer in place, the entire persistence approach—including both the persistence API and the storage infrastructure—should be able to change without modifications to the abstraction layer or any of the layers that depend on it. There are patterns that can help with the implementation of a proper abstraction layer, the most popular of which is the *Data Access Objects (DAO)* pattern. Some frameworks, including iBATIS, implement this pattern for you. We discuss the iBATIS DAO framework in chapter 11.

The persistence framework

The persistence framework is responsible for interfacing with the driver (or interface). The persistence framework will provide methods for storing, retrieving, updating, searching, and managing data. Unlike the abstraction layer, a persistence framework is generally specific to one class of storage infrastructure. For example, you might find a persistence API that deals exclusively with XML files for storing data. However, with most modern enterprise applications, a relational database is the storage infrastructure of choice. Most popular languages come with standard APIs for accessing relational databases. JDBC is the standard framework for Java applications to access databases, while ADO.NET is the standard database persistence framework for .NET applications. The standard APIs are general purpose and as a result are very complete in their implementation, but also very verbose and repetitive in their use. For these reasons many frameworks have been built on top of the standard ones to extend the functionality to be more specific, and therefore more powerful. iBATIS is a persistence framework that deals exclusively with relational databases of all kinds and supports both Java and .NET using a consistent approach.

The driver or interface

The storage infrastructure can be as simple as a comma-delimited flat file or as complex as a multimillion-dollar enterprise database server. In either case, a software driver is used to communicate with the storage infrastructure at a low level. Some drivers, such as native file system drivers, are very generic in functionality but specific to a platform. You will likely never see a file input/output (I/O) driver, but you can be sure that it is there. Database drivers, on the other hand, tend to be complex and differ in implementation, size, and behavior. It is the job of the persistence framework to communicate with the driver so that these differences are minimized and simplified. Since iBATIS only supports relational databases, that is what we'll focus on in this book.

1.2.5 The relational database

iBATIS exists entirely to make accessing relational databases easier. Databases are complex beasts that can involve a lot of work to use them properly. The database is responsible for managing data and changes to that data. The reason we use a database instead of simply a flat file is that a database can offer a lot of benefits, primarily in the areas of integrity, performance, and security.

Integrity

Integrity is probably the most important benefit, as without it not much else matters. If our data isn't consistent, reliable, and correct, then it is less valuable to us—or possibly even useless. Databases achieve integrity by using strong data types, enforcing constraints, and working within transactions.

Databases are strongly typed, which means that when a database table is created, its columns are configured to store a specific type of data. The database management system ensures that the data stored in the tables are valid for the column types. For example, a table might define a column as `VARCHAR(25) NOT NULL`. This type ensures that the value is character data that is not of a length greater than 25. The `NOT NULL` part of the definition means that the data is required and so a value must be provided for this column.

In addition to strong typing, other constraints can be applied to tables. Such constraints are usually broader in scope in that they deal with more than just a single column. A constraint usually involves validation of multiple rows or possibly even multiple tables. One type of constraint is a `UNIQUE` constraint, which ensured that for a given column in a table a particular value can be used only once. Another kind of constraint is a `FOREIGN KEY` constraint, which ensures that the value in one column of a table is the same value as a similar column in another table. Foreign key constraints are used to describe relationships among tables, and so they are imperative to relational database design and data integrity.

One of the most important ways a database maintains integrity is through the use of transactions. Most business functions will require many different types of data, possibly from many different databases. Generally this data is related in some way and therefore must be updated consistently. Using transactions, a database management system can ensure that all related data is updated in a consistent fashion. Furthermore, transactions allow multiple users of the system to update data concurrently without colliding. There is a lot more to know about transactions, so we'll discuss them in more detail in chapter 8.

Performance

Relational databases help us achieve a greater level of performance that is not easily made possible using flat files. That said, database performance is not free and it can take a great deal of time and expertise to get it right. Database performance can be broken into three key factors: design, software tuning, and hardware.

The number one performance consideration for a database is design. A bad relational database design can lead to inefficiencies so great that no amount of software tuning or extra hardware can correct it. Bad designs can lead to deadlocking, exponential relational calculations, or simply table scans of millions of rows. Proper design is such a great concern that we'll talk more about it in section 1.3.

Software tuning is the second-most important performance consideration for large databases. Tuning a relational database management system requires a person educated and experienced in the particular RDBMS software being used. Although some characteristics of RDBMS software are transferable across different products, generally each product has intricacies and sneaky differences that require a specialist for that particular software. Performance tuning can yield some great benefits. Proper tuning of a database index alone can cause a complex query to execute in seconds instead of minutes. There are a lot of parts to an RDBMS, such as caches, file managers, various index algorithms, and even operating system considerations. The same RDBMS software will behave differently if the operating system changes, and therefore must be tuned differently. Needless to say, a lot of effort is involved with tuning database software. Exactly how we do that is beyond the scope of this book, but it is important to know that this is one of the most important factors for improving database performance. Work with your DBA!

Large relational database systems are usually very demanding on computer hardware. For this reason, it is not uncommon that the most powerful servers in a company are the database servers. In many companies the database is the center of their universe, so it makes sense that big investments are made in hardware for databases. Fast disk arrays, I/O controllers, hardware caches, and network interfaces are all critical to the performance of large database management systems. Given that, you should avoid using hardware as an excuse for bad database design or as a replacement for RDBMS tuning. Hardware should not be used to solve performance problems—it should be used to meet performance requirements. Further discussion of hardware is also beyond the scope of this book, but it is important to consider it when you're working with a large database system. Again, work with your DBA!

Security

Relational database systems also provide the benefit of added security. Much of the data that we work with in everyday business is confidential. In recent years, privacy has become more of a concern, as has security in general. For this reason, even something as simple as a person's full name can be considered confidential because it is potentially "uniquely identifiable information." Other information—

for example, such as social security numbers and credit card numbers—must be protected with even higher levels of security such as strong encryption. Most commercial-quality relational databases include advanced security features that allow for fine-grained security as well as data encryption. Each database will have unique security requirements. It's important to understand them, as the application code must not weaken the security policy of the database.

Different databases will have different levels of integrity, performance, and security. Generally the size of the database, the value of the data, and the number of dependents will determine these levels. In the next section we'll explore different database types.

1.3 Working with different database types

Not every database is so complex that it requires an expensive database management system and enterprise class hardware. Some databases are small enough to run on an old desktop machine hidden in a closet. All databases are different. They have different requirements and different challenges. iBATIS will help you work with almost any relational database, but it is always important to understand the type of database you're working with.

Databases are classified more by their relationships with other systems than by their design or size. However, the design and size of a database can often be driven by its relationships. Another factor that will affect the design and size of a database is the *age* of the database. As time passes, databases tend to change in different ways, and often the way that these changes are applied are less than ideal. In this section, we'll talk about four types of databases: application, enterprise, proprietary, and legacy.

1.3.1 Application databases

Application databases are generally the smallest, simplest, and easiest databases to work with. These databases are usually the ones that we developers don't mind working with, or perhaps even like working with. Application databases are usually designed and implemented alongside the application as part of the same project. For this reason, there is generally more freedom in terms of design and are therefore more capable of making the design *right* for our particular application. There is minimal external influence in an application database, and there are usually only one or two interfaces. The first interface will be to the application, and the second might just be a simple reporting framework or tool like Crystal Reports. Figure 1.4 shows an application database and its relationships at a very high level.

Figure 1.4 Application database relationships

Application databases are sometimes small enough that they can be deployed to the same server as the application. With application databases there is more infrastructure freedom as well.

With small application databases, it is generally easier to convince companies to buy into using cheaper open source RDBMS solutions such as MySQL or PostgreSQL instead of spending money on Oracle or SQL Server. Some applications may even use an embedded application database that runs within the same virtual environment as the application itself, and therefore does not require a separate SQL at all.

iBATIS works very well as a persistence framework for application databases. Because of the simplicity of iBATIS, a team can get up to speed very quickly with a new application. For simple databases, it's even possible to generate the SQL from the database schema using the administrative tools that come with your RDBMS. Tools are also available that will generate all of the iBATIS SQL Map files for you.

1.3.2 Enterprise databases

Enterprise databases are larger than application databases and have greater external influence. They have more relationships with other systems that include both dependencies, as well as dependents. These relationships might be web applications and reporting tools, but they might also be interfaces to complex systems and databases. With an enterprise database, not only are there a greater number of external interfaces, but the way that the interfaces work is different too. Some interfaces might be nightly batch load interfaces, while others are real-time transactional interfaces. For this reason, the enterprise database itself might actually be composed of more than one database. Figure 1.5 depicts a high-level example of an enterprise database.

Enterprise databases impose many more constraints on the design and use of the database. There is a lot more to consider in terms of integrity, performance, and security. For this reason, enterprise databases are often split up to separate concerns and isolate requirements. If you tried to create a single database to meet all the requirements of an enterprise system, it would be extremely expensive and complex, or it would be completely impractical or even impossible.

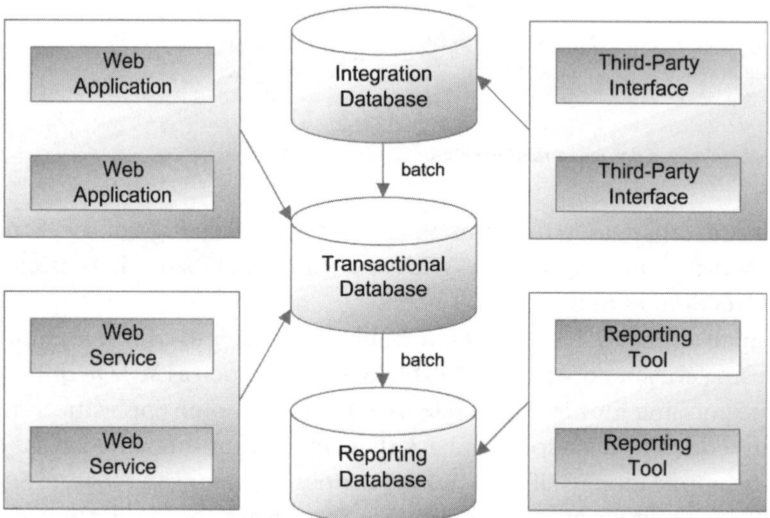

Figure 1.5 An example of enterprise database architecture

In the example depicted by figure 1.5, the requirements have been separated in terms of horizontal and nonfunctional requirements. That is, the databases have been separated into integration concerns, online transactional concerns, and reporting concerns. Both the integration database and the reporting database interface with the transactional system via a batch load, which implies that for this system it is acceptable to have reports that are not exactly up-to-date and that the transactional database only requires periodic updates from third-party systems. The advantage is that the transactional system has a great deal of load lifted from it and can have a simpler design as well. Generally it is not practical to design a database that is efficient for integration, transactions, and reporting. There are patterns for each that ensures the best performance and design. However, it is sometimes a requirement to have near real-time integration and reporting functions. For that reason this kind of design may not work. You might instead find that your enterprise database has to be partitioned vertically by business function.

Regardless of your enterprise database design, it's easy to appreciate the difference between an application database and an enterprise database. It's important to understand the particular limitations of your environment to ensure that your application uses the database effectively and is a good neighbor to other applications that are using the same database.

iBATIS works extremely well in an enterprise database environment. It has a number of features that make it ideal for working with complex database designs and large data sets. iBATIS also works well with multiple databases and does not assume that any type of object is coming from only one database. It also supports complex transactions that require multiple databases to be involved in a single transaction. Furthermore, iBATIS isn't only useful for online transactional systems, but works very well for both implementing reporting and integration systems.

1.3.3 Proprietary databases

If you've been working with software for any length of time, you've no doubt heard of the "build versus buy" debate. That is, should we build our own solution to a business problem, or buy a package that claims to solve the problem already. Often the cost is about the same (otherwise there would be no debate), but the real trade-off is between time to implement and the fit to the problem. Custom-built software can be tailored to an exact fit to business need, but takes more time to implement. Packages can be implemented very quickly, but sometimes don't quite meet every need. For that reason, when a choice is made to buy a package, businesses often decide that they can get the best of both worlds by digging into the proprietary database of the software to "extend" it just for the features that are missing.

We could discuss the horror stories of such a scenario, but it's probably better just to know that such proprietary databases were likely not meant to be touched by third parties. The designs are often full of assumptions, limitations, nonstandard data types, and other warning signs that can be easily read as "Enter at Your Own Risk." Regardless of the warning signs, businesses will do amazing things to save a few dollars. So software developers get stuck with navigating the jungle that is the proprietary database.

iBATIS is an excellent persistence layer for interfacing with proprietary databases. Often such databases allow for read-only access, which you can feel confident about when using iBATIS because you can restrict the kinds of SQL that are run. iBATIS won't perform any magical updates to the database when they aren't expected. If updates are required, proprietary databases are often very picky about how the data is structured. iBATIS allows you to write very specific update statements to deal with that.

1.3.4 Legacy databases

If ever there were a bane of a modern object-oriented developer's existence, it would be the legacy database. Legacy databases are generally the prehistoric remains of what was once an enterprise database. They have all of the complexities, intricacies, and dependencies of an enterprise database. In addition, they have battle scars from years of modifications, quick fixes, cover-ups, workarounds, bandage solutions, and technical limitations. Furthermore, legacy databases are often implemented on older platforms that are not only outdated but are sometimes totally unsupported. There may not be adequate drivers or tools available for modern developers to work with.

iBATIS can still help with legacy databases. As long as there's an appropriate database driver available for the system you're working with, iBATIS will work the same way it does for any database. In fact, iBATIS is probably one of the best persistence frameworks around for dealing with legacy data, because it makes no assumptions about the database design and can therefore deal with even the most nightmarish of legacy designs.

1.4 How iBATIS handles common database challenges

On modern software projects databases are often considered legacy components. They have a history of being difficult to work with for both technical and nontechnical reasons. Most developers probably wish that they could simply start over and rebuild the database entirely. If the database is to remain, some developers might just wish that the DBAs responsible for it would take a long walk off a short pier. Both of these cases are impractical and unlikely to ever happen. Believe it or not, databases are usually the way they are for a reason—even if the reason isn't a good one. It may be that the change would be too costly or there may be other dependencies barring us from changing it. Regardless of why the database is challenged, we have to learn to work effectively with all databases, even challenged ones. iBATIS was developed mostly in response to databases that had very complex designs or even poor designs. The following sections describe some common database challenges and how iBATIS can help with them.

1.4.1 Ownership and control

The first and foremost difficulty with databases in a modern enterprise environment is not technical at all. It is simply the fact that most enterprises separate the ownership and responsibility for the database from the application development teams. Databases are often owned by a separate group within the enterprise altogether. If you're lucky, this group may work with your project team to help deliver the software. If you're unlucky, there will be a wall between your project team and the database group, over which you must volley your requirements and hope that they are received and understood. It's a sad truth, but it happens all the time.

Database teams are often difficult to work with. The primary reason is that they are under enormous pressure and are often dealing with more than one project. They often deal with multiple and sometimes even conflicting requirements. Administration of database systems can be difficult and many companies consider it a mission-critical responsibility. When an enterprise database system fails, corporate executives will know about it. For this reason, database administration teams are cautious. Change control processes are often much stricter for database systems than they are for application code. Some changes to a database might require data migration. Other changes may require significant testing to ensure that they don't impact performance. Database teams have good reasons for being difficult to work with, and therefore it's nice to be able to help them out a bit.

iBATIS allows a lot of flexibility when it comes to database design and interaction. DBAs like to be able to see the SQL that is being run and can also help tune complex queries, and iBATIS allows them to do that. Some teams that use iBATIS even have a DBA or data modeler maintain the iBATIS SQL files directly. Database administrators and SQL programmers will have no problem understanding iBATIS, as there is no magic happening in the background and they can see the SQL.

1.4.2 Access by multiple disparate systems

A database of any importance will no doubt have more than one dependent. Even if it is simply two small web applications sharing a single database, there will be a number of things to consider. Imagine a web application called Web Shopping Cart, which uses a database that contains Category codes. As far as Web Shopping Cart is concerned, Category codes are static and never change, so the application caches the codes to improve performance. Now imagine that a second web application called Web Admin is written to update Category codes. The Web Admin application is a separate program running on a different server. When Web Admin updates a category code, how does Web Shopping Cart know when to flush its cache of Category codes? This is a simple example of what is sometimes a complex problem.

Different systems might access and use the database in different ways. One application might be a web-based e-commerce system that performs a lot of database updates and data creation. Another might be a scheduled batch job for loading data from a third-party interface that requires exclusive access to the database tables. Still another might be a reporting engine that constantly stresses the database with complex queries. One can easily imagine the complexity that is possible.

The important point is that as soon as a database is accessed by more than one system, the situation heats up. iBATIS can help in a number of ways. First of all, iBATIS is a persistence framework that is useful for all types of systems, including transactional systems, batch systems, and reporting systems. This means that regardless of what systems are accessing a given database, iBATIS is a great tool. Second, if you are able to use iBATIS, or even a consistent platform like Java, then you can use distributed caches to communicate among different systems. Finally, in the most complex of cases, you can easily disable iBATIS caching and write specific queries and update statements that behave perfectly, even when other systems using the same database do not.

1.4.3 Complex keys and relationships

Relational databases were designed and intended to follow a set of strict design rules. Sometimes these rules are broken, perhaps for a good reason, or perhaps not. Complex keys and relationships are usually the result of a rule being broken, misinterpreted, or possibly even overused. One of the relational design rules requires that each row of data be uniquely identified by a primary key. The simplest database designs will use a meaningless key as the primary key. However, some database designs might use what is called a *natural* key, in which case a part of the real data is used as the key. Still more complex designs will use a composite key of two or more columns. Primary keys are also often used to create relationships between other tables. So any complex or erroneous primary key definitions will propagate problems to the relationships between the other tables as well.

Sometimes the primary key rule is not followed. That is, sometimes data doesn't have a primary key at all. This complicates database queries a great deal as it becomes difficult to uniquely identify data. It makes creating relationships between tables difficult and messy at best. It also has a performance impact on the database in that the primary key usually provides a performance-enhancing index and is also used to determine the physical order of the data.

In other cases, the primary key rule might be overdone. A database might use composite natural keys for no practical reason. Instead the design was the result of taking the rule too seriously and implementing it in the strictest sense possible. Creating relationships between tables that use natural keys will actually create some duplication of real data, which is always a bad thing for database maintainability. Composite keys also create more redundancy when used as relationships, as multiple columns must be carried over to the related table to uniquely identify a single row. In these cases flexibility is lost because both natural keys and composite keys are much more difficult to maintain and can cause data-migration nightmares.

iBATIS can deal with any kind of complex key definition and relationship. Although it is always best to design the database properly, iBATIS can deal with tables with meaningless keys, natural keys, composite keys, or even no keys at all.

1.4.4 Denormalized or overnormalized models

Relational database design involves a process of eliminating redundancy. Elimination of redundancy is important to ensure that a database provides high performance and is flexible and maintainable. The process of eliminating redundancy in a data model is called *normalization*, and certain levels of normalization can be achieved. Raw data in tabular form generally will contain a great deal of redundancy and is therefore considered denormalized. Normalization is a complex topic that we won't discuss in great detail here.

When a database is first being designed, the raw data is analyzed for redundancy. A database administrator, a data modeler, or even a developer will take the raw data and normalize it using a collection of specific rules that are intended to eliminate redundancy. A denormalized relational model will contain redundant data in a few tables, each with a lot of rows and columns. A normalized model will have minimal or no redundancy and will have a greater number of tables, but each table will have fewer rows and columns.

There is no perfect level of normalization. Denormalization does have advantages in terms of simplicity and sometimes performance as well. A denormalized model can allow data to be stored and retrieved more quickly than if the data were normalized. This is true simply because there are fewer statements to issue, fewer joins to calculate, and generally less overhead. That said, denormalization should always be the exception and not the rule. A good approach to database design is to begin with a "by the book" normalized model. Then the model can be denormalized as needed. It is much easier to denormalize the database after the fact than it is to renormalize it. So always start new database designs with a normalized model.

It is possible to overnormalize a database, and the results can be problematic. Too many tables create a lot of relationships that need to be managed. This can include a lot of table joins when querying data, and it means multiple update statements are required to update data that is very closely related. Both of these characteristics can have a negative impact on performance. It also means that it's harder to map to an object model, as you may not want to have such fine-grained classes as the data model does.

Denormalized models are problematic too, possibly more so than overnormalized models. Denormalized models tend to have more rows and columns. Having too many rows impacts performance negatively in that there is simply more data to search through. Having too many columns is similar in that each row is bigger and therefore requires more resources to work with each time an update or a query is performed. Care must be taken with these *wide* tables to ensure that only columns that are required for the particular operation are included in the update or query. Furthermore, a denormalized model can make efficient indexing impossible.

iBATIS works with both denormalized models and overnormalized models. It makes no assumptions about the granularity of your object model or database, nor does it assume that they are the same or even remotely alike. iBATIS does the best job possible of separating the object model from the relational model.

1.4.5 Skinny data models

Skinny data models are one of the most notorious and problematic abuses of relational database systems. Unfortunately, they're sometimes necessary. A skinny data model basically turns each table into a generic data structure that can store sets of name and value pairs, much like a properties file in Java or an old-school INI (initialization) file in Windows. Sometimes these tables also store metadata such as the intended data type. This is necessary because the database only allows one type definition for a column. To better understand a skinny data model, consider the following example of typical address data, shown in table 1.2.

Table 1.2 Address data in typical model

ADDRESS_ID	STREET	CITY	STATE	ZIP	COUNTRY
1	123 Some Street	San Francisco	California	12345	USA
2	456 Another Street	New York	New York	54321	USA

Obviously this address data could be normalized in a better way. For example, we could have related tables for COUNTRY, STATE and CITY, and ZIP. But this is a simple and effective design that works for a lot of applications. Unless your requirements are complex, this is unlikely to be a problematic design.

If we were to take this data and arrange it in a skinny table design, it would look like table 1.3.

Table 1.3 Address data in a skinny model

ADDRESS_ID	FIELD	VALUE
1	STREET	123 Some Street
1	CITY	San Francisco
1	STATE	California
1	ZIP	12345

Table 1.3 Address data in a skinny model *(continued)*

ADDRESS_ID	FIELD	VALUE
1	COUNTRY	USA
2	STREET	456 Another Street
2	CITY	New York
2	STATE	New York
2	ZIP	54321
2	COUNTRY	USA

This design is an absolute nightmare. To start, there is no hope of possibly normalizing this data any better than it already is, which can only be classified as first normal form. There's no chance of creating managed relationships with COUNTRY, CITY, STATE, or ZIP tables, as we can't define multiple foreign key definitions on a single column. This data is also difficult to query and would require complex subqueries if we wanted to perform a query-by-example style query that involved a number of the address fields (e.g., searching for an address with both street and city as criteria). When it comes to updates, this design is especially poor in terms of performance; inserting a single address requires not one, but five insert statements on a single table. This can create greater potential for lock contention and possibly even deadlocks. Furthermore, the number of rows in the skinny design is now five times that of the normalized model. Due to the number of rows, the lack of data definition, and the number of update statements required to modify this data, effective indexing becomes impossible.

Without going further, it's easy to see why this design is problematic and why it should be avoided at all costs. The one place that it is useful is for dynamic fields in an application. Some applications have a need to allow users to add additional data to their records. If the user wants to be able to define new fields and insert data into those fields dynamically while the application is running, then this model works well. That said, all known data should still be properly normalized, and then these additional dynamic fields can be associated to a parent record. The design still suffers all of the consequences as discussed, but they are minimized because most of the data (probably the important data) is still properly normalized.

Even if you encounter a skinny data model in an enterprise database, iBATIS can help you deal with it. It is difficult or maybe even impossible to map classes to a skinny data model, because you don't know what fields there might be. You'd have better luck mapping such a thing to a hashtable, and luckily iBATIS supports that. With iBATIS, you don't necessarily have to map every table to a user-defined class. iBATIS allows you to map relational data to primitives, maps, XML, and user-defined classes (e.g., JavaBeans). This great flexibility makes iBATIS extremely effective for complex data models, including skinny data models.

1.5 Summary

iBATIS was designed as a hybrid solution that does not attempt to solve every problem, but instead solves the most important problems. iBATIS borrows from the various other methods of access. Like a stored procedure, every iBATIS statement has a signature that gives it a name and defines its inputs and outputs (encapsulation). Similar to inline SQL, iBATIS allows the SQL to be written in the way it was supposed to be, and to use language variables directly for parameters and results. Like Dynamic SQL, iBATIS provides a means of modifying the SQL at runtime. Such queries can be dynamically built to reflect a user request. From object/relational mapping tools, iBATIS borrows a number of concepts, including caching, lazy loading, and advanced transaction management.

In an application architecture, iBATIS fits in at the persistence layer. iBATIS supports other layers by providing features that allow for easier implementation of requirements at all layers of the application. For example, a web search engine may require paginated lists of search results. iBATIS supports such features by allowing a query to specify an offset (i.e., a starting point) and the number of rows to return. This allows the pagination to operate at a low level, while keeping the database details out of the application.

iBATIS works with databases of any size or purpose. It works well for small application databases because it is simple to learn and quick to ramp up. It is excellent for large enterprise applications because it doesn't make any assumptions about the database design, behaviors, or dependencies that might impact how our application uses the database. Even databases that have challenging designs or are perhaps surrounded by political turmoil can easily work with iBATIS. Above all else, iBATIS has been designed to be flexible enough to suit almost any situation while saving you time by eliminating redundant boilerplate code.

In this chapter we've discussed the philosophy and the roots of iBATIS. In the next chapter we'll explain exactly what iBATIS is and how it works.

2 What is iBATIS?

This chapter covers

- When to use iBATIS
- When not to use iBATIS
- Getting started
- Future direction

In the previous chapter we discussed in detail the philosophy behind iBATIS and how the framework came to be. We also stated that iBATIS is a hybrid solution that borrows ideas from various other methods of working with a relational database. So what exactly is iBATIS? This chapter will answer that question.

iBATIS is what is known as a *data mapper*. In his book *Patterns of Enterprise Application Architecture* (Addison-Wesley Professional, 2002), Martin Fowler describes the Data Mapper pattern as follows:

> *A layer of Mappers*[1] *that moves data between objects and a database while keeping them independent of each other and the mapper itself.*

Martin does a good job of distinguishing between data mapping and metadata mapping, which is where an object/relational mapping tool fits in. Such a tool maps the tables and columns of the database to the classes and fields of the application. That is, an object relational mapper maps database metadata to class metadata. Figure 2.1 shows an object/relational mapping between a class and a database table. In this case, each field of the class is mapped to a single corresponding column in the database.

iBATIS is different in that it does not directly tie classes to tables or fields to columns, but instead maps the parameters and results (i.e., the inputs and outputs) of a SQL statement to a class. As you'll discover throughout the rest of the book, iBATIS is an additional layer of indirection between the classes and the tables, allowing it more flexibility in how classes and tables can be mapped, without requiring any changes to the data model or the object model. The layer of indirection we're talking about is in fact SQL. This extra layer of indirection allows iBATIS to do a better job of isolating the database design from the object model. This means relatively few dependencies exist between the two. Figure 2.2 shows how iBATIS maps data using SQL.

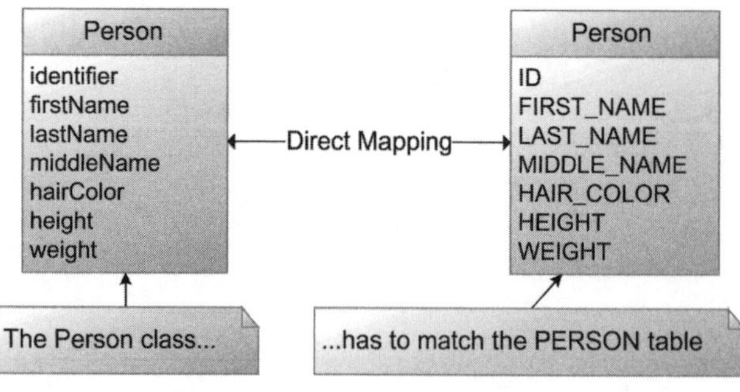

Figure 2.1
Object/relational mapping

[1] Mapper: An object that sets up a communication between two independent objects.
—Martin Fowler in *Patterns of Enterprise Architecture*

Person
identifier
firstName
lastName
middleName
hairColor
height
weight

```
SELECT
  ID           as identifier,
  FIRST_NAME   as firstName,
  LAST_NAME    as lastName
  MIDDLE_NAME  as middleName,
  HAIR_COLOR   as hairColor,
  HEIGHT       as height,
  WEIGHT       as weight
FROM PERSON
WHERE ID = #identifier#
```

Person
ID
FIRST_NAME
LAST_NAME
MIDDLE_NAME
HAIR_COLOR
HEIGHT
WEIGHT

Figure 2.2 iBATIS SQL mapping

As you can see in figure 2.2, the mapping layer of iBATIS is actual SQL. iBATIS lets you write your SQL. iBATIS takes care of mapping the parameters and results between the class properties and the columns of the database table. For this reason, and to eliminate any confusion around the various mapping approaches, the iBATIS team often refers to the data mapper as a SQL mapper.

2.1 Mapping SQL

Any SQL statement can be viewed as a set of inputs and outputs. The inputs are the parameters, typically found in the `WHERE` clause of the SQL statement. The outputs are the columns found in the `SELECT` clause. Figure 2.3 depicts this idea.

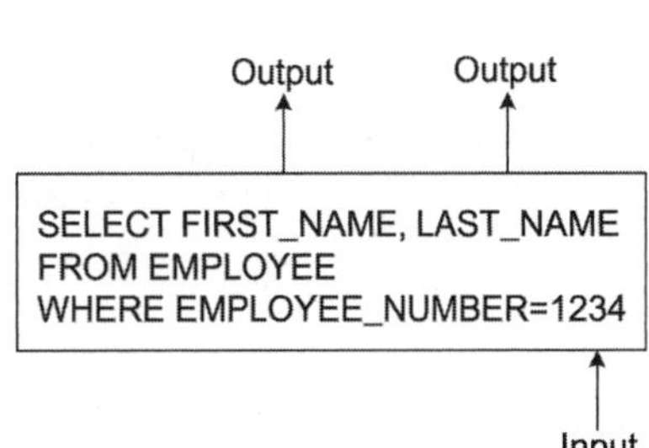

Figure 2.3 SQL can be viewed as inputs and outputs.

The advantage to this approach is that the SQL statement leaves a great deal of flexibility in the hands of the developer. One can easily manipulate the data to match the object model without changing the underlying table design. Furthermore, developers can actually introduce multiple tables or results from built-in database functions or stored procedures. The full power of SQL is at their fingertips.

iBATIS maps the inputs and outputs of the statement using a simple XML descriptor file. Listing 2.1 shows an example of this.

Listing 2.1 A sample SQL mapping descriptor

```
<select id="getAddress"
      parameterClass="int"
      resultClass="Address">
SELECT
      ADR_ID           as id,
      ADR_DESCRIPTION  as description,
      ADR_STREET       as street,
      ADR_CITY         as city,
      ADR_PROVINCE     as province,
      ADR_POSTAL_CODE  as postalCode
  FROM ADDRESS
  WHERE ADR_ID = #id#
</select>
```

Here we can see a SQL SELECT statement that returns address data. From the <select> element we can see that it takes an Integer object as a parameter, which is marked by the #id# token in the WHERE clause. We can also see that the result is an object instance of the Address class, which is assumed to contain the properties of the same name as the aliases assigned to each column in the SELECT clause. For example, the alias *id* would be mapped to a property of the Address class also called id. Believe it or not, that is all it takes to map a SQL statement that receives an integer as a parameter and returns an Address object as output. The Java code used to execute this statement would be

```
Address address = (Address) sqlMap.queryForObject("getAddress",
                                                    new Integer(5));
```

The SQL mapping approach is a very portable concept that can be applied to any full-featured programming language. For example, the C# code from iBATIS.NET is nearly identical:

```
Address address = (Address) sqlMap.QueryForObject("getAddress", 5);
```

Of course there are more advanced options for mapping, especially around results. But we'll discuss those in greater detail in part 2, "iBATIS basics." Right now, it's more important to understand the features and benefits of iBATIS and how it works.

2.2 How it works

More than anything else, iBATIS is an alternative to writing JDBC and ADO.NET code. APIs like JDBC and ADO.NET are powerful, but tend to be verbose and repetitive. Consider the JDBC example in listing 2.2.

Listing 2.2 Example of well-written JDBC code

```
public Employee getEmployee (int id) throws SQLException {
    Employee employee = null;
    String sql = "SELECT * FROM EMPLOYEE " +
                 "WHERE EMPLOYEE_NUMBER = ?";        Our SQL is buried here
    Connection conn = null;
    PreparedStatement ps = null;
    ResultSet rs = null;
    try {
      conn = dataSource.getConnection();
      ps = conn.prepareStatement(sql);
      ps.setInt(1, id);
      rs = ps.executeQuery();
      employee = null;
      while (rs.next()) {
        employee = new Employee();
        employee.setId(rs.getInt("ID"));
        employee.setEmployeeNumber(rs.getInt("EMPLOYEE_NUMBER"));
        employee.setFirstName(rs.getString("FIRST_NAME"));
        employee.setLastName(rs.getString("LAST_NAME"));
        employee.setTitle(rs.getString("TITLE"));
      }
    } finally {
      try {
        if (rs != null) rs.close();
      } finally {
        try {
          if (ps != null) ps.close();
        } finally {
          if (conn != null) conn.close();
        }
      }
    }
    return employee;
  }
```

It's easy to see the overhead created by the JDBC API. Every line is necessary, though, so there's no easy way to reduce it. At best, a few of the lines can be extracted into utility methods, most notably the closing of resources such as the `PreparedStatement` and the `ResultSet`.

Under the hood, iBATIS will run nearly the same JDBC code. iBATIS will get a connection to the database, set the parameters, execute the statement, retrieve the results, and close all of the resources. However, the amount of code that you need to write is significantly reduced. Listing 2.3 shows the code needed for iBATIS to run the exact same statement.

Listing 2.3 iBATIS, which is much less verbose than JDBC

```
<select id="getEmployee"
            parameterClass="java.lang.Integer"
            resultClass="Employee">
       SELECT ID                  as id,
            EMPLOYEE_NUMBER       as employeeNumber,
            FIRST_NAME            as firstName,
            LAST_NAME             as lastName,
            TITLE                 as title
      FROM EMPLOYEE
      WHERE EMPLOYEE_NUMBER = #empNum#
</select>
```

There is no comparison. The iBATIS code is more concise and easier to read, and thus easier to maintain. We'll discuss more of the benefits of iBATIS later in this chapter. But for now, you're probably wondering how this gets executed from the Java code. As you've seen in earlier examples,, it's a very simple single line of code:

```
Employee emp = (Employee) sqlMap.queryForObject("getEmployee",
                                              new Integer(5));
```

There's nothing to it. This line of code executes the statement, sets the parameters, and retrieves the results as a real Java object. The SQL is encapsulated and externalized neatly in an Extensible Markup Language (XML) file. iBATIS manages all of the resources behind the scenes, and the net effect is the same as the JDBC code we saw earlier in listing 2.2.

This begs the question, does iBATIS work the same way for all systems? Is it best suited for a particular kind of application? The next few sections will answer that, starting with how well iBATIS works with small applications.

2.2.1 iBATIS for small, simple systems

Small applications often work with only a single database, and they often have a fairly simple user interface and domain model. The business logic is very basic, or perhaps nonexistent for some simple CRUD (Create, Read, Update, Delete) applications. There are three reasons why iBATIS works well with small applications.

First, iBATIS itself is small and simple. It doesn't require a server or any sort of middleware. No additional infrastructure is required at all. iBATIS has no third-party dependencies. A minimal installation of iBATIS consists of only two JAR files that total about 375KB of disk space. There is no setup beyond the SQL Mapping files themselves, so in a matter of minutes you can have a working persistence layer.

Second, iBATIS does not impose on the existing design of the application or the database. Therefore, if you have a small system that is already partially implemented or perhaps even released, it is still easy to refactor the persistence layer to use iBATIS. Because iBATIS is simple, it won't overcomplicate the architecture of the application at all. The same might not be true of object/relational mapping tools or code generators that make assumptions about the design of either the application or the database.

Finally, if you've been working with software for any length of time, you'll likely agree that it's almost inevitable that any *small* piece of software will one day become a large piece of software. All successful software has a tendency to grow. It's a good thing, then, that iBATIS is also very good for large systems, and that it can grow to meet the needs of even enterprise-class applications.

2.2.2 iBATIS for large, enterprise systems

iBATIS was designed for enterprise-class applications. More than anything, iBATIS has a great number of advantages in this area over other solutions. The original creator of iBATIS has only ever had the *luxury* of working applications ranging from large-scale to enterprise-class systems. These systems typically involved not one, but many databases, none of which he had control over. In chapter 1 we discussed various types of databases, including enterprise databases, proprietary databases, and legacy databases. iBATIS was written largely in response to the need to deal with such databases. As a result, iBATIS has a great many features that lend themselves well to the enterprise environment.

The first reason has been stated in other areas, but is so important that it cannot be overstated: *iBATIS does not make any assumptions about the design of your database or your object model.* Regardless of how mismatched these two designs are, iBATIS will work with the application. Furthermore, iBATIS does not make assumptions about the architecture of your enterprise system. If you have partitioned your database vertically by business function, or horizontally by technology, iBATIS will still allow you to effectively work with that data and integrate it into your object-oriented application.

Second, iBATIS has features that allow it to effectively work with very large data sets. iBATIS supports features like row handlers that allow batch processing of very large record sets, one record at a time. It also supports fetching a range of results, allowing you to fetch only the data absolutely necessary for your immediate needs. If you have 10,000 records and only want records 500 to 600, then you can easily fetch just those records. iBATIS supports driver hints that allow it to perform such operations very efficiently.

Finally, iBATIS allows you to map your objects to the database in multiple ways. It's pretty rare that an enterprise system functions only in a single mode. Many enterprise-class systems need to perform transactional functions throughout the day and perform batch functions during the night. iBATIS allows you to have the same class mapped in multiple ways to ensure that each function is supported in the most efficient way possible. iBATIS also supports multiple fetch strategies. That is, you can choose to have some data loaded lazily, while other complex object graphs are loaded with a single SQL join to avoid serious performance problems.

This sounds a lot like a sales pitch. So while we're in the mood, why don't we go into some reasons why you want to use iBATIS? We'll do exactly that in section 2.5. To be fair, a little later in section 2.5 we'll discuss some times when you may *not* want to use iBATIS.

2.3 Why use iBATIS?

There are a great many reasons to use iBATIS in nearly any system. As you learned earlier in this chapter, a framework like iBATIS offers opportunities to inject architectural benefits into your application. Here we'll discuss these benefits and the features that make them possible.

2.3.1 Simplicity

iBATIS is widely regarded as being one of the simplest persistence frameworks available today. Simplicity is at the heart of the design goals of the iBATIS team, and it takes priority over nearly everything else. This simplicity is achieved by maintaining a very solid foundation upon which iBATIS is built: JDBC and SQL. iBATIS is easy for Java developers because it works like JDBC, only with much less code. Almost everything you knew about JDBC applies to iBATIS as well. You can almost think of iBATIS as JDBC code described in XML format. That said, iBATIS includes a number of other architectural benefits that JDBC does not have, which we'll discuss next. iBATIS is also easy to understand for database administrators and SQL programmers. iBATIS configuration files can be easily understood by nearly anyone with any SQL programming experience.

2.3.2 Productivity

The primary purpose of any good framework is to make the developer more productive. Generally a framework exists to take care of common tasks, reduce boilerplate code, and solve complex architectural challenges. iBATIS succeeds in making developers more productive. In one case study presented at a Java Users Group in Italy (www.jugsardegna.org/vqwiki/jsp/Wiki?IBatisCaseStudy), Fabrizio Gianneschi found that iBATIS reduced the amount of code in the persistence layer by a significant 62 percent. This savings was primarily due to the fact that no JDBC code had to be written. The SQL was still handcoded, but as you saw earlier in this chapter, the SQL is not the problem—it's the JDBC API, and ADO.NET is no different.

2.3.3 Performance

The topic of performance will spark debate among framework authors, users, and even commercial software vendors. The fact is, at a low level all frameworks incur some sort of overhead. Generally, if you compare handcoded JDBC to iBATIS and iterate it 1,000,000 times in a `for` loop, you'll likely see a performance hit in favor of JDBC. Fortunately, this is not the kind of performance that matters in modern application development. What is much more significant is how you fetch data from the database, when you fetch it, and how often. For example, using a paginated list of data that dynamically fetches records from the database can significantly increase the performance of the application because you aren't unnecessarily loading potentially thousands of records from the database at once. Similarly, using features like lazy loading will avoid loading data that isn't necessarily used in a given use case. On the other hand, if you know for certain that you have to load a complex object graph that involves a large amount of data from a number of tables, loading it using a single SQL statement will improve performance greatly. iBATIS supports a number of performance optimizations that we'll discuss in more detail later. For now, it is important to know that iBATIS can usually be configured and used in such a way that is simple, yet it performs as well as JDBC, or possibly better. Another important consideration is that not all JDBC code is well written. JDBC is a complex API that requires a lot of care to code correctly. Unfortunately, much JDBC code is poorly written and therefore will not even perform as well as iBATIS at a low level.

2.3.4 Separation of concerns

With typical JDBC code, it was not uncommon to find database resources such as connections and result sets strewn throughout the application at all layers. We've all seen the nasty applications with database connections and statements in JSP pages, results being iterated over, and HTML in between it all. It's truly nightmarish. In chapter 1 we discussed the importance of application layering. We saw how the application is layered at a high level and also how the persistence layer is layered internally. iBATIS helps to support this layering by managing all of the persistence-related resources, such as database connections, prepared statements, and result sets. It provides database-independent interfaces and APIs that help the rest of the application remain independent of any persistence-related resources. With iBATIS, you're always working only with true objects and never with arbitrary result sets. iBATIS actually makes it hard to break layering best practices.

2.3.5 Division of labor

Some database administrators love their database so much that they won't let anyone else write the SQL for it. Others are just so good at it that everyone else wants them to write the SQL. Whatever the reason, it's always nice to leverage the strengths in your development team. If you have someone who is particularly good at writing SQL but not so hot at writing Java or C#, then let them write the SQL unimpeded. iBATIS allows this to happen. Because the SQL statements are largely separated from the application source code, SQL programmers can write the SQL the way it was meant to be written, without having to worry about string concatenation. Even if the same developers write both the Java code and the SQL, a common request from DBAs while performance tuning a database is "Show me the SQL." This is not an easy thing to do with JDBC, as the SQL is often wound up in a series of concatenated strings or perhaps even dynamically built from a combination of iteration and conditionals. With an object relational mapper the situation is even worse, as you usually have to run the application and log the statements, and once you find them, you may not be able to do anything to change them. iBATIS allows full freedom to enable anyone to develop, view, and change the SQL statements run against the database.

2.3.6 Portability: Java, .NET, and others

iBATIS is a very portable concept. Because of its relatively simple design, it can be implemented for nearly any language or platform. At the time of this writing, iBATIS supports the three most popular development platforms: Java, Ruby, and C# for Microsoft .NET.

The configuration files aren't entirely compatible across the platforms at this time, but there are plans to make that more of a reality. More important, the *concept* and *approach* are very portable. This allows you to be consistent in the design of all of your applications. iBATIS works with more languages and more types of applications than any other framework, regardless of the design of the application. If consistency across your applications is important to you, then iBATIS will work very well for you.

2.3.7 Open source and honesty

Earlier we called this section a "sales pitch." The truth is, iBATIS is free, open source software. We don't make a dime on it whether you use it or not. You've already bought the book, so we've made as much money as we're going to. That said, one of the greatest advantages of open source software is *honesty*. We have no reason to stretch the truth or lie to you. We'll be very up-front and say that iBATIS isn't the perfect solution for all problems. So let's do something that is rarely done in commercial software documentation. Let's discuss some reasons why you may not want to use iBATIS, and suggest alternatives where appropriate.

2.4 When not to use iBATIS

Every framework is built around rules and constraints. Lower-level frameworks like JDBC provide a flexible and complete feature set, but they are harder and more tedious to use. High-level frameworks like object/relational mapping tools are much easier to use and save you a lot of work, but they are built with more assumptions and constraints that make them applicable to fewer applications.

iBATIS is a mid-level framework. It's higher level than JDBC, but lower level than an object relational mapper. That puts iBATIS in a unique position that makes it applicable to a unique set of applications. In the previous sections we discussed why iBATIS is useful in various types of applications, including small, rich client applications and large, enterprise, web applications—and everything in between. So when does iBATIS not fit? The next few sections detail situations where iBATIS is not the best solution and offer recommendations for alternatives.

2.4.1 When you have full control…forever

If you are guaranteed to have full control of your application design and database design, then you are a very lucky person indeed. This is rare in an enterprise environment or any business where the core competency is not software development. However, if you work at a software company that develops a shrink-wrapped product for which you have full design control, then you might be in this situation.

When you have full control, you have a good reason to use a full object/relational mapping solution such as Hibernate. You can fully leverage the design benefits and productivity gains that an object relational mapper can provide. There will probably not be any interference from an enterprise database group, or a legacy system to integrate with. Furthermore, the database is probably deployed with the application, which places this into the category of an application database (see chapter 1). A good example of a packaged application that uses Hibernate is JIRA from Atlassian. They supply their issue-tracking software as a shrink-wrapped product over which they have full control.

It's important to consider where the application will be in the future, though. If there is any chance that the database could fall out of the control of the application developers, then you might want to carefully consider the impacts that could have on your persistence strategy.

2.4.2 When your application requires fully dynamic SQL

If the core functionality of your application is the dynamic generation of SQL, then iBATIS is the wrong choice. iBATIS supports very powerful dynamic SQL features that in turn support advanced query capability and even some dynamic update functions. However, if every statement in your system is dynamically generated, then you're better off sticking with raw JDBC and possibly building your own framework.

Much of the power of iBATIS is that it allows you complete freedom to manually write and manipulate SQL directly. This advantage is quickly lost when the majority of your SQL is built dynamically from some SQL generator class.

2.4.3 When you're not using a relational database

There are JDBC drivers available for more than relational databases. There are JDBC drivers for flat files, Microsoft Excel spreadsheets, XML, and other types of data stores. Although some people have been successful using such drivers with iBATIS, we don't recommend them for the majority of users.

iBATIS doesn't make many assumptions about your environment. But it does expect that you're using a real relational database that supports transactions and relatively typical SQL and stored procedure semantics. Even some well-known databases don't support very key features of a relational database. Early versions of MySQL did not support transactions, and therefore iBATIS did not work well with it. Luckily today MySQL does support transactions and has a fairly compliant JDBC driver.

If you're not using a real relational database, we recommend that you stick with raw JDBC or even a lower-level file I/O API.

2.4.4 When it simply does not work

iBATIS has a lot of great features that continue to be implemented as the needs of the community grow. However, iBATIS does have a direction as well as design goals that will sometimes conflict with the needs of some applications. People do amazing things with software, and there have been cases where iBATIS simply did not work because of a complex requirement. Although we may have been able to add features to support the requirement, it would have added significant complexity or perhaps would have changed the scope of the iBATIS framework. As a result, we would not change the framework. To support these cases, we try to offer pluggable interfaces so that you can extend iBATIS to meet nearly any need. The simple fact is, sometimes it just doesn't work. In these cases it's best to find a better solution, rather than try to twist iBATIS (or any framework) into something that it is not.

So instead of continuing to discuss the whys and why nots, let's look at a simple example.

2.5 iBATIS in five minutes

The iBATIS framework is a very simple one, and getting started with it is equally simple. How simple? Well, simple enough that we can build an entire application that uses iBATIS in five minutes—not a big Enterprise Resource Planning (ERP) solution or massive e-commerce website, but a simple command-line tool to execute a SQL statement from an iBATIS SQL Map and output the results to the console. The following example will configure a simple static SQL statement to query a simple database table and write it to the console like this:

```
java -classpath <…> Main

Selected 2 records.
{USERNAME=LMEADORS, PASSSWORD=PICKLE, USERID=1, GROUPNAME=EMPLOYEE}
{USERNAME=JDOE, PASSSWORD=TEST, USERID=2, GROUPNAME=EMPLOYEE}
```

Not exactly the prettiest data output, but you get the picture of what it is going to do. In the next few sections, we will walk through the steps to get you from nothing to this level of functionality.

2.5.1 *Setting up the database*

For the purpose of the sample application, we will use a MySQL database. The iBATIS framework works with any database, as long as it has a JDBC-compliant driver. You simply need to supply a driver class name and a JDBC URL in the configuration.

Setting up a database server is beyond the scope of this book, so we will only provide you with what you need to do on the assumption that the database is already set up and functional. Here is the MySQL script that creates the table we will use and adds some sample data to it:

```
#
# Table structure for table 'user'
#

CREATE TABLE USER_ACCOUNT (
  USERID          INT(3) NOT NULL AUTO_INCREMENT,
  USERNAME        VARCHAR(10) NOT NULL,
  PASSSWORD       VARCHAR(30) NOT NULL,
  GROUPNAME       VARCHAR(10),
  PRIMARY KEY     (USERID)
);

#
# Data for table 'user'
#

INSERT INTO USER_ACCOUNT (USERNAME, PASSSWORD, GROUPNAME)
      VALUES ('LMEADORS', 'PICKLE', 'EMPLOYEE');
INSERT INTO USER_ACCOUNT (USERNAME, PASSSWORD, GROUPNAME)
      VALUES ('JDOE', 'TEST', 'EMPLOYEE');
COMMIT;
```

If you have a different database server already set up with other data that you would like to execute some SQL queries over, feel free to use it for the example. You will need to modify the query in the `SqlMap.xml` file to have your SQL in it and will also need to modify the `SqlMapConfig.xml` file to configure iBATIS to use your database instead. To make it work, you have to know the driver name, the JDBC URL, and a username and password to connect with.

2.5.2 *Writing the code*

Because this application is our first full example, and an introduction to using iBATIS, the code will be much simpler than a real application would be. We discuss type safety and exception handling later, so we will not be considering those topics here. Listing 2.4 contains the complete code.

Listing 2.4 Main.java

```
import com.ibatis.sqlmap.client.*;
import com.ibatis.common.resources.Resources;

import java.io.Reader;
import java.util.List;
                                                        Configures
                                                            iBATIS
public class Main {
    public static void main(String arg[]) throws Exception {
        String resource = "SqlMapConfig.xml";
        Reader reader = Resources.getResourceAsReader (resource);
      SqlMapClient sqlMap = SqlMapClientBuilder.buildSqlMapClient(reader);
        List list = sqlMap.queryForList("getAllUsers", "EMPLOYEE");
        System.out.println("Selected " + list.size() + " records.");
        for(int i = 0; i < list.size(); i++) {
            System.out.println(list.get(i));          Prints the results
        }
    }                                          Executes the statement
}
```

That's it! We've configured iBATIS, executed the statement, and printed the results in about 10 lines of Java code. That's all the Java code required for a fully functional iBATIS application. Later, we will refine how things happen, but for now, let's move on to the basics of the configuration.

2.5.3 Configuring iBATIS (a preview)

Since we cover the configuration of iBATIS in depth in the next chapter, we discuss it only briefly here. You won't find much in the way of explanation of the options here, but we cover the essential information.

First, let's look at the `SqlMapConfig.xml` file. This is the starting point for iBATIS, and ties all of the SQL Maps together. Listing 2.5 contains the `SqlMapConfig.xml` file for our simple application.

Listing 2.5 The SQL map configuration for the simplest iBATIS application ever written

```
<?xml version="1.0" encoding="UTF-8" ?>

<!DOCTYPE sqlMapConfig
    PUBLIC "-//ibatis.apache.org//DTD SQL Map Config 2.0//EN"
     "http://ibatis.apache.org/dtd/sql-map-config-2.dtd">
```

1 Provides DOCTYPE and DTD for validation

```
<sqlMapConfig>
  <transactionManager type="JDBC" >
```

```
    <dataSource type="SIMPLE">
      <property name="JDBC.Driver"
                value="com.mysql.jdbc.Driver"/>
      <property name="JDBC.ConnectionURL"
                value="jdbc:mysql://localhost/test"/>
      <property name="JDBC.Username"
                value="root"/>
      <property name="JDBC.Password"
                value="blah"/>
    </dataSource>
  </transactionManager>
  <sqlMap resource="SqlMap.xml" />
</sqlMapConfig>
```

❷ **Provides name of built-in transaction manager**

❸ **Provides your SQL Maps**

As you may have guessed, this is where we tell iBATIS how to connect to the database and which SQL Map files are available. Since it is an XML document, we need to provide a doctype and DTD for validation ❶. SIMPLE is the name of a built-in transaction manager ❷. Here is where you provide the name of your JDBC driver, the JDBC URL, a username, and a password that lets you connect to the database. Then you provide your SQL Maps ❸. Here, we only have one SQL Map, but you can have as many as you want. There are a few other things you can do here, but we cover them all in the next chapter.

Now that you have seen the main configuration file, let's take a look at the `SqlMap.xml` file (listing 2.6). This is the file that contains the SQL statement that we will be running.

Listing 2.6 The simplest SQL Map ever

```
<?xml version="1.0" encoding="UTF-8" ?>
<!DOCTYPE sqlMap PUBLIC "-//ibatis.apache.org//DTD SQL Map 2.0//EN"
    "http://ibatis.apache.org/dtd/sql-map-2.dtd">

<sqlMap>
    <select id="getAllUsers" parameterClass="string"
                             resultClass="hashmap">
        SELECT * FROM USER_ACCOUNT WHERE GROUPNAME = #groupName#
    </select>
</sqlMap>
```

In the XML code in listing 2.6, we're accepting a String parameter (`parameterClass`) for the `GROUPNAME` parameter, and mapping the results (`resultClass`) to a HashMap.

WARNING Using a Map (e.g., HashMap, TreeMap) as your domain model is not recommended, but this does show the level of mapping flexibility that iBATIS provides. You don't necessarily always need a JavaBean to map to—you can map directly to Maps and primitives as well.

Believe it or not, you have now seen all of the code and configuration required to use iBATIS. We have intentionally spread it out for printing, but even with that, it is only about 50 lines of code, including Java and XML. But the more important point is that 45 of the 50 lines are configuration and are only written once in an application, not for every single statement. As you saw earlier in this chapter, JDBC can end up costing you 50 lines of code or more per statement.

2.5.4 Building the application

Usually when building a large application, you will use something like Ant to make it simpler. Because this is only one class, we are not going to bother building an Ant script for it. To build it, the only JAR files you need on the classpath are `ibatis-common-2.jar` and `ibatis-sqlmap-2.jar`, so we will just key them in on the command line to the Java compiler:

```
javac -classpath <your-path>ibatis-common-2.jar;
<your-path>ibatis-sqlmap-2.jar Main.java
```

Of course, that should all be on one line, and instead of `<your-path>`, you should substitute the actual path to the JAR files. If everything is OK, there should be no output from the compiler to the screen, but a `Main.class` file should be created in the current directory.

2.5.5 Running the application

We will have a few more JARs when we run the application, but not many. To run our application, the only JAR files we need on the classpath are `ibatis-common-2.jar`, `ibatis-sqlmap-2.jar`, `commons-logging.jar`, and our JDBC driver (in this case, `mysql-connector-java.jar`), so next enter this command:

```
java -classpath <your-path>;mysql-connector.jar;commons-logging.jar;
                ibatis-common-2.jar;ibatis-sqlmap-2.jar;.
                Main
```

Again, as with the compilation, this should all go on one line, and `<your-path>` should be replaced with the actual paths on your system.

The program should run and tell you how many records were selected, and then output the data in a rough format, something like this:

```
Selected 2 records.
{USERID=1, USERNAME=LMEADORS, PASSSWORD=PICKLE, GROUPNAME=EMPLOYEE}
{USERID=2, USERNAME=JDOE, PASSSWORD=TEST, GROUPNAME=EMPLOYEE}
```

The iBATIS framework is designed to be very flexible. It can be a very lightweight and simple framework that simply executes SQL and returns data, or it can be used to do much more.

One key to that flexibility is in the proper configuration of the framework. In the next chapter, we are going to look at the two main types of configuration files, and then we'll look at some patterns for solving difficult situations through the use of configuration.

NOTE The configuration files are very standard XML documents. That means that if you have a modern XML editor, the Document Type Definition (DTD) can be used to validate the document, and in some cases even provide code completion while editing.

You've now seen iBATIS in its simplest form. Before we continue, let's talk a bit about where iBATIS is going, so that you can be confident in your decision to use it.

2.6 The future: where is iBATIS going?

iBATIS has gained a great deal of momentum in recent months. As a result, the team has grown, the product has moved, and we've started talking about supporting new platforms. Let's discuss the future in more detail.

2.6.1 Apache Software Foundation

Recently iBATIS became a part of the Apache Software Foundation. We chose to move to Apache because we believe in their mission and respect their attitude. Apache is more than a bunch of servers and infrastructure; it's a system and a true home for open source software. Apache focuses on the community that surrounds software rather than the technology behind it, because without a community the software is a dead project.

What this means to iBATIS users is that iBATIS is not under the direction of a single entity, nor is it dependent on a single entity. Nobody owns iBATIS—it belongs to the community. Apache is there to protect the software and ensure that it stays that way. That said, the Apache license does not restrict the use of open source software as some licenses such as the GPL might. The Apache license is not a *viral* license, which means that you can use the software freely in a commercial environment without worrying about being compliant with unreasonable conditions.

Although Apache doesn't focus on infrastructure, they do have some very good infrastructure. Currently iBATIS makes use of Subversion source control (SVN), Atlassian's JIRA for issue tracking, Atlassian's Confluence for collaborative wiki documentation, and Apache's mailing list servers for communication among the development team, users, and the community in general.

Apache has what it takes to protect iBATIS and ensure that it will be around for as long as there are people who want to use it.

2.6.2 Simpler, smaller, with fewer dependencies

Unlike some frameworks, the iBATIS project has no goals to branch out into new areas and take over the world. iBATIS is a very focused project and with each release we only hope to make it smaller and simpler and maintain independence from third-party libraries.

We believe that iBATIS has much room for innovation. There are a lot of new technologies and design approaches that iBATIS can benefit from to make configuration more concise and easier to work with. For example, both C# and Java have attribute (a.k.a. annotation) functionality built in. In future versions, iBATIS will likely leverage this to reduce the amount of XML needed to configure the framework.

There is also a lot of room for tools development. The iBATIS design lends itself well to graphical tools such as integrated development environments. It is also possible for iBATIS configurations to be generated from database schemas, for which there are already tools available. You can see examples of some of the tools on our website at http://ibatis.apache.org.

2.6.3 More extensions and plug-ins

iBATIS already has a number of extension points. We'll talk about them in detail in chapter 12. You can already implement your own transaction manager, data source, cache controllers, and more. But we have a goal to make iBATIS even more extendible. We'd like to see a pluggable design at nearly every layer of JDBC architecture, meaning you'd be able to implement your own `ResultSet` handlers and SQL execution engines. This would help us support more complex or legacy systems that operate in a proprietary way. It would also enable developers to take greater advantage of customized features of particular databases or application servers.

2.6.4 Additional platforms and languages

As you've noticed in both chapters 1 and 2, we've discussed iBATIS for .NET and Java. The remainder of this book will focus mostly on the Java APIs, but most of the information is transferable to the .NET platform as well. We'll also discuss

.NET in more detail in appendix. iBATIS has been implemented for Ruby as well, but Ruby is a significantly different language, and therefore iBATIS for Ruby is quite different as well. We'll not discuss the Ruby implementation here.

In addition to Java and C#, the iBATIS team has discussed implementing iBATIS in other languages, including PHP 5 and Python. We believe that iBATIS can contribute significant value to almost any platform where the choices are limited to a low-level database API and a high-level object/relational mapping tool. iBATIS can fill the middle ground and again allow you to implement all of your applications in a consistent way across the board.

We've also discussed drafting a specification that would make it easier to migrate iBATIS to different platforms and ensure reasonable consistency. Of course, we'd like iBATIS to take full advantage of unique language and platform features, but we'd also like to see some level of similarity to ensure that they can all be called iBATIS and be recognizable to developers experienced with iBATIS in another language.

2.7 Summary

In this chapter you learned that iBATIS is a unique data mapper that uses an approach called SQL mapping to persist objects to a relational database. iBATIS is consistently implemented in both Java and .NET, and there is significant value in a consistent approach to persistence in your applications.

You also learned how iBATIS works. Generally, under the hood iBATIS will run well-written JDBC or ADO.NET code that would otherwise be hard to maintain when coded manually. You found that when compared to JDBC, iBATIS code is less verbose and easier to code.

We discussed how iBATIS, despite its simple design, is a very appropriate framework for both small and large enterprise applications alike. iBATIS has many features that support enterprise-level persistence requirements. Features such as row handlers allow large data sets to be processed efficiently, one record at a time, to ensure that you don't completely drain the system memory.

We also discussed a number of important features that distinguish iBATIS from the competition, and we made a strong case for using iBATIS. These features include the following:

- *Simplicity*—iBATIS is widely regarded as the simplest persistence framework available.
- *Productivity*—Concise code and simple configuration reduces the code to 62 percent of the corresponding JDBC code.
- *Performance*—Architectural enhancements like join mapping speed up data access.
- *Separation of concerns*—iBATIS improves design to ensure future maintainability.
- *Division of labor*—iBATIS helps break up the work to allow teams to leverage expertise.
- *Portability*—iBATIS can be implemented for any full-featured programming language.

After our sales pitch, we admitted that iBATIS is not a silver bullet, because no framework is. We discussed situations where iBATIS would likely not be the ideal approach. For example, if you have full control over the application and the database now and forever, then a full-blown object relational mapper is probably a better choice. On the other hand, if your application works primarily with dynamically generated SQL code, then raw JDBC is the way to go. We also mentioned that iBATIS is primarily designed for relational databases, and if you are using flat files, XML, Excel spreadsheets, or any other nonrelational technology, then you're better off with a different API altogether.

Finally, we ended the chapter by discussing the future of iBATIS. The team has a lot of great design goals for the future, and the Apache Software Foundation will ensure that there is an energetic community capable of supporting it for years to come.

Part 2

iBATIS basics

As you saw in part 1, iBATIS was built on a foundation of simplicity. If you're familiar with JDBC, XML, and SQL, there is very little more you need to learn. This section will tie together the basic features of iBATIS, including installation, configuration, statements, and transactions. It sounds like a lot to learn, but iBATIS simplifies the usual challenges in these areas and these five chapters will have you up and running very quickly.

3 Installing and configuring iBATIS

This chapter covers

- Getting iBATIS
- iBATIS vs. JDBC
- Configuration basics

Installing iBATIS is a quick and simple process. Because it is a library, and not an application, there is no installation process, but you do need to go through a few steps to use iBATIS in your application.

If you are familiar with Java and JDBC, then you will probably read all you need to get up and running in the next paragraph or two. Just in case, we provide an overview of the process that you can read through, and then the rest of the chapter gives more details on the installation process.

To get iBATIS, you have two choices. You can either download a binary distribution and unzip it into a directory, or check out a copy of the source from the Subversion repository and build it. In either case, you will have the same set of files when you are done.

Once you have a build of the distribution, you simply need to add the required JAR files to your application's classpath. If you are using JDK 1.4 or later, there are only two required files:

- `ibatis-common-2.jar`—Shared iBATIS classes[1]
- `ibatis-sqlmap-2.jar`—The iBATIS SQL mapping classes

Those two JAR files contain the most important iBATIS functionality and will be enough for nearly any application that uses iBATIS. Notice that there are no required dependencies on third-party libraries. This is intentional to avoid conflicts with various versions of other frameworks—a welcome benefit for anyone who's been bitten by version conflicts in the past. There are optional JAR files that enable certain features; these will be discussed later in this chapter.

That is all there is to it! You are now ready to start using iBATIS in your application. If that was enough detail, you can skip ahead to section 3.3 to see if there are any other dependencies you may need for other features in iBATIS, or you can jump to section 3.6 and see how to configure iBATIS. If you need more information, the next few sections go into greater detail.

3.1 Getting an iBATIS distribution

As we mentioned earlier, you have two choices for procuring an iBATIS distribution: you can download the ready-to-use prebuilt binary distribution or you can get the source from the Subversion repository and build the distribution from that. Both methods produce the same result—a finished distribution that can be

---

[1] By the time you read this, the common jar file may be merged into a single JAR file with the sqlmap classes, thus reducing the classpath requirement to a single JAR file and further simplifying deployment.

used to add iBATIS to your application, and full source code with debugging information available when necessary.

3.1.1 Binary distribution

This approach is the quickest and easiest way to get started with iBATIS. Because the distribution comes prebuilt, you can simply download it, unpack it, and get started using it.

NOTE The binary distribution of iBATIS is currently available at http://ibatis.apache.org.

The binary distribution of iBATIS contains the precompiled JAR files required to use iBATIS, all of the relevant Java source code that was used to build it, and the basic documentation as well.

3.1.2 Building from source

If you are interested in enhancing the framework, fixing a bug, or if you just want to build it from source so that you know exactly what you have, you can obtain a copy from the Subversion repository and build it yourself from that source. Chapter 12 will delve into the details of building iBATIS in the context of extending the framework, so this section will be somewhat brief, but you should find enough information to get you started.

NOTE The Subversion (or SVN) repository that is referred to here is the version control system used by all new Apache projects. Subversion is a replacement for the Concurrent Version System (CVS) that has been used on many open source projects in the past. The purpose of SVN is to provide an environment where changes to the framework can be made without fear of losing source code (because each developer has a copy of it, and the server has multiple copies of it).

If you want to learn more about Subversion, its home page is http://subversion.tigris.org/.

The Subversion repository for iBATIS is currently located at http://svn.apache.org/repos/asf/ibatis/.

Digging into the repository

The Subversion repository includes both a batch file for Windows and a bash shell script for Linux to build the entire iBATIS distribution. This means that, once you have the source, the only requirement is that you have a JDK installed and that you have `JAVA_HOME` set properly.

All of the requirements for building iBATIS are in the repository either as JAR files or as stub classes that satisfy the compile-time requirements. The repository has the top-level directories shown in table 3.1.

Table 3.1 The directory structure of the source code as available from the Apache Subversion source control system

Directory	Purpose
build	This is where you will find the Ant script used to build the framework, and where the build will put everything that it builds.
devlib	Compile-time requirements that can be included in an Apache project are in this directory.
devsrc	Compile-time requirements that are unavailable for distribution in an Apache project, or are just too big to include in the repository. For those requirements, we have dummy versions of them in the repository that "look like" the application programming interfaces (APIs) and allow us to build iBATIS.
doc	This is where you will find the project documentation.
javadoc	JavaDoc is a tool for generating API documentation in HTML format from doc comments in source code, and this is where example configuration files are placed for the build process.
src	This is where you will find the actual code for the framework. In chapter 12 we will look at the structure of the application in more detail.
test	Unit testing is one way to test the correctness of code. The iBATIS framework uses JUnit for automated unit testing during the build process. The build procedure will run the tests and generate reports based on the results.
tools	Tools that are useful for working with iBATIS are here. For example, you'll find the Abator tool in this directory.

Running the build

To build iBATIS, you need to run `build.bat` (for Windows), or `build.sh` (for Linux or Macintosh). The build process will do the following:

1. Clear out the directories that the build puts its files into.
2. Compile all of the source code.
3. Instrument the compiled classes.
4. Run the unit tests.
5. Build the unit-test and coverage reports.
6. Build the JavaDoc-generated documentation.
7. Build the JAR files for distribution.
8. Zip all of that into a single file, ready for use as the binary distribution.

While it is not necessary to understand the steps that are being performed at this point, we will go over them quickly so that you have some idea of what is happening as the messages fly by on the screen.

The first step is required to make sure that previous builds do not affect the current build—each time you run it, it starts with a clean slate.

The second step is obvious (the code has to be compiled), but the third one may not be. What happens here is that the compiled code is copied and instrumented by a coverage-tracking tool called EMMA. This will be explained shortly.

Next, the unit tests are run over the framework components. As mentioned earlier, this is to verify that the components work as expected at a low level (i.e., when you call a method with known inputs, you see the expected results).

The compatibility tests are used to verify that users who are using version 1.*x* of the framework are able to replace it with version 2.*x* without rewriting their application.

The reports generated by the build process are intended to provide two pieces of information: first, the JUnit report shows the tests that were run and whether or not they were successful. The entry point for those reports is `reports\junit\index.html` (relative to the build directory), and is useful when you are making changes to the framework and want to see if the tests were successful. The second report, which is located at `reports\coverage\coverage.html`, shows coverage for the tests that were run. *Code coverage* is a measure used in software testing that describes the degree to which the source code of a program has been tested. In other words, it shows how effective the tests were. The coverage reports show four statistics:

- *Class coverage*—Which classes have been tested?
- *Method coverage*—Which methods have been tested?
- *Block coverage*—Which blocks of code have been tested?
- *Line coverage*—Which lines of code have been tested?

If you do make a change in the framework, be sure that that you check the test reports to make sure that the existing tests are successful and that the unit tests have been modified to adequately test your change. Once that is done, feel free to upload the changes to the Apache issue-tracking system (JIRA), and if it is something that needs to be added to the framework, one of the committers will try to include it in the next distribution.

So, now that you built a distribution, what do you have? Read on to find out!

3.2 Distribution contents

Regardless of how you get the distribution (unzip or build), you will end up with the same set of seven JAR and ZIP files. A JAR file is a Java archive and is how most Java libraries are distributed—it is actually just a ZIP file with extra information in it. The important files in the distribution are shown in table 3.2.

Table 3.2 The most important files in the iBATIS distribution

File	Purpose
ibatis-common-2.jar	This file contains common components that are used in both the SQL Map and DAO frameworks. In the near future (by the time this book ships) these common classes may be merged into a single JAR file along with the SQL mapper classes currently found in the ibatis-sqlmap-2.jar file.
ibatis-sqlmap-2.jar	This file contains the SQL Map framework components.
ibatis-dao-2.jar	This file contains the DAO framework components.
user-javadoc.zip	This file contains a limited set of the JavaDoc documentation for the project that is specifically trimmed down for people who are only working with the framework, not on the framework.
dev-javadoc.zip	This file contains all of the JavaDoc documentation for the project.
ibatis-src.zip	This file contains the entire source used to build the framework JAR files.

You can begin to see of how lightweight the iBATIS framework is by how few dependencies and files are required. That said, the framework has some optional functionality that can be enabled by including other frameworks such as cglib, a common bytecode enhancement framework that you will learn more about in the next section.

3.3 Dependencies

There are other features of iBATIS that you will probably want to configure, such as bytecode enhancement for lazy loading, which we look at next. Furthermore, in the rest of the book we will be exploring the capabilities of the iBATIS framework. Many of those features will require other open source or commercial packages to make them work properly. To enable those additional features, you will need to fulfill their dependencies and configure iBATIS to use them. This section provides a brief overview of these features.

3.3.1 *Bytecode enhancement for lazy loading*

Bytecode enhancement is a technique that modifies your code at runtime, based on configuration or other rules that you define. For example, the iBATIS framework allows you to relate SQL queries with other SQL queries. It is easy to imagine a situation where you may have a list of customers, a list of orders for each customer (as part of that customer object), and a list of line items as part of the order objects. In that case, you can define your SQL map so that all of those lists are related and loaded from the database automatically, but only if they are actually requested by the application.

NOTE If you are familiar with O/RM tools, you may be thinking that this is the same functionality that they provide. While the functionality is similar, the iBATIS framework does something a bit more flexible. While O/RM tools allow you to relate tables and views only, the iBATIS framework allows you to relate any number of queries, not just database objects.

This functionality is very useful, and can save you some coding in cases where you have related queries. However, if you have 1,000 customers who each have 1,000 orders with 25 line items, the combined data would consist of 25,000,000 objects. Needless to say, this has grown to a point where it is not feasible to have it all in memory at once.

Lazy loading is intended to deal with these kinds of situations. What iBATIS lets you do is load only the data that you actually need.

So, in the previous example, you could reconfigure the SQL map to load the related lists lazily. Therefore, when your user is looking at the list of customers, only the list of 1,000 customers is in memory. The information to load the other lists is kept available, but the data is not loaded until it is actually requested. In other words, the order information is not loaded until the user clicks on a customer to see that customer's orders. At that point, the framework loads that customer's list of 1,000 orders; none of the others are loaded. If the user then clicks on an order to drill down more, only the 25 line items on the selected order are loaded.

So, by making a configuration change and not changing a single line of code, we have gone from 25,000,000 objects to 2,025. This means our application runs in about one ten-thousandth of the time as it did in the original configuration.

3.3.2 *Jakarta Commons Database Connection Pool*

Because iBATIS is a tool for simplifying interaction with a database, connecting to a database is obviously a requirement. Creating new connections on demand can be a time-consuming process (in some cases, taking seconds to complete).

Instead, iBATIS uses a pool of connections that are kept open and shared by all users of the application.

Many vendors provide pooled versions of their drivers, but one problem is that the features and configuration of the pools are as varied as the implementations.

The Jakarta Commons Database Connection Pool (DBCP) project is a wrapper that makes it possible to easily use any JDBC driver as part of a connection pool.

3.3.3 Distributed caching

Caching data in a multiuser environment can be tricky. Caching data in a multi-server environment makes the multiuser environment look simple.

To deal with this problem, iBATIS provides an implementation of caching that uses the OpenSymphony cache (OSCache). OSCache can be configured to cluster across multiple servers to provide scalability and fail-over support.

Now that we've looked at some of the features you can configure in iBATIS, let's add it to your application!

3.4 Adding iBATIS to your application

Once you've configured iBATIS, the only change required to make it available to your application is to add it (and any other dependencies you choose) to your compile-time and runtime classpaths. Let's start with a look at the classpath.

Every computer system needs a way to find what it needs to work. Just like the `$PATH` variable on Linux or `%PATH%` variable on Windows, Java has a path that it uses to find its required components that is called the *classpath*.

In the early days of Java, you would set a `CLASSPATH` environment variable. While this still works, it is messy because it is inherited by every Java application on the system.

The Java Runtime Environment (JRE) also has a special `lib/ext` directory that can be used, but this is not recommended except for a few special cases because all classes in this directory are shared by all applications that use the JRE. We recommend that you don't put iBATIS in that directory.

So how do you make iBATIS available to your application? There are a couple of ways.

3.4.1 Using iBATIS with a stand-alone application

For a stand-alone application, you can set the classpath in a startup script. This is a reasonable approach used by many applications. For example, if you have a stand-alone application that is console based, you would add the iBATIS JARs to the classpath in Linux using the `-cp` switch, like this:

```
java -cp ibatis-sqlmap-2.jar:ibatis-common-2.jar:. MyMainClass
```

If you are using iBATIS in an application server, consult the documentation that comes with the server for the appropriate way to add iBATIS to the classpath for your application.

3.4.2 Using iBATIS with a web application

When setting up a web application, you should put the iBATIS JAR files in the web application's `WEB-INF/lib` directory.

NOTE It may be tempting to put the iBATIS jars into a shared location. For example, with Tomcat, those would be the `shared/lib` or `common/lib` directories. However, putting JARs like this in a shared location is generally a bad idea unless it is required for some reason (like a JDBC driver that is being used by a JNDI data source).

One reason that putting jar files in a shared location is a bad idea is that upgrading becomes riskier. For example, in an environment where you have 10 applications sharing a JAR file, if you need to upgrade the JAR for one application, you have to test it for all 10 that use it. In addition, there are classloader issues to consider. The exact same bytecode loaded by two different classloaders are considered by Java to be different classes. This means that static variables are not shared, and if you try to cast one to the other, you will get a `ClassCastException`, even though the classes are identical. Another classloader issue that you would likely encounter is the matter of how the classloader finds resources. For example, if the `common/lib` classloader in Tomcat loads iBATIS, it cannot see a configuration file in a web application using that classloader.

To sum it up: if you put your iBATIS JAR anywhere but in the `WEB-INF/lib` directory of your web application and it does not work, do not bother posting a question to the mailing lists. The first thing you will be told is to move it to the `WEB-INF/lib` directory.

3.5 iBATIS and JDBC

A deep definition of JDBC is beyond the scope of this book, but we will cover it from a high level to provide a foundation for the rest of the book.

Sun's JDBC API is the standard for database connectivity for the Java programming language. JDBC is one part of the Java technology that allows you to realize the "write once, run anywhere" promise, because all database interaction uses JDBC to access data.

Sun's biggest contribution to JDBC is not in the implementations but in the interfaces. Vendors are required to implement connectivity to their database according to the interfaces defined by JDBC. If they do not, developers are unlikely to use them, because (in the Java world at least) vendor lock-in is considered an anti-pattern to be avoided.

The JDBC API borrows many concepts from Microsoft's ODBC API, and has been a core component of Java since version 1.1, which was released in 1997. In 1999, version 2 of the JDBC API was released, and in 2002, version 3 was released. Version 4 is being designed now as part of JCP-221.

The iBATIS framework currently requires at least version 2 of the API, but is compatible with version 3 as well.

With that brief introduction to JDBC, let's take a look at a few issues you need to be aware of when using it without iBATIS.

3.5.1 Releasing JDBC resources

When using JDBC, it is easy to acquire resources and forget to properly release them. While the garbage collection process may eventually release them, this can take time and is not guaranteed. If these objects do not get released, the application eventually runs out of available resources and crashes. The iBATIS framework helps to manage these resources by removing the burden of managing them from the application developer. Instead of worrying about what resources are being allocated and released, developers can focus on the data they need and how to get it. However, developers can still manage these resources manually if they so choose.

3.5.2 SQL injection

Another common problem (more prevalent in web applications) is that of *SQL injection*, which is a way of using an application to execute SQL in a way that was not intended by the developer. If an application uses string concatenation to build SQL statements without properly escaping the parameters, a malicious user can pass in parameters that will change the query. Take the example of a query like `select * from product where id = 5`. If the 5 comes directly from the user, and is concatenated to `select * from product where id =` then the user could pass in `5 or 1=1` to change the meaning of the SQL statement. It would be even worse if the user passed in `5; delete from orders`, which would dutifully select the one record, then clean out your orders table. With flexibility comes risk, and therefore using iBATIS incorrectly can still expose your application to a SQL injection attack. However, iBATIS makes it easier to protect the application by always using `PreparedStatements` that are not susceptible to this type of attack.

Only statements that use the explicit SQL string substitution syntax are at risk in iBATIS. Consider this quick example. The following statement allows for a dynamic table name and column name:

```
SELECT * FROM $TABLE_NAME$ WHERE $COLUMN_NAME$ = #value#
```

Such a statement is flexible and useful in some situations, but exposes you to SQL injection and should therefore be used judiciously. This is not an iBATIS problem, as you'd have the same problem no matter how you executed such a statement. Always be sure to validate user input that will have an impact on dynamically constructed SQL statements.

3.5.3 Reducing the complexity

While JDBC is a very powerful tool, it is also a very low-level API. To help better understand where iBATIS fits in your application, let's draw an analogy.

Years ago, to create a web application with Java, you would have to start at the HTTP level, and write an application that listened to a port and responded to requests. After a few years of this, Sun provided us with a Servlet specification that we could use as a starting point so that we would not have to do this sort of socket- and port-level development. Not long after that came the Struts framework, which took web development with Java to the next level.

Most Java developers today would never seriously consider writing a web-based application starting at the HTTP protocol or even with straight Servlets—instead they would get a Servlet container like Tomcat and use it with the Struts framework (or something similar like Spring or WebWork).

To draw a parallel to persistence, when Java 1.0 came out, there was no JDBC specification. Developers doing database work had to figure out how to talk directly to the database via its native network protocols. With the release of version 1.1 of Java, JDBC entered the picture, and we were given a starting point for working with databases instead of having to work with sockets and ports. The iBATIS framework is to database development what Struts is to HTTP. Although you could write applications by opening a port to the database server or using straight JDBC, it is much simpler to write your application using a tool like iBATIS and letting it deal with `Connection`, `Statement`, and `ResultSet` objects instead of mixing them into your business logic.

Just as Struts does, iBATIS provides you with an abstraction to suppress a great deal of complexity that comes along with the lower-level components that it uses. It does not completely remove them from your application, but it lets you avoid dealing with them until you need to.

As an example of the complexity that iBATIS takes care of for you, let's look at the pattern for properly allocating and ensuring the release of a JDBC connection:

```
Connection connection = null;
try {
  connection = dataSource.getConnection();
  if (null == connection){
    // kaboom
  } else {
    useConnection(connection);
  }
} catch (SQLException e) {
  // kaboom
}finally{
  if (null != connection) {
    try {
      connection.close();
    } catch (SQLException e) {
      // kaboom
    }
  }
 }
```

That is almost 20 lines of code to simply get a `Connection` object, use it, and then close it properly. Beyond that, the same pattern is required for safely working with `Statement` and `ResultSet` objects. When you consider what is required to implement many of the features using plain JDBC that iBATIS handles for you—such as getting a connection to the database, parameter and result mapping, lazy loading, and caching—it becomes clear that it would take a great deal of careful coding. Luckily, iBATIS is a lot easier to configure and work with, as you'll see in the remainder of this and the next few chapters.

3.6 iBATIS configuration continued

In chapter 2, we looked very briefly at how to configure iBATIS (so briefly, in fact, that if you haven't read that section, don't worry about it). In this section, we build on that basic configuration by creating the SQL Map configuration file. This file is the brain of iBATIS, as shown in figure 3.1.

In this figure, we have the `SqlMapConfig` file at the top, which is where we define global configuration options, and also reference the individual `SqlMaps` themselves. The `SqlMaps` in turn define the mapped statements that will be used in conjunction with input that your application provides to interact with the database.

Let's take a closer look at how you'd use this configuration file.

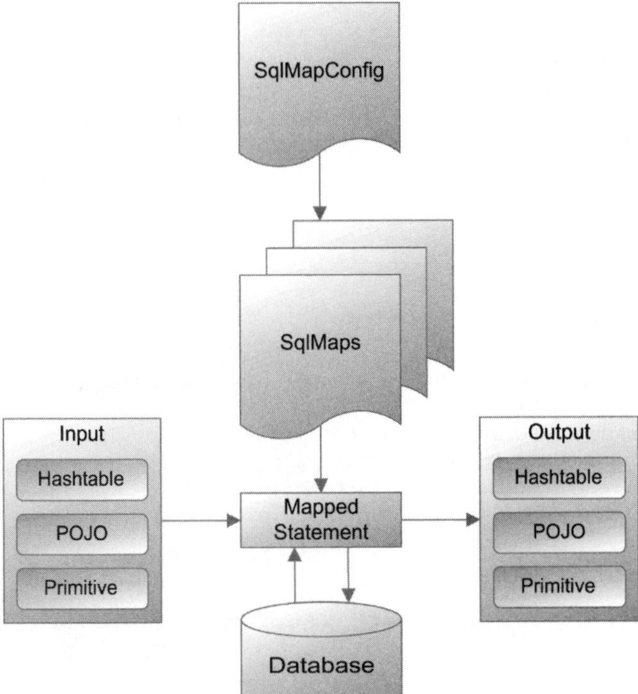

Figure 3.1 Conceptual iBATIS configuration hub with SqlMapConfig at the head of it all

3.6.1 The SQL Map configuration file

The SQL Map configuration file (`SqlMapConfig.xml`) is the central hub for configuring iBATIS, as you can see in the conceptual diagram in figure 3.1. Everything from the database connection to the actual `SqlMaps` to be used is supplied to the framework by this file.

> **NOTE** The main configuration file is commonly named `SqlMapConfig.xml`. Although it does not have to use that name, we will follow the convention here.

Listing 3.1 shows an example configuration file that we will discuss in the following sections.

Listing 3.1 SqlMapConfig.xml

```
<?xml version="1.0" encoding="UTF-8" ?>
<!DOCTYPE sqlMapConfig
    PUBLIC "-//ibatis.apache.org//DTD SQL Map Config 2.0//EN"
    "http://ibatis.apache.org/dtd/sql-map-config-2.dtd">
```

```
<sqlMapConfig>

  <properties resource="db.properties" />

  <settings                                    ❶ Global configuration options
    useStatementNamespaces="false"
    cacheModelsEnabled="true"
    enhancementEnabled="true"
    lazyLoadingEnabled="true"
    maxRequests="32"
    maxSessions="10"
    maxTransactions="5"
  />

  <transactionManager type="JDBC" >    ❷ Transaction manager
    <dataSource type="SIMPLE">
      <property name="JDBC.Driver" value="${driver}"/>
      <property name="JDBC.ConnectionURL" value="${url}"/>
      <property name="JDBC.Username" value="${user}"/>
      <property name="JDBC.Password" value="${pword}"/>
    </dataSource>
  </transactionManager>                          References to ❸
                                                  SqlMap files
  <sqlMap resource="org/apache/mapper2/ii15/SqlMap.xml" />

</sqlMapConfig>
```

In the next few sections, we will explore the options at ❶ in listing 3.1, as well as describe the transaction manager ❷. In the next three chapters (4, 5, and 6), we will examine mapped statements that are defined in ❸. Then in chapter 7, we will come back and talk about transactions in detail.

3.6.2 The <properties> element

The `<properties>` element allows you to provide a list of name/value pairs outside of the main configuration file that can be used to further generalize the configuration. This is useful when deploying an application, because you can have the shared configuration in one place but isolate values that vary depending on the environment in a properties file.

There are two ways to specify the properties file to be used, each of which is an attribute of the `<properties>` element. The choices are

- `resource`—A resource (or file) on the classpath
- `url`—A Uniform Resource Locator (URL)

When using the `resource` attribute, the classloader will attempt to locate that resource on the application's classpath. This is called a *resource*, because we are using a classloader to read it. The Java documentation refers to resources when accessing data this way, because while it may just be a file on the local files system, it is just as possible that it is an entry in a JAR file, possibly even on a different computer.

The `url` attribute is handled by the `java.net.URL` class, so it can be any valid URL that it understands and can use to load data.

In our earlier example, we used the `<properties>` element to keep the database configuration details out of our XML file and put them in a simple properties file called `db.properties` that exits on our classpath. This separation is useful for a number of reasons, not the least of which is simplicity. Let's assume that our `db.properties` file contained the following four property definitions:

```
driver=com.mysql.jdbc.Driver
url=jdbc:mysql://localhost/test
user=root
pword=apple
```

We refer to the properties file with the following line taken from our previous example:

```
<properties resource="db.properties" />
```

Finally, we use the properties by name using a syntax that will be familiar to many people:

```
<property name="JDBC.Driver" value="${driver}"/>
<property name="JDBC.ConnectionURL" value="${url}"/>
<property name="JDBC.Username" value="${user}"/>
<property name="JDBC.Password" value="${pword}"/>
```

At this point you should be thinking to yourself, "Gee, that looks just like the way every other tool uses properties!"

3.6.3 The <settings> element

The `<settings>` element is a bit of a grab bag of configuration options. You set these options by inserting attributes into the `<settings>` element. Several settings are available, and each of them is global to this SQL Map instance.

lazyLoadingEnabled

Lazy loading is a technique in which you load only the information that is essential, and defer the loading of other data until it is specifically requested. In other words, you want to have the application do as little as possible until it is absolutely required.

In the previous chapter, we talked about an example where you had 1,000 customer accounts with 1,000 orders each, and 25 items on each order. Loading all of that data would require creating 25,000,000 objects, and keeping them in memory. Using lazy loading we reduce that requirement to a number closer to 2,500, which is one ten-thousandth of the original number.

The `lazyLoadingEnabled` setting is used to indicate whether or not you want to use lazy loading when you have related mapped statements (which we will talk about in section 6.2.2). Valid values are `true` or `false`, and the default value is `true`.

In our sample `SqlMapConfig.xml` file earlier, lazy loading is enabled.

cacheModelsEnabled

Caching is a performance-enhancement technique where recently used data is kept in memory based on the assumption that it will be needed again in the future. The `cacheModelsEnabled` setting is used to indicate whether or not you want iBATIS to use caching. As with most of the values of the `<settings>` element, valid values are `true` or `false`.

In our earlier example, caching is enabled, which is the default. To take advantage of caching, you must also configure cache models for your mapped statements, which are introduced in section 9.1.

enhancementEnabled

The `enhancementEnabled` setting is used to indicate whether or not you want to use cglib optimized classes to improve performance with lazy loading. Again, valid values are `true` or `false`, and the default value is `true`.

> **NOTE** cglib is a runtime code generation library that allows iBATIS to optimize certain functions, like the setting of JavaBeans properties. Also, it allows you to lazily load concrete classes and thus avoid having to create an interface for the lazy loaded type. You can get cglib from http://cglib.sourceforge.net/. As with any performance enhancement, you should probably avoid using it unless you are sure you need it.

In our previous example, we are allowing enhancements, but if cglib is not on the classpath, the enhancements will be silently disabled.

useStatementNamespaces

The `useStatementNamespaces` setting is used to tell iBATIS to require qualified names for mapped statements. Valid values are `true` or `false`, and the default value is `false`.

In other words, when the SQL maps are defined (see the section 4.2.1 for more information on that), the map name is to be used to qualify the mapped statement.

So, for example, you may have a SQL map named `Account`, with mapped statements named `insert`, `update`, `delete`, and `getAll`. When you want to insert an account, you would call the `Account.insert` mapped statement when namespaces are used. You can have as many mapped statements (in other maps) named `insert` as needed, and the names will not collide.

While you could accomplish the same thing using names like `insertAccount`, using namespaces can be very helpful when working with large systems, because it helps in finding statements if they are not organized logically.

maxRequests (deprecated)

A request is any SQL operation—an insert, update, delete, or a stored procedure call. In our example, we are scaling back and only allow 32 requests to be active at one time instead of the default value of 512.

maxSessions (deprecated)

A session is a thread-level mechanism that is used to track information about a group of related transactions and requests. In our example, we allow only 10 sessions at any time, instead of the default value of 128.

maxTransactions (deprecated)

A transaction is just what it appears: a database transaction. As with `maxRequests`, we have reduced the number of active transactions to 5 from the default value of 32.

> **NOTE** These settings are complicated to understand, but luckily they are deprecated. In future versions of iBATIS, you won't need to configure them manually. So, for the most part, you should simply never modify them. The default settings will work for most systems of a reasonable scale. If you do modify the settings, always ensure that `maxRequests` is larger than `maxSessions`, and that `maxSessions` is larger than `maxTransactions`. A simple rule of thumb is to keep the ratios the same. Also note that none of these settings directly impacts the number of connections in your connection pool or any other resources that your application server is responsible for managing.

OK, that is all you need to know about the `<settings>` element. Let's move on—we are almost done!

3.6.4 The <typeAlias> elements

Nobody likes to type in a name like `org.apache.ibatis.jgamestore.domain.Account` if they do not have to. The `<typeAlias>` element lets you define an alias such as `Account` that can be used in place of that fully qualified class name.

In our example, we do not have a real use for this yet, but we will soon. We can demonstrate how it works by providing an alias that we will use later in our SQL Map.

To create that alias, insert an element like this:

```
<typeAlias alias="Account"
  type="org.apache.ibatis.jgamestore.domain.Account" />
```

This `Account` alias is available any time after it is defined in the configuration process. You can use either the fully qualified name or the alias to tell iBATIS what you want to use any time you have to supply a data type.

The framework defines several type aliases to save developers from having to add them manually, as shown in table 3.3.

Table 3.3 Built-in type alias definitions that save you from having to type some of these very long class names

Alias	Type
Transaction manager aliases	
JDBC	com.ibatis.sqlmap.engine.transaction.jdbc.JdbcTransactionConfig
JTA	com.ibatis.sqlmap.engine.transaction.jta.JtaTransactionConfig
EXTERNAL	com.ibatis.sqlmap.engine.transaction.external.ExternalTransactionConfig
Data types	
string	java.lang.String
byte	java.lang.Byte
long	java.lang.Long
short	java.lang.Short
int	java.lang.Integer
integer	java.lang.Integer
double	java.lang.Double
float	java.lang.Float
boolean	java.lang.Boolean
date	java.util.Date
decimal	java.math.BigDecimal
object	java.lang.Object
map	java.util.Map
hashmap	java.util.HashMap

Table 3.3 Built-in type alias definitions that save you from having to type some of these very long class names *(continued)*

Alias	Type
Data types *(continued)*	
list	java.util.List
arraylist	java.util.ArrayList
collection	java.util.Collection
iterator	java.util.Iterator
Data source factory types	
SIMPLE	com.ibatis.sqlmap.engine.datasource.SimpleDataSourceFactory
DBCP	com.ibatis.sqlmap.engine.datasource.DbcpDataSourceFactory
JNDI	com.ibatis.sqlmap.engine.datasource.JndiDataSourceFactory
Cache controller types	
FIFO	com.ibatis.sqlmap.engine.cache.fifo.FifoCacheController
LRU	com.ibatis.sqlmap.engine.cache.lru.LruCacheController
MEMORY	com.ibatis.sqlmap.engine.cache.memory.MemoryCacheController
OSCACHE	com.ibatis.sqlmap.engine.cache.oscache.OSCacheController
XML result types	
Dom	com.ibatis.sqlmap.engine.type.DomTypeMarker
domCollection	com.ibatis.sqlmap.engine.type.DomCollectionTypeMarker
Xml	com.ibatis.sqlmap.engine.type.XmlTypeMarker
XmlCollection	com.ibatis.sqlmap.engine.type.XmlCollectionTypeMarker

The built-in type aliases are real time-savers, but remember that you can also define your own to simplify things even more.

3.6.5 The <transactionManager> element

Because iBATIS is about making database access simpler, it will deal with database transactions for you. While transaction management will be discussed in greater detail in chapter 8, what it means for now is that when you are using iBATIS, some sort of transaction manager implementation is required. There are several predefined transaction managers that you can choose from. The `type` attribute of the `<transactionManager>` element is used to specify which transaction manager should be used. Several implementations are provided out of the box, as listed in table 3.4.

Table 3.4 Built-in transaction managers

Name	Description
JDBC	Used to provide simple JDBC-based transaction management. For most cases, this is all you need.
JTA	Used to provide container-based transaction management in your application.
EXTERNAL	Used to provide no transaction management, and assumes that the application will manage the transactions instead of iBATIS.

NOTE You may recognize the names of those transaction managers from the previous table. They are simply type aliases for the fully qualified names of the classes that implement them. This is a common pattern in the iBATIS configuration files.

Another setting that is available for the transaction manager is the `commitRequired` attribute. This can be set to either `true` or `false`, and the default value is `false`. This attribute is primarily used in situations where a commit or rollback is required before a connection can be released.

For some operations (like selects and stored procedure calls) transactions are not normally required, and are generally ignored. Some drivers (like the Sybase driver, for instance) will not release a connection until any transactions that were started for that connection are either committed or rolled back. In those cases, the `commitRequired` attribute can be used to force that to happen even if nothing has happened that would normally require a transaction.

The <property> elements

Each transaction manager can have different configuration options. Because of that, the iBATIS framework uses the `<property>` element to allow you to specify any number of named values that can be supplied to the transaction manager implementation.

The <dataSource> element

In Java, the standard method for working with a connection pool is by using a `javax.sql.DataSource` object. The `<dataSource>` element of the transaction manager has a type attribute that tells iBATIS what class to instantiate and use for its data source factory. The name of this element is a bit misleading, because it does not really define a `DataSource`, but a `DataSourceFactory` implementation, which will be used to create the actual `DataSource`.

Three data source factory implementations come with iBATIS; each is listed in table 3.5, along with a brief description. These will be discussed in more detail in chapter 8.

Table 3.5 Data source factories

Name	Description
SIMPLE	The simple data source factory is just that. It is used to configure a data source that has a simple connection pool built into it, and everything it needs is included with the iBATIS framework except the actual JDBC driver.
DBCP	The DBCP data source factory is for using the Jakarta Commons Database Connection Pool implementation.
JNDI	The JNDI data source factory is used to allow iBATIS to share a container-based data source that is located via JNDI.

Similar to the `<transactionManager>` element, the `<dataSource>` element can have any number of properties passed to it for configuration using nested property elements.

3.6.6 The <typeHandler> element

The iBATIS framework uses type handlers to convert data from the JDBC database-specific data types to your application data types, so you can create an application that uses a database in a way that makes the database as transparent as possible. A type handler is essentially a translator—it takes a result set column and translates it into a bean property.

In most cases, these components are very simple, like the `StringTypeHandler` that simply calls the result set's `getString` method and returns it as a String. In other cases, you may have more complex translation requirements. For example, if your database does not have a Boolean data type, you may use a single character with `Y` and `N` values to indicate `true` and `false` in the database, but then translate that character to Boolean in your application classes.

In chapter 12, you will learn more about how to build custom type handlers to deal with these sorts of situations, so we will not go into much more detail here. To deal with this situation, you need to create two classes: a custom type handler and a type handler callback.

If you write a custom type handler, you need to tell iBATIS how and when to use them. You do that by using the `<typeHandler>` element and telling it what it is translating between: the `jdbcType` and the `javaType`. In addition, the callback class that is used to manage the type handler is required.

Note that in most cases you'll never need to write a custom type handler. iBATIS has prebuilt type handlers to deal with 99 percent of the cases. Usually a custom type handler is only necessary if you're using an odd database or driver that does not support the typical type mapping common to most databases. Avoid writing custom type handlers if you can, to keep your application simple.

3.6.7 The <sqlMap> element

The last section of the `SqlMapConfig.xml` file is where we configure the `<sqlMap>` elements. This is where you start to get into the real "heavy lifting" that iBATIS can do for you.

The `<sqlMap>` element is actually one of the simplest elements in this file, because it only requires one of two attributes to be set.

The `resource` attribute is used if you want to put your SQL Map files on the Java classpath and refer to them that way. Generally, this is the easiest way, because they can be stored in a JAR file or a WAR file, and simply referenced relative to the root of the classpath.

In other cases, you may want to be more explicit about the location of the files. In those cases, you can use the `url` attribute. This attribute can use the `java.net.URL` class to resolve the location of the file, so you can use any URL value that can be understood by that class.

3.7 Summary

Installing iBATIS is a very simple process. In this chapter, we looked at the two ways to get the framework and what to do with it once you have it. Because iBATIS was designed to be simple to use, it has very few dependencies and can be extended to use other tools very easily.

While JDBC is a very powerful API, it is also a low-level API, and writing solid code that uses it can be difficult. With iBATIS you can step back from the complexity of dealing with database components, and focus more on the business problems that you are trying to solve.

We looked at a simple iBATIS configuration—quite possibly the simplest case ever written! In the next chapter, we will examine how to configure it in more detail and how to make it fit into your application perfectly.

In this chapter, we also explored the iBATIS configuration files. When using any framework it is essential to have a solid understanding of the fundamentals. This chapter provided just that—an understanding of the fundamentals or a quick reference guide.

Put a bookmark in this chapter and return to it when you get stuck. If you do not find the answer here, you are likely to find a pointer to another chapter where the answer can be found.

The Java API that we will examine in the next few chapters is pretty small in scope, but the framework will behave differently based on how you configure it. We will cover every configuration option again in the next few chapters in much greater detail and with more context and code examples.

4 Working with mapped statements

This chapter covers

- JavaBeans
- Using the iBATIS API
- Mapped statements
- Using parameters and results

In previous chapters we looked at how to configure iBATIS `SqlMaps`, and you saw an example of a mapped statement. You should now have a foundation on which to start building more of the database access layer for an application.

This chapter and the next examine mapped statements in greater detail, and discuss using SQL maps to create them. In this chapter, we first look at mapped statements in general and what you need to know to use them. Then we explain how to get data out of the database using mapped statements that return typed objects (JavaBeans), and how to pass in parameters to limit the data being returned. In chapter 5, you will learn how to update a database with mapped statements.

4.1 Starting with the basics

There are a few conceptual challenges to understand before getting started with iBATIS. You will need to have a basic understanding of Java development using JavaBeans. You will also need to know what iBATIS makes available in terms of the types of SQL statements you can use, and the API that you need to use to execute those statements.

As mentioned before, iBATIS is not an object/relational mapping (O/RM) tool; it is a query mapping tool. Because of that, the API that we will be looking at is not the only API you have available. You can still use any other API you want to create the beans that your application will use or to access your database. So, if you find that you are unable to accomplish something with iBATIS, you can still use the straight JDBC API without too much concern about the repercussions. Keep that freedom in mind as we look at what iBATIS does make available—while it does not solve every problem, it does attempt to simplify most of your data access chores.

4.1.1 Creating JavaBeans

While the use of JavaBeans is not required by iBATIS, we do recommend using them in most (but not all) cases. If you are new to Java, creating JavaBeans is quite simple: a JavaBean is a reusable component that can be developed and then assembled to create more sophisticated components and applications. The JavaBean specification (all 114 pages of it) is freely available from Sun. A simple search at http://java.sun.com should yield this document.

We do not have that many pages to spare here, so we will try to condense the specification down to something more relevant to iBATIS.

What makes a bean?

Essentially, the JavaBean specification is a set of rules for defining components for use with Java. We have those rules to make it possible for tool creators (like the people who work on iBATIS) to know how to interact with the components that we use in our applications. Think of the specification as a middle-ground common language for framework developers and application developers.

The only rules in the specification that apply to iBATIS are the ones that concern property naming. Property names are defined in a JavaBean by a pair of methods that the specification refers to as *accessor methods.* Here is the pattern for creating accessor methods for a property named `value`:

```
public void setValue(ValueType newValue);
public ValueType getValue();
```

These accessor methods define a simple property named `value` with a lowercase *v.* Java bean properties should always start with a lowercase letter, with very few exceptions. The types for the two methods should always be the same. If you have a setter that accepts a Long, and a getter that returns an Integer, you will have problems. Always make them the same.

Property names with multiple words are named using a pattern known as camel case (or camelCase), which means that uppercase letters are used to separate the words:

```
public void setSomeValue(ValueType newValue);
public ValueType getSomeValue();
```

When creating properties for JavaBeans, it's important to remember that abbreviations are generally treated as words, not individual letters. For example, the abbreviation URL would become a property named `url`, and the methods `getUrl` and `setUrl` would be used to access that property.

Another oddity in the specification is that property names with the second letter capitalized are treated differently. If the second letter of the property name is uppercase, then the name after the get or set part of the method for that property is used as the property name, and the case is left unchanged. We will clarify this confusing rule in table 4.1 (which also shows get and set methods for the properties listed).

Properties of type boolean (the primitive) are allowed to use `isProperty` for the getter, but if the type is Boolean (the object, or boxed version), then the standard `getProperty` name is required instead.

Table 4.1 Sample JavaBean property names and methods

Property name/type	Get method	Set method
`xcoordinate`/Double	`public Double getXcoordinate()`	`public void setXcoordinate (Double newValue)`
`xCoordinate`/Double	`public Double getxCoordinate()`	`public void setxCoordinate (Double newValue)`
`XCoordinate`/Double	`public Double getXCoordinate()`	`public void setXCoordinate (Double newValue)`
`Xcoordinate`/Double	Not allowed	Not allowed
`student`/Boolean	`public Boolean getStudent()`	`public void setStudent(Boolean newValue)`
`student`/boolean	`public boolean getStudent()` `public boolean isStudent()`	`public void setStudent(boolean newValue)`

Indexed properties are properties that represent an array of values. For example, if you have an `Order` bean, you may want an indexed property for the `OrderItem` objects associated with that `Order`. According to the specification, the signatures for the get and set methods for it would be

```
public void setOrderItem(OrderItem[] newArray);
public OrderItem[] getOrderItem();
public void setOrderItem(int index, OrderItem oi);
public OrderItem getOrderItem(int index);
```

In our experience, overloading bean properties (as the specification suggests, and as demonstrated in the previous example of indexed properties) is not very well supported by most tools and can often cause a great deal of confusion for developers. It is also not immediately clear by looking at the names what the difference is between the two `getOrderItem()` methods. For that reason, we prefer to use the following signatures instead:

```
public void setOrderItemArray(OrderItem[] newArray);
public OrderItem[] getOrderItemArray();
public void setOrderItem(int index, OrderItem oi);
public OrderItem getOrderItem(int index);
```

Here's another (nonstandard, but more functional) way to implement set methods:

```
public BeanType setProperty(PropType newValue){
      this.property = newValue;
      return this;
};
```

The reason for having the setter return the bean instance is so that you can chain calls to the setters:

```
myBean.setProperty(x)
      .setSomeProperty(y);
```

For two properties, it is not all that useful, but if you have a bean in which you have more, it can save you some typing.

Bean navigation

When using tools that are bean aware, properties are often referred to using something called *dot notation,* which means that instead of calling getters and setters, you refer to the properties defined by them. The property name is determined by using the rules discussed earlier. Table 4.2 contains some examples.

Table 4.2 Bean navigation examples

Java code	Dot notation
anOrder.getAccount().getUsername()	anOrder.account.username
anOrder.getOrderItem().get(0).getProductId()	anOrder.orderItem[0].productId
anObject.getID()	anObject.ID
anObject.getxCoordinate()	anObject.xCoordinate

If you have a bean and want to see the names of the properties of that bean, the following sample method will use the built-in Java `Introspector` class to output them:

```
public void listPropertyNames(Class c)
    throws IntrospectionException {
  PropertyDescriptor[] pd;
  pd = Introspector.getBeanInfo(c).getPropertyDescriptors();
  for(int i=0; i< pd.length; i++) {
    System.out.println(pd[i].getName()
        + " (" + pd[i].getPropertyType().getName() + ")");
  }
}
```

This example uses the `Introspector` class to get an array of `PropertyDescriptor` objects for a bean, and then walks through that array to display the name and type of the properties that the bean exposes, which can be a useful troubleshooting aid.

4.1.2 The SqlMap API

Now that you have an understanding of what JavaBeans are, we can start to look at the API that iBATIS gives you for working with them. The `SqlMapClient` interface has over 30 methods on it, and we will get to all of them in the coming chapters. But for now, let's look only at the parts of it that we will be using in this chapter.

The queryForObject() methods

The `queryForObject()` methods are used to get a single row from the database into a Java object, and come with two signatures:

- `Object queryForObject(String id, Object parameter) throws SQLException;`
- `Object queryForObject(String id, Object parameter, Object result) throws SQLException;`

The first version is the more commonly used one, and creates the returned object for you if it has a default constructor (and throws a runtime exception if it does not).

The second form accepts an object that will be used as the return value—after running the mapped statement the properties will be set on it instead of creating a new object. The second form is useful if you have an object that cannot be easily created because of a protected constructor or the lack of a default constructor.

Something to remember when using `queryForObject()` is that if the query returns more than one row, this method will throw an exception, because it checks to make sure that only one row is returned.

The queryForList() methods

The `queryForList()` methods are used to get one or more rows from the database into a List of Java objects, and like `queryForObject()`, they also come in two versions:

- `List queryForList(String id, Object parameter) throws SQLException;`
- `List queryForList(String id, Object parameter, int skip, int max) throws SQLException;`

The first method returns all of the objects that are returned by the mapped statement. The second returns only a subset of them—it skips ahead up to the number indicated by the `skip` parameter, and returns only `max` rows from the query. So, if you have a mapped statement that returns 100 rows but you only want the first set of 10 rows, you can pass in 0 for `skip` and 10 for `max` to get them. If you want the second set of 10 records, you can repeat the call with a value of 10 for `skip` to get the next 10 rows.

The queryForMap() methods

The `queryForMap()` methods return a Map (instead of a List) of one or more rows from the database as Java objects. Just like the other query methods, it has two forms as well:

- `Map queryForMap(String id, Object parameter, String key) throws SQLException;`
- `Map queryForMap(String id, Object parameter, String key, String value) throws SQLException;`

The first method will execute a query and return a Map of objects, where the key to the objects is identified by the property named by the `key` parameter, and the value objects are the complete objects from the mapped statement. The second form will return a similar Map, but the objects will be the property of the objects identified by the `value` parameter.

This is one of those times when an example is worth a thousand words. Let's consider an example where you have a mapped statement that returns a set of accounts. By using the first method, you could create a Map that had the `accountId` property as the key to the map and the full account bean as the value. Using the second method, you could create a Map that had the `accountId` property as the key to the map, and only the account name as the value:

```
Map accountMap = sqlMap.queryForMap(
    "Account.getAll",
    null,
    "accountId");
System.out.println(accountMap);
accountMap = sqlMap.queryForMap(
    "Account.getAll",
    null,
    "accountId",
    "username");
System.out.println(accountMap);
```

Now that you have seen all the portions of the API that you need to start using iBATIS, let's take a look at the different ways in which you can create mapped statements.

4.1.3 Mapped statement types

Before you can use the `SqlMap` API that you just learned about, you need to know how to create mapped statements to make it work. In the previous example, we called a mapped statement named `Account.getAll`, but we did not talk about where it came from (except in chapter 2, where we did our simple application). This was an example of a `<select>` mapped statement.

There are several types of mapped statements, each with its own purpose and set of attributes and child elements. This may sound obvious, but generally it is best to use the statement type that matches what you are trying to do (i.e., use an `<insert>` to insert data instead of an `<update>` statement, or the more generic `<statement>` type), because the specific types are more descriptive, and in some cases provide additional functionality (as is the case with `<insert>` and its `<selectKey>` child element—which we'll cover in section 5.2).

Table 4.3 contains each type of mapped statement (and two other related XML elements that we will discuss later) as well as some additional information about them.

Table 4.3 Mapped statement types and related XML elements

Statement type	Attributes	Child elements	Uses	More details
<select>	id parameterClass resultClass parameterMap resultMap cacheModel	All dynamic elements	Selecting data	Section 4.2; chapter 8
<insert>	id parameterClass parameterMap	All dynamic elements selectKey	Inserting data	Section 5.2; chapter 8
<update>	id parameterClass parameterMap	All dynamic elements	Updating data	Section 5.3; chapter 8
<delete>	id parameterClass parameterMap	All dynamic elements	Deleting data	Section 5.3; chapter 8
<procedure>	id parameterClass resultClass parameterMap resultMap xmlResultName	All dynamic elements	Calling a stored procedure	Section 5.5; chapter 8

Table 4.3 Mapped statement types and related XML elements *(continued)*

Statement type	Attributes	Child elements	Uses	More details
<statement>	id parameterClass resultClass parameterMap resultMap cacheModel xmlResultName	All dynamic elements	Catching all statement types that can be used to execute nearly anything	Section 6.3.1; chapter 8
<sql>	id	All dynamic elements	Not really a mapped statement, but used to make components that can be used in mapped statements	Section 4.2; chapter 8
<include>	refid	None	Not really a mapped statement, but used to insert components created with the `<sql>` type into mapped statements	Section 4.2

In this chapter, we focus on the `<select>` mapped statement type. In addition to the mapped statement types, two additional elements are included in table 4.3 that are commonly used to build mapped statements: the `<sql>` element and the `<include>` element. These elements work together to create and insert components into mapped statements. You will find them useful when you have complex SQL fragments that you want to be able to reuse without duplicating them.

The `<sql>` element is used to create text fragments that can be grouped together to create complete SQL statements. For example, you may have a query with a complex set of conditions for the `WHERE` section. If you need to select a record count using the same complex set of conditions but do not want to duplicate them, you can put them into a `<sql>` fragment and include them in the query that does the count, as well as in the query that returns the actual data. Listing 4.1 contains a simple example.

Listing 4.1 An example of the <sql> and <include> tags

```
<sql id="select-order">                    <-- (1) Gets all columns
  select * from order
</sql>
                                            (2) Gets count
<sql id="select-count">                    <--
  select count(*) as value from order
```

```
</sql>

<sql id="where-shipped-after-value">     ❸ Includes orders shipped after date
  <![CDATA[
  where shipDate > #value:DATE#
  ]]>
</sql>

<select                                  ❹ Gets all columns for orders shipped after date
  id="getOrderShippedAfter"
  resultClass="map">
  <include refid="select-order" />
  <include refid="where-shipped-after-value" />
</select>

<select                                  ❺ Gets count of orders shipped after date
  id="getOrderCountShippedAfter"
  resultClass="int">
  <include refid="select-count" />
  <include refid="where-shipped-after-value" />
</select>
```

While listing 4.1 is a fairly trivial example, it shows the technique clearly without making it overly complex. We define three SQL fragments: one to get all the columns from a table ❶, another to get a count of the rows returned from a query ❷, and one more ❸ for the condition to use to filter that data. We then build two mapped statements that return the full objects, `getOrderShippedAfter` ❹, and the count, `getOrderCountShippedAfter` ❺, using those fragments. In this case it would have been easier to just duplicate the SQL code, but the process of duplication becomes much more error-prone when you start to use more complex operations or dynamic SQL (see chapter 8 for more on Dynamic SQL use) in a SQL fragment.

4.2 Using <select> mapped statements

Selecting data from a database is one of the most fundamental uses of an application. The iBATIS framework makes most `SELECT` statements effortless, and provides many features to make it possible to access virtually any data you want out of your database.

4.2.1 Using inline parameters with the # placeholders

So far, all of the previous examples have been unrealistically simple, because rarely do you want to execute a query without any selection criteria. Inline parameters are an easy way to start adding selection criteria to your mapped statements and can be designated by using one of two different methods.

The first method is by using the hash (#) syntax. Here is an example using that syntax to pass a simple inline parameter in to get a single `Account` bean out by its `accountId` value:

```
<select id="getByIdValue" resultClass="Account">
  select
    accountId,
    username,
    password,
    firstName,
    lastName,
    address1,
    address2,
    city,
    state,
    postalCode,
    country
  from Account
  where accountId = #value#
</select>
```

The `#value#` string in this mapped statement is a placeholder that tells iBATIS that you are going to pass in a simple parameter that it needs to apply to the SQL before executing it. This mapped statement could be called this way:

```
account = (Account) sqlMap.queryForObject(
    "Account.getByIdValue",
    new Integer(1));
```

Let's take a few minutes to look into what the iBATIS framework does with this statement. First, it looks up the mapped statement named `Account.getByIdValue`, and transforms the `#value#` placeholder into a prepared statement parameter:

```
select
  accountId,
  username,
  password,
  firstName,
  lastName,
  address1,
  address2,
  city,
  state,
  postalCode,
  country
from Account
where accountId = ?
```

Next, it sets the parameter to 1 (from the Integer passed to `queryForObject()` as the second parameter above), and finally executes the prepared statement. It then takes the resulting row, maps it to an object, and returns it.

While this may seem like low-level information, it is important to understand what is happening here. One of the most frequently asked questions regarding iBATIS is: "How do I use `LIKE` in my `WHERE` clauses?" Looking at the previous statement, it is obvious why the parameter that is coming in has to have the wildcards in it, and why they cannot be inserted into the SQL statement easily. There are three possible solutions to that dilemma:

- The value of the parameter passed in has to have the SQL wildcard characters in it.
- The text to search for has to be part of a SQL expression (e.g., `'%' || #value# || '%'`) that can be parameterized.
- The substitution syntax (which is the next topic, in section 4.2.2) has to be used instead.

4.2.2 Using inline parameters with the $ placeholders

Another way to use inline parameters is with the substitution ($) syntax, which is used to insert a value directly into the SQL before it is turned into a parameterized statement. *Use this approach with caution, as it may leave you open to SQL injection, and it may cause performance problems if overused.*

This is one approach to handling `LIKE` operators. Here is an example:

```
<select id="getByLikeCity" resultClass="Account">
  select
    accountId,
    username,
    password,
    firstName,
    lastName,
    address1,
    address2,
    city,
    state,
    postalCode,
    country
  from Account
  where city like '%$value$%'
</select>
```

The difference between this statement and the last one is how iBATIS handles the parameter passed into the statement. This statement is called the same way:

```
accountList = sqlMap.queryForList(
    "Account.getByLikeCity",
    "burg");
```

This time, iBATIS turns the statement into this:

```
select
  accountId,
  username,
  password,
  firstName,
  lastName,
  address1,
  address2,
  city,
  state,
  postalCode,
  country
from Account
where city like '%burg%'
```

No parameters are set, because the statement is already complete, but one important thing to remember when using this technique is that it makes your application more susceptible to SQL injection attacks.

4.2.3 A quick look at SQL injection

A SQL injection attack is one where a malicious user passes specially formed data to an application to make it do something it is not supposed to do. For example, in the latter case, if a user provided this text:

```
burg'; drop table Account;--
```

it would turn our simple little `select` statement into this more nefarious set of statements:

```
select
  accountId,
  username,
  password,
  firstName,
  lastName,
  address1,
  address2,
  city,
  state,
  postalCode,
  country
from Account
where city like '%burg';drop table Account;--%'
```

Now your clever user has managed to select all the records in the database that end in `burg`, which is no big deal. But he also managed to drop a table from your database (and only one, if you are lucky—if he is a real clever user, he will realize that this is a one-chance deal and drop multiple tables). The `--` at the end of the string tells the database to ignore anything that comes after the `drop table` statement, so no error is thrown.

If this happens in a real application in a production environment because of your code, it is going to be a very bad day at the office. As we mentioned earlier, use substitution syntax with caution.

4.2.4 Automatic result maps

You may have already noticed that in our examples we did not define any result maps, but we did define result classes. This works through the automatic result mapping done by iBATIS, which creates a result map on the fly and applies it to the mapped statement the first time it is executed.

There are three ways to use this feature: single-column selection, fixed-column list selection, and dynamic-column list selection.

WARNING If you do not provide either a result map or a result class, iBATIS will execute your statement and simply return nothing. This is a behavior that has been in iBATIS since the earliest days, and has caused many cases of heartburn. Unfortunately, some users use `select` statements to do inserts and updates, and while this may seem like a bad idea, we have left this in to avoid breaking working applications.

If you only want to get a single column out of a query, you can use the alias `value` as a shortcut to accomplish that:

```
<select id="getAllAccountIdValues"
  resultClass="int">
  select accountId as value
  from Account
</select>

List list = sqlMap.queryForList(
  "Account.getAllAccountIdValues", null);
```

This returns all of the `accountId` values in the Account table as a List of simple Integer objects.

If you need multiple columns, you can tell iBATIS to use the column names as bean property names, or as Map keys using automatic result mapping.

When mapping in this way to a bean, there is one caveat to remember: if the column you are selecting exists in the database but does not exist in the bean you are mapping to, you will get no error, no warning, and no data—the data will simply be quietly ignored. When mapping to a `Map` object, the problem is similar: while you will still get the data, it will not be where you expect it to be.

If you want a firmer approach to data mapping, look at using external result maps (in section 4.3.1).

In spite of these two potential issues, automatic mapping works well in cases where you are willing to let the framework do the mapping for you, and when you do not mind paying the price when the mapping is done the first time.

If the list of fields being selected in the statement can change at runtime, dynamic result mapping can also be used. Listing 4.2 shows an example of a query using dynamic result mapping.

Listing 4.2 Dynamic result mapping example

```
<select id="getAccountRemapExample"
  remapResults="true"                      <-- 1 Remaps results when mapped statement executes
  resultClass="java.util.HashMap" >
  select
    accountId,
    username,
    <dynamic>                              <-- 2 Contains simple Dynamic SQL to demonstrate technique
      <isEqual
        property="includePassword"
        compareValue="true" >
          password,
      </isEqual>
    </dynamic>
    firstName,
    lastName
  from Account
  <dynamic prepend=" where ">              <-- 2
    <isNotEmpty property="city">
      city like #city#
    </isNotEmpty>
    <isNotNull
      property="accountId"
      prepend=" and ">
        accountId = #accountId#
    </isNotNull>
  </dynamic>
</select>
```

The example in listing 4.2 uses the `remapResults` attribute ❶ combined with Dynamic SQL ❷ to demonstrate how to change the data returned from a mapped statement on the fly. While Dynamic SQL is not covered until chapter 8, this example uses it to create a mapped statement where the value of the `includePassword` property determines the fields that are in the results. Depending on its value, you may or may not get the password field back in your results. One thing to be aware of is that the performance hit for determining a result map each and every time a statement is run may be prohibitive, so use this feature only when it is an absolute requirement.

4.2.5 Joining related data

There are times when you want to join multiple data tables into a single "flattened-out" structure for reporting or other purposes. The iBATIS framework makes this completely effortless, because it maps SQL statements to objects, not tables to objects. There is literally no difference between mapping a single-table select and a multitable select.

In chapter 7, we will look at how to perform more advanced multitable operations for the purpose of providing lists of child objects that are related to their containing objects—such as a list of orders details for an order.

For now, we will simply restate that there is literally no difference between mapping a single-table select and a multitable select.

We have talked about how SQL is similar to a function in that it has input values and, based on those input values, it produces output values. In the next section, let's see how you provide those input values.

4.3 Mapping parameters

There are two ways to map parameters into your mapped statements: inline mapping and external mapping. Using inline parameter mapping means that you give iBATIS some hints as to what you want, and let it figure out the details. External parameter mapping, on the other hand, is more explicit—you tell iBATIS exactly what you want it to do.

4.3.1 External parameter maps

You can specify up to six attributes when using an external parameter map. If you do not specify them, iBATIS will try to decide on reasonable values using reflection, but this takes time and may not be as accurate. Table 4.4 lists the attributes that are available for mapping parameters, and briefly describes how each is used.

Table 4.4 Parameter mapping attributes

Attribute	Description
`property`	The `property` attribute of the parameter map is the name of a JavaBean property or Map entry of the parameter object passed to a mapped statement. The name can be used more than once, depending on the number of times it is needed in the statement. For example, if the same property is being updated in the set clause of a SQL `UPDATE` statement, and is also used as part of the key in the `WHERE` clause, the name can be referenced twice in the mapped statement.
`javaType`	The `javaType` attribute is used to explicitly specify the Java property type of the parameter to be set. Normally this can be derived from a JavaBean property through reflection, but certain mappings such as Map and XML mappings cannot provide the type to the framework. In those cases, if the `javaType` is not set and the framework cannot otherwise determine the type, the type is assumed to be `Object`.
`jdbcType`	The `jdbcType` attribute is used to explicitly specify the database type of the parameter. Some JDBC drivers are not able to identify the type of a column for certain operations without explicitly telling the driver the column type. A perfect example of this is the `PreparedStatement.setNull(int parameterIndex, int sqlType)` method. This method requires the type to be specified. Some drivers will allow the type to be implicit by simply sending `Types.OTHER` or `Types.NULL`. However, the behavior is inconsistent and some drivers need the exact type to be specified. For such situations, iBATIS allows the type to be specified using the `jdbcType` attribute of the `parameterMap` property element. This attribute is normally only required if the column can be set to null. Another reason to use the type attribute is to explicitly specify date types when the Java type may be ambiguous. For example, Java only has one Date value type (`java.util.Date`), but most SQL databases usually have at least three different types. Because of this you might want to specify explicitly that your column type is DATE versus DATETIME. The `jdbcType` attribute can be set to any string value that matches a constant in the JDBC `Types` class.

Table 4.4 Parameter mapping attributes *(continued)*

Attribute	Description
`nullValue`	The `nullValue` attribute can be set to any valid value based on property type. The `nullValue` attribute is used to specify an outgoing null value replacement. What this means is that when the value is detected in the JavaBeans property or Map entry, a NULL will be written to the database (the opposite behavior of an inbound null value replacement). This allows you to use a "magic" null number in your application for types that do not support null values (e.g., int, double, float, etc.). When these types of properties contain a matching null value (e.g., –9999), a NULL will be written to the database instead of the value.
`mode`	This attribute is used exclusively for stored procedure support. It is covered in detail in section 5.5.2.
`typeHandler`	If you want to specify a type handler (instead of letting iBATIS select one based on the `javaType` and `jdbcType` attributes), you can do that here. More commonly, this is used to provide a custom type handler, which will be covered in chapter 12.

While inline parameter mapping in iBATIS works well for most mapped statements, if you want to improve performance or encounter a case where things are not working as expected, an external parameter map may be just what you need. In chapter 5, we will look at a full-blown external parameter map, but for our purposes here, that is not needed.

4.3.2 Inline parameter mapping revisited

In the beginning of section 4.2, we talked about using inline parameter mapping in its simplest form to tell iBATIS the names of properties that we wanted to substitute into your query at runtime. In addition to that, you can provide some of the attributes that external parameter maps allow, such as the database type and a null value placeholder for your parameters, by separating the parameter name, the type, and the null value placeholder with colon characters. The database type is commonly required when you use null-capable columns in your database. The reason for this is that the JDBC API uses this method to send null values to the database:

```
public void setNull(
  int parameterIndex,
  int sqlType);
```

If you do not tell iBATIS what the type is, then it will use `java.sql.Types.OTHER` for the second parameter, and some drivers do not allow that (for example, the Oracle driver currently does not) and you will get an error in that case.

TIP If you see an unexpected 1111 number in your log when you get an error with an inline parameter map and null values, chances are good that the problem is that your driver does not like null values without an explicit type. The integer value used for OTHER is 1111.

To tell iBATIS what the type is with an inline parameter, you add the type name from java.sql.Types after the property name and separate them with a colon character. Here is an example of a mapped statement that specifies a database type:

```
<select id="getOrderShippedAfter"
        resultClass="java.util.HashMap">
  select *
  from order
  where shipDate > #value:DATE#
</select>
```

NOTE Remember that we are working with XML. In the previous example, had we wanted to create a statement named getOrderShippedBefore and make the condition shipDate < #value:DATE# we would have had to use < instead of <, because in XML, the less-than symbol means you are starting a new element. A CDATA section could also be used, but be careful with Dynamic SQL (chapter 9) and CDATA, because Dynamic SQL tags in a CDATA section will not be parsed. Generally, you can get away with > in XML, but it is probably better to be safe and use the > entity instead.

Null value replacement lets you treat "magic numbers" in your Java code as null values in your database. Developing with "magic numbers" is a bad design for most applications (in fact, we cannot think of a single case where it is the *right* thing to do), and is only supported as a way for people to start using iBATIS in spite of poor model design. If you need to have a null value in your database, you should map it to a null value in your Java model as well.

In current releases of iBATIS, you can specify any value for the parameter map using a name=value syntax. For example, the following example is equivalent to the previous one:

```
<select id="getOrderShippedAfter" resultClass="hashmap">
  select *
  from "order"
  where shipDate > #value,jdbcType=DATE#
</select>
```

Remember that an inline parameter map is just a shortcut to creating a parameter map. If you get an error with a mapped statement telling you there was an error with the parameter map YourNamespace.YourStatement-InlineParameterMap, look at the inline parameter mapping for the statement YourStatement in the namespace

`YourNamespace`. That is where the error is occurring. If you do not define a parameter map, that does not necessarily mean that one does not exist.

4.3.3 Primitive parameters

As we saw with result mapping, primitive values can only be used if they are wrapped in another object (this assumes that you are not using Java 5, in which case you can pass in primitive parameters anywhere you want to because of the "autoboxing" feature). If you want to pass a primitive value into iBATIS, you can do it by using a bean (see section 4.3.2) or by using one of the primitive wrapper classes (i.e., Integer, Long, etc.).

NOTE Arrays of primitive types can be passed into iBATIS, but using arrays is beyond the scope of this chapter. For information related to using arrays with Dynamic SQL, see section 8.2.5.

OK, now let's move on and not be so primitive...

4.3.4 JavaBean and Map parameters

Although there is a difference between bean and Map parameters, the syntax is identical when you are working with them. The difference lies in the behavior of the two when the parameter maps are loading.

If you create a parameter map with a bean and attempt to refer to a property that does not exist, you will get an immediate failure when the parameter map is loaded. This is a good thing, because it helps you keep from letting users find the bugs—you will find them yourself.

If you do the same thing with a Map, there is no way for iBATIS to know that the property does not exist (because the Map is built at runtime instead of at compile time), so there is no way for it to help you identify a potential failure.

This brings up an important point: early failure is a good thing. Every bug you see and correct before releasing your application is a bug that does not impact your users. Fewer bugs sent to your users means that your users are more productive, and the value of your software increases.

OK, so now that we have input values nailed down, let's move on to getting the output values that you need.

4.4 Using inline and explicit result maps

Inline result maps are great, because they are super easy to use, and in most cases work well enough.

Explicit result maps are also valuable in iBATIS because they provide higher performance, tighter configuration validation, and more precise behavior. When using explicit result mapping, there are very few surprises at runtime. Table 4.5 describes the attributes available for explicit result maps.

Table 4.5 Result map attributes

Attribute	Description
`property`	The `property` attribute of the result map is the name of a JavaBean property or Map entry of the result object that will be returned by the mapped statement. The name can be used more than once depending on the number of times it is needed to populate the results.
`column`	The `column` attribute is used to provide the name of the column in the `ResultSet` that will be used to populate the property.
`columnIndex`	As an optional (minimal) performance enhancement, the `columnIndex` attribute can be used to provide the index of the column in the `ResultSet` instead of the column name. This is not likely necessary in 99 percent of applications and sacrifices maintainability and readability for performance. Depending on your JDBC driver, you may or may not experience any performance increase.
`jdbcType`	The `jdbcType` attribute is used to explicitly specify the database column type of the `ResultSet` column that will be used to populate the property. Although result maps do not have the same difficulties with null values as parameter maps do, specifying the type can be useful for certain mapping types, such as Date properties. Because Java only has one Date value type and SQL databases may have many (usually at least three), specifying the date may become necessary in some cases to ensure that dates (or other types) are set correctly. Similarly, a VARCHAR, CHAR, or CLOB may populate String types, so specifying the type might be needed in those cases too. Depending on your driver, you may not need to set this attribute.
`javaType`	The `javaType` attribute is used to explicitly specify the Java property type of the property to be set. Normally this can be derived from a JavaBeans property through reflection, but certain mappings such as Map and XML mappings cannot provide the type to the framework. If the `javaType` is not set and the framework cannot otherwise determine the type, the type is assumed to be Object.

Table 4.5 Result map attributes *(continued)*

Attribute	Description
nullValue	The nullValue attribute specifies the value to be used in place of a NULL value in the database. So if a NULL is read from the ResultSet, the JavaBean property will be set to the value specified by the nullValue attribute instead of NULL. The nullValue attribute can be any value, but must be appropriate for the property type.
select	The select attribute is used to describe a relationship between objects so that iBATIS can automatically load complex (i.e., user-defined) property types. The value of the statement property must be the name of another mapped statement. The value of the database column (the column attribute) that is defined in the same property element as this statement attribute will be passed to the related mapped statement as the parameter. Therefore the column must be a supported, primitive type. This will be discussed in more detail in chapter 5.

So, now that you know what the attributes are, how do you use them? Keep reading to find out.

4.4.1 Primitive results

The Java language has eight primitive types (boolean, char, byte, short, int, long, float, and double), each with its corresponding wrapper class (`Boolean`, `Char`, `Byte`, `Short`, `Integer`, `Long`, `Float`, and `Double`).

While iBATIS does not allow you to get a primitive result directly, it does allow you to get wrapped primitive results. For example, if you want a count of orders for a customer, you can do it as an Integer, but not as a primitive int, as the next example shows:

```
Integer count = (Integer)sqlMap.queryForObject(
  "Account.getOrderCountByAccount",
  new Integer(1));

  <select
    id="getOrderCountByAccount"
    resultClass="java.lang.Integer" >
    select count(*) as value
    from order
    where accountId = #value#
  </select>
```

If we had used a bean for the results, that bean could have an int property to receive the results, as in the following example:

```
public class PrimitiveResult {
  private int orderCount;
  public int getOrderCount() {
    return orderCount;
  }
  public void setOrderCount(int orderCount) {
    this.orderCount = orderCount;
  }
}

<resultMap id="primitiveResultMapExample"
  class="PrimitiveResult">
  <result property="orderCount"
    column="orderCount" />
</resultMap>

<select id="getPrimitiveById"
  resultMap="primitiveResultMapExample">
  select count(*) as orderCount
  from order
  where accountId = #accountId#
</select>
```

So, the bottom line is this: iBATIS can map results into any type, but because it only returns Object instances, primitive values must be wrapped in one of the following: a simple value wrapper, a bean, or a Map.

NOTE Again, if you are able to use J2SE 5, this is not completely true. Methods such as `queryForObject()` still return an instance of Object. You cannot cast Object directly to a primitive (such as int or long), but you can cast it to the boxed type (Integer or Long), then let the compiler unbox that into the primitive type. In this case, however, there is a caveat: if the returned Object is null, the value of the boxed type will also be null. When that situation arises, the application will throw a `NullPointerException` because the unboxed type cannot be null.

Sometimes (most of the time, actually) you will want to get more than just a single column from your SQL statement. In those cases, you will want to put your results into a JavaBean or Map.

4.4.2 JavaBean and Map results

The iBATIS framework will allow you to use either Map or bean objects for result mapping (in addition to the primitive wrapper classes—`Integer`, `Long`, etc.). Both approaches have their advantages and disadvantages, which are summarized in table 4.6.

Table 4.6 Advantages and disadvantages of JavaBeans and Maps as data structures

Approach	Advantage	Disadvantage
Bean	Performance Strong typing at compile time Compile-time name checking Refactoring support in IDE Less type casting	More code (get/set)
Map	Less code	Slower No compile-time check Weakly typed More runtime errors No refactoring support

As a general rule, using a bean is the recommended practice for domain data (i.e., getting an account or order out of the database for editing), whereas using a Map is recommended for less critical and more dynamic data (i.e., a report or other output methods).

When creating a result map, if you map a field to a property that does not exist, you will get an exception immediately when the result map is loaded. This early failure loading the SQL Map is a good thing, because it means that you catch the error before your users see it.

On the other hand, if you map a column that does not exist to a property that does exist, you experience a rather nasty runtime failure when trying to get the data. This is a good reason to have lots of unit tests around your DAO layer (see chapter 13 for more of these sorts of best practices with iBATIS).

4.5 Summary

In this chapter, we delved into the basics of JavaBeans, the SQL Map API, and mapping statements. As you become more familiar with the topics presented here, creating mapping statements will become as easy as any other development tasks you perform, and just like anything else, the more you do it, the easier it will be.

If you want to tighten down your application and eliminate as many runtime errors as possible, be explicit! Use explicit parameter and result maps as well as strongly typed beans for both parameters and results. This will also make your application start faster (because iBATIS will not be trying to figure it all out on the fly), run faster, and use less memory.

In the next chapter, we will explore the nonquery aspects of iBATIS as we finish up looking at all of the essential operations required for database maintenance.

5 Executing nonquery statements

This chapter covers

- More of the iBATIS API
- Inserting data
- Updating and deleting data
- Using stored procedures

Running a query over your database is definitely worthwhile, but most applications also need to get data into the database. In this chapter, we explore some of the ways to populate your database using the iBATIS framework. We build on the concepts introduced in chapter 4, so if you are new to iBATIS and have not read that chapter yet, you may want to take a quick look. Nearly all of the parameter-mapping information (and result-mapping information too, to a small extent) from chapter 4 will apply to nonquery mapped statements as well.

5.1 The building blocks for updating data

In chapter 4, you learned about all of the available statement types and the parts of the API relevant to basic queries. Here we look at the API that you will commonly use for executing nonquery statements, and review the mapped statement types for updating your database.

5.1.1 The SqlMap API for nonquery SQL statements

We save the topic of advanced ways to update your database for the next chapter, so for now, let's stick to the basics of `insert`, `update`, and `delete`—the three methods that you will most often use to update your database. We cover each of these methods in more detail later in this chapter, but right now, we offer a brief introduction, which may be enough for you to get started using them.

The insert method

As you may have guessed, the `insert` method is used to execute mapped statements that correspond to the SQL `insert` statement:

```
Object insert(String id, Object parameterObject)
                                    throws SQLException;
```

The `insert` method takes two parameters: the name of the mapped statement to execute, and the parameter object to be used to build the `insert` statement that will insert your data into the database.

Of the three methods that are generally used to update your database, the `insert` method is unusual in that it returns `Object` (see section 5.2.3).

The update method

The `update` method is used to execute mapped statements that correspond to SQL `update` statements:

```
int update(String id, Object parameterObject)
                                    throws SQLException;
```

As with the insert method, the update method takes two parameters: the name of the mapped statement to execute, and the parameter object to be used in providing the values for completing the mapped statement. The returned value is the number of rows affected by the update statement (when the specific JDBC driver supports this).

The delete method

The delete method is almost identical to the update method, but instead of being used to execute update SQL statements, it is used to execute delete statements:

```
int delete(String id, Object parameterObject)
                                throws SQLException;
```

The same two parameters are used for delete as were used for the other two methods: the name of the mapped statement to execute, and the parameter object that will be used to complete the mapped statement. The value returned by this method is the number of rows deleted by it.

5.1.2 Nonquery mapped statements

Table 5.1 is a subset of table 4.3 from chapter 4. There are three primary mapped statement types commonly used to update the database, and two other top-level configuration elements that can be used to create them.

Table 5.1 Mapped statement types for updating data (and related XML elements)

Mapped statement type	Attributes	Child elements	Uses	More details
<insert>	id parameterClass parameterMap	All dynamic elements <selectKey>	Inserting data	Section 5.2; chapter 8
<update>	id parameterClass parameterMap	All dynamic elements	Updating data	Section 5.3; chapter 8
<delete>	id parameterClass parameterMap	All dynamic elements	Deleting data	Section 5.3; chapter 8
<procedure>	id parameterClass resultClass parameterMap resultMap xmlResultName	All dynamic elements	Calling a stored procedure	Section 5.5; chapter 8

Table 5.1 Mapped statement types for updating data (and related XML elements) *(continued)*

Mapped statement type	Attributes	Child elements	Uses	More details
<sql>	id	All dynamic elements	Not really a mapped statement, but used to make components that can be used in mapped statements	Section 4.2; chapter 8
<include>	refid	None	Not really a mapped statement, but used to insert components created with the `<sql>` type into mapped statements	Section 4.2

For more information on the `<sql>` and `<include>` elements, refer to section 4.1.3 in the previous chapter.

Now that you have the building blocks, let's look at how you can put them together.

5.2 Inserting data

Inserting data into your database is not exactly the same as selecting data, but the process is very similar. Regardless of whether you use inline or external parameter mapping (both of which are explained in detail in the previous chapter—see sections 4.3.1 and 4.3.2), they work just like they do with all other mapped statements.

5.2.1 Using inline parameter mapping

Inline parameter mapping lets you very quickly build your mapped statements by providing hints in your markup that tell iBATIS how you want it to map your input to your mapped statement. Here is an example of an `insert` statement using inline parameter mapping:

```
<insert id="insertWithInlineInfo">
   insert into account (
     accountId,
     username, password,
     memberSince,
     firstName, lastName,
     address1, address2,
     city, state, postalCode,
     country, version
   ) values (
```

```
    #accountId:NUMBER#,
    #username:VARCHAR#, #password:VARCHAR#,
    #memberSince:TIMESTAMP#,
    #firstName:VARCHAR#, #lastName:VARCHAR#,
    #address1:VARCHAR#, #address2:VARCHAR#,
    #city:VARCHAR#, #state:VARCHAR#, #postalCode:VARCHAR#,
    #country:VARCHAR#, #version:NUMBER#
  )
</insert>
```

That was the mapped statement, and here is the code used to execute it (from a unit test):

```
Account account = new Account();
account.setAccountId(new Integer(9999));
account.setUsername("inlineins");
account.setPassword("poohbear");
account.setFirstName("Inline");
account.setLastName("Example");
sqlMapClient.insert("Account.insertWithInlineInfo", account);
```

While this mapped statement will work, it can become verbose and difficult to maintain once you reach the point where you have a few different versions of the `insert` statement as well as some `update` statements, and you throw in a couple dozen queries. When that happens, an external parameter map may help simplify the maintenance of your SQL Map files.

5.2.2 Using an external parameter map

Along with providing the same functionality as inline parameter mapping, using an external parameter map has the added benefit of improved performance and additional validation at load time (which means that fewer errors slip through the cracks during testing for your users to find at runtime).

Here is an example of an `insert` statement that uses an external parameter map. The following code is functionally identical to the previous example, but uses an external parameter map instead of an inline one:

```
<parameterMap id="fullParameterMapExample" class="Account">
  <parameter property="accountId" jdbcType="NUMBER" />
  <parameter property="username" jdbcType="VARCHAR" />
  <parameter property="password" jdbcType="VARCHAR" />
  <parameter property="memberSince" jdbcType="TIMESTAMP" />
  <parameter property="firstName" jdbcType="VARCHAR" />
  <parameter property="lastName" jdbcType="VARCHAR" />
  <parameter property="address1" jdbcType="VARCHAR" />
  <parameter property="address2" jdbcType="VARCHAR" />
  <parameter property="city" jdbcType="VARCHAR" />
  <parameter property="state" jdbcType="VARCHAR" />
```

```
    <parameter property="postalCode" jdbcType="VARCHAR" />
    <parameter property="country" jdbcType="VARCHAR" />
    <parameter property="version" jdbcType="NUMBER" />
  </parameterMap>

  <insert id="insertWithExternalInfo"
      parameterMap="fullParameterMapExample">
    insert into account (
      accountId,
      username, password,
      memberSince
      firstName, lastName,
      address1, address2,
      city, state, postalCode,
      country, version
    ) values (
      ?,?,?,?,?,?,?,?,?,?,?,?,?,?
    )
  </insert>
```

While that does not look any less verbose than the inline version, the difference becomes more apparent when you start including additional statements. Not only will they be simplified (because you do not need to specify the types for each property), but the centralized maintenance also means that when you make changes to the parameter map, you only have to do it once.

For example, everywhere that the `memberSince` property is passed in, it is automatically handled as a TIMESTAMP database type. If later, we decide that DATE is adequate (because we do not need to know the number of seconds since an account was created), we do it in exactly one place—the parameter map.

Another added benefit to this approach is that the inline parameter map does not need to be generated dynamically when first called.

In both of the previous examples, the code to call the statements is identical (except for the name of the mapped statement in our example):

```
sqlMap.insert("Account.insertWithInlineInfo", account);
sqlMap.insert("Account.insertWithExternalInfo", account);
```

The difference between inline and explicit parameter maps is maintenance cost and performance—both are improved by using externally defined parameter maps.

5.2.3 Autogenerated keys

With any database, the ability to uniquely identify a row in a table is absolutely critical. Nearly all databases include the means to automatically generate primary key values for newly inserted rows. While this is convenient, it can be problematic when you're inserting a record into a database if you need to know the primary key after the insert completes.

Most database vendors provide a way to determine the last-generated key for the current session using standard SQL to facilitate using this functionality from a stored procedure. Several database vendors (including Oracle and PostgreSQL) also provide a way to generate identity values without inserting a column. Also, with JDBC 3.0, the API was modified to allow fetching generated keys when inserting data.

If you design your database to use generated primary keys, you can use iBATIS to get those generated keys back into your object by using the `<selectKey>` element, which is a special child element of the `<insert>` element. There are two patterns you can follow with this approach, and the choice will be driven by the key-generation technique you are using.

The first approach is to fetch the key after you have inserted the record and the database has generated the key. Be aware that you will need to ensure that the driver you are using is guaranteed to return the key generated by the last `insert` statement you performed. For example, if two threads execute `insert` statements nearly simultaneously, the order of the execution could be `[insert for user #1]`, `[insert for user #2]`, `[selectKey for user #1]`, `[selectKey for user #2]`. If the driver simply returns the last-generated key (globally), then the `[selectKey for user #1]` will get the generated key for user #2, which would wreak havoc in the application. Most drivers should work fine for this, but be sure to test this if you are not absolutely certain whether yours does or not. Also, be aware that triggers may also cause problems with this approach. For example, with Microsoft SQL Server, the `@@identity` value is affected by triggers, so if you insert a record into a table with a trigger that inserts a record that also generates a key value, the value returned by `@@identity` will be the generated key for the record inserted by the trigger, not the generated key for the first record you inserted. In that case, you would want to use the `SCOPE_IDENTITY` function instead.

The second approach to consider is fetching the key before you insert the record. This method entails more work if you are inserting records using an interactive database tool, because you have to allocate a key value before inserting a record. However, this strategy avoids the potential risks associated with threading and getting the key after it has been inserted, and is generally the safest since it requires very few assumptions in the code. With the first method, there are potential issues that could cause things to not work as expected. With this approach, all we need is a guarantee that the generated key is unique when we get it. We do not require it to be managed by the database for the session; we just need it generated and passed back to us.

In both cases, iBATIS can help make this easier for you. The <selectKey> element makes this task transparent to your application (at least in the calling code). The signature for the insert method is:

```
Object insert(
    String id,
    Object parameterObject
) throws SQLException;
```

The reason that the insert method returns an Object is so that you can get the key that was generated. For example, if you had this mapped statement and code in your application that uses the second approach explained earlier:

```
<insert id="insert">
  <selectKey
    keyProperty="accountId"
    resultClass="int">
    SELECT nextVal('account_accountid_seq')
  </selectKey>
  INSERT INTO Account (
    accountId, username, password
  ) VALUES(
    #accountId#, #username#, #password#)
</insert>

Integer returnValue = (Integer) sqlMap.insert(
  "Account.insert", account);
```

the returnValue variable would contain your generated key. But there is more—the keyProperty attribute in the <selectKey> element tells iBATIS to get the value and set it on the object to be inserted. This means that if you want, you can even ignore the returned value, because the object that was inserted already has the key value set for you.

Something to remember is that the <selectKey> element defines a mapped statement, and this mapped statement has access to the same parameter map that the containing insert statement does. So, in the previous example, if you wanted to select the sequence to use for inserted records, you could do so by using this mapped statement:

```
<insert id="insertSequence">
  <selectKey keyProperty="accountId" resultClass="int">
    SELECT nextVal(#sequence#)
  </selectKey>
  INSERT INTO Account (
```

```
    accountId, username, password
  ) VALUES(
    #accountId#, #username#, #password#)
</insert>
```

That mapped statement would expect a property named `sequence` which would contain the name of the sequence to be used for the inserted record.

In the previous examples, we acquired the key by fetching the next value from a sequence and setting it on the object before the record was inserted. On the other hand, if we were using Microsoft SQL Server, we might use this mapped statement instead:

```
<insert id="insert">
  INSERT INTO Account (
    username, password
  ) VALUES(
    #username#, #password#)
  <selectKey
    keyProperty="accountId"
    resultClass="int">
    SELECT SCOPE_IDENTITY()
  </selectKey>
</insert>
```

This example lets the database create the key when we insert the record, then fetches the generated key and sets it onto the object that was passed into the `insert` method. As far as your application is concerned, there is no difference at all between these two mapped statements.

Earlier, we touched on the API that the JDBC 3.0 specification exposes to get generated keys. At this point, iBATIS does not support this API, because only a limited numbers of JDBC drivers support it. As more and more begin to implement it, it will be an option for using automatically generated keys as well.

5.3 Updating and deleting data

Now that we can insert rows into our database and figure out what the generated keys are for the inserted data, let's take a look at updating and deleting data.

While the insert method returns an object, both the `update` and `delete` methods return a primitive integer value (or, an int value to be more correct) which indicates how many records were updated or deleted by the mapped statement.

The iBATIS framework allows you to affect either single or multiple rows in your database, depending on your need, with a single SQL statement. This is one of the differentiating factors between it and most object relational mapping tools, which generally only allow single record changes.

5.3.1 Handling concurrent updates

One thing that iBATIS does not currently implement is any sort of record locking to manage concurrent modifications to the same data. You can use one of several techniques to handle concurrent updates, such as using a timestamp or version number on rows in the database. For example, if you have an account table defined thusly:

```
CREATE TABLE account (
  accountid serial NOT NULL,
  username varchar(10),
  passwd varchar(10),
  firstname varchar(30),
  lastname varchar(30),
  address1 varchar(30),
  address2 varchar(30),
  city varchar(30),
  state varchar(5),
  postalcode varchar(10),
  country varchar(5),
  version int8,
  CONSTRAINT account_pkey PRIMARY KEY (accountid)
)
```

you can increment the version column in the record when you update it, and use both the `accountId` and `version` fields in the `where` clause of the `update` statement. When the update runs, if the record that is being updated has not been changed by another user, then the update will be successful because the version number has not been changed, and the mapped statement will return the expected record count of one. If it returns zero, and no exception is thrown, then you know that someone else updated the data since you read it from the database. How you proceed in your application once you have this information is up to you.

5.3.2 Updating or deleting child records

It is not unusual for an object model to include components that also contain child objects. For example, an `Order` object may contain a list or array of `OrderItem` objects that represent the items that were ordered.

Because the iBATIS framework is primarily a SQL mapping tool, it does not manage these sorts of relationships when updating the database. As a result, this functionality is something that must be handled in the data layer of your application rather than in iBATIS. The code to accomplish this is pretty simple:

```
public void saveOrder(SqlMapClient sqlMapClient, Order order)
throws SQLException {
  if (null == order.getOrderId()) {
    sqlMapClient.insert("Order.insert", order);
  } else {
    sqlMapClient.update("Order.update", order);
  }

  sqlMapClient.delete("Order.deleteDetails", order);

  for(int i=0;i<order.getOrderItems().size();i++) {
    OrderItem oi = (OrderItem) order.getOrderItems().get(i);
    oi.setOrderId(order.getOrderId());
    sqlMapClient.insert("OrderItem.insert", oi);
  }
}
```

While this code works adequately, it does not provide for any sort of transaction isolation, so if the update of the last `OrderItem` fails, all of the other data is left in an inconsistent state because the transactions happen on each insert or update. In addition, performance is hindered because each statement is committed as soon as it happens. In the next section, you will learn how to resolve both of those issues using batch updates.

5.4 Running batch updates

Batch updates are one way to improve performance with iBATIS. By creating a batch of statements, the driver can perform such tasks as compression to improve performance.

One important tip for using batched statements is to wrap the batch in a single transaction. If you fail to do so, a new transaction will be started for each statement, and performance will suffer as the batch size grows.

In section 5.2.2, we saw one way to update an object that contained child objects. There were two issues with that solution: performance and data integrity. To remedy the second issue, we could simply wrap the method in a transaction and roll it back if anything threw an exception while doing the update.

This would also improve performance, but we can improve it further if we also execute the statements in a batch:

```
public void saveOrder(SqlMapClient sqlMapClient, Order order)
throws SQLException {
  sqlMapClient.startTransaction();
  try {
    if (null == order.getOrderId()) {
      sqlMapClient.insert("Order.insert", order);
```

```
      } else {
        sqlMapClient.update("Order.update", order);
      }
      sqlMapClient.startBatch();

      sqlMapClient.delete("Order.deleteDetails", order);

      for (int i=0;i<order.getOrderItems().size();i++) {
        OrderItem oi = (OrderItem) order.getOrderItems().get(i);
        oi.setOrderId(order.getOrderId());
        sqlMapClient.insert("OrderItem.insert", oi);
      }
      sqlMapClient.executeBatch();
      sqlMapClient.commitTransaction();
    } finally {
      sqlMapClient.endTransaction();
    }
  }
```

You may have noticed that we did not start the batch until after the parent record was already updated (or potentially inserted). The reason is that when you are using a batched set of statements, database-generated keys will not be generated until you execute the batch by calling the `executeBatch()` method. In simpler terms, this means that if you are using `selectKey` statements to update your inserted objects with system-generated keys, they will return null for the generated keys, and nothing will work as expected. Here is an example:

```
sqlMapClient.startBatch();
sqlMapClient.insert("Account.insert", account);
order.setAccountId(account.getAccountId());    // error!
sqlMapClient.insert("Order.insert", order);
sqlMapClient.executeBatch();
```

In that example, everything looks right: we insert the account, set the generated key onto the order, and then we insert the order. However, none of the SQL statements execute until you call the `executeBatch()` method. So, when the third line executes, the account still has a null value for the `accountId` property. When the fourth line executes, the object passed to the `insert` method has a null `accountId`, too, creating an orphaned record in the order table.

Keep in mind also that batched statements only reuse the `PreparedStatement` objects if they are exactly the same as the previous mapped statements. This can be problematic if you have many mapped statements that you are executing, and they occur in an order that causes them not to be reused. If you can, execute statements that are the same all together.

NOTE This behavior is almost a bug—not quite, but almost. If you do not care about the order that the statements get executed in, one person did manage to hack the `SqlExecutor` class to make it reuse the prepared statements out of order. However, this is not yet supported in iBATIS.

Some people use batched statements to insert a group of records that differ only by a value that can be easily determined. One example is a system that inserted up to 200 records that represented tickets in the database. The tickets differed only by the database-generated primary key, and a ticket number had a starting value and was incremented for each ticket inserted. A loop in the DAO was used to accomplish the job, but a stored procedure would have been a faster and cleaner solution.

While running statements in batch mode may improve performance slightly, using a stored procedure (section 5.5) will generally provide more of an improvement if the statements can be grouped into a stored procedure easily. For example, we could implement a `deleteOrder` method using the same approach as with the update example earlier. However, to delete an order and its related order items, all we need to know is the identity of the order, which in this case is just an integer. Deleting the order and its children would be faster and easier using a stored procedure than the equivalent iBATIS code would be.

5.5 Working with stored procedures

Stored procedures are blocks of code that execute in the database server process. While most stored procedures are written in a database-specific language that is generally based on SQL, some vendors are now allowing other languages (e.g., Oracle allows stored procedures in Java, Microsoft has planned support for stored procedures in C#, and PostgreSQL allows nearly any language).

5.5.1 Considering the pros and cons

Stored procedures are often seen as an enemy by Java developers, because they are platform specific (database platform specific, not necessarily operating system specific), which offends the sensibilities of some Java developers.

As developers who are more interested in solving problems than using a particular solution, we find stored procedures to be a compelling option for optimization and also for encapsulating the solutions to complex data-centric problems.

Don't be an extremist!

There are two polar extremes in discussing when to use stored procedures. On one end, you have Java purists who believe that stored procedures are never to be used by applications (and for that matter, there are even some who believe that SQL itself should not be used). On the other end, you have the database purists who believe that every single database interaction should be performed through a stored procedure.

The simple fact of the matter is that the old adage that "Purists are always wrong" applies here, because both extremes are wrong. Stored procedures are a tool, and should be viewed as nothing more and nothing less than that. As an analogy, let's look at the carpenter: he uses a hammer, a tape measure, and a saw. While he could use a hammer to measure a board, a tape measure does a much better job of it (and the same can be said for using the saw to drive nails). Every job has a tool that is the most appropriate, and every tool has a job that it was designed to do. Any time you use the wrong tool for a job, it does not work very well.

Using the right tool for the job

Such is the case with SQL, stored procedures, and application code. Some operations are accomplished very well by simple SQL, others by stored procedures, and still others by application code.

For example, consider a case in which you have to query a handful of tables for a report. Grabbing all of the data from all of the tables and then filtering and joining it all back together in application code makes very little sense. Creating a stored procedure for a simple query also adds complexity with very little added value. Putting that SQL into an iBATIS mapped statement and running it that way is a quick, easy, and efficient solution to the problem in this case.

Now, for a more complex report that has to do multiple subqueries and left joins to gather the data from tables with millions of rows in them, a stored procedure makes much more sense. Using a stored procedure, you have many more options available for optimization.

For an application where you want to use Dynamic SQL, mapped statements are also very useful. In chapter 8, we have an example of using Dynamic SQL where the SQL statement is built using Java, a stored procedure, and a mapped statement with dynamic elements in it. We won't spoil the surprise, but if you just can't wait to find out, skip ahead to section 8.5 and take a look.

Another consideration with stored procedures is that they can be called to do updates and return data. This can cause issues when transactions are not committed because the method used to call the procedure does not normally require a commit. In those cases, the transaction manager needs to be configured to always commit, even after read operations, or you have to manually manage the transactions yourself, as in the following example:

```
try {
  sqlMapClient.startTransaction();
  sqlMapClient.queryForObject("Account.insertAndReturn", a);
  sqlMapClient.commitTransaction();
} finally {
  sqlMapClient.endTransaction();
}
```

Transactions are covered in more detail in chapter 7, so if you have more questions about them, that is the best place to go.

5.5.2 IN, OUT, and INOUT parameters

So far, the only parameters that we have seen are input only—you pass them into iBATIS, and (with the exception of the `<selectKey>` element) what you pass in remains unchanged. With stored procedures, you are given three types of parameters: `IN`, `OUT`, and `INOUT`.

`IN` parameters are very simple to use with iBATIS and stored procedures. They are passed into the procedure just as you would pass a parameter into any other mapped statement. Here is a simple stored procedure that accepts two `IN` parameters and returns a value:

```
CREATE OR REPLACE FUNCTION max_in_example
  (a float4, b float4)
  RETURNS float4 AS
$BODY$
BEGIN
  if (a > b) then
    return a;
  else
    return b;
  end if;
END;
$BODY$
LANGUAGE 'plpgsql' VOLATILE;
```

Here is the parameter map, mapped statement, and Java code to use this procedure:

```
<parameterMap id="pm_in_example" class="java.util.Map">
  <parameter property="a" />
  <parameter property="b" />
</parameterMap>
<procedure id="in_example" parameterMap="pm_in_example"
                           resultClass="int" >
  { call max_in_example(?, ?) }
</procedure>


//  Call a max function
```

```
Map m = new HashMap(2);
m.put("a", new Integer(7));
m.put("b", new Integer(5));
Integer val =
      (Integer)sqlMap.queryForObject("Account.in_example", m);
```

INOUT parameters are parameters that are passed into a procedure and can be changed by the procedure, as in the following example, which takes two numbers and swaps them. Here is the code for the procedure (in Oracle PL/SQL):

```
create procedure swap(a in out integer, b in out integer) as
   temp integer;
begin
   temp := a;
   a := b;
   b := temp;
end;
```

Here is the parameter map, mapped statement, and Java code to use it:

```
<parameterMap id="swapProcedureMap" class="java.util.Map">
  <parameter property="a" mode="INOUT" />
  <parameter property="b" mode="INOUT" />
</parameterMap>

<procedure id="swapProcedure" parameterMap="swapProcedureMap">
  { call swap(?, ?) }
</procedure>

//  Call swap function
Map m = new HashMap(2);
m.put("a", new Integer(7));
m.put("b", new Integer(5));
Integer val =
      (Integer) sqlMap.queryForObject("Account.in_example", m);
```

OUT parameters are a bit more peculiar. They are similar to results (as in resultMap results), but are passed in like parameters. The value passed in is ignored and then replaced with a return value from the stored procedure. An OUT parameter can return anything from a single value (as in our next example) to a complete set of records (as in the case of an Oracle REFCURSOR).

Here is an example of a somewhat trivial stored procedure that uses two IN parameters and an OUT parameter (Oracle PL/SQL):

```
create or replace procedure maximum
  (a in integer, b in integer, c out integer) as
begin
  if (a > b) then c := a; end if;
  if (b >= a) then c := b; end if;
end;
```

This procedure accepts three parameters and returns void. However, the third parameter is out only, so depending on which of the other two parameters is greater, it is replaced with one of them. To call this using iBATIS, you would create a parameter map and a mapped statement:

```
<parameterMap id="maxOutProcedureMap" class="java.util.Map">
  <parameter property="a" mode="IN" />
  <parameter property="b" mode="IN" />
  <parameter property="c" mode="OUT" />
</parameterMap>
<procedure id="maxOutProcedure"
          parameterMap="maxOutProcedureMap">
  { call maximum (?, ?, ?) }
</procedure>

//  Call maximum function
Map m = new HashMap(2);
m.put("a", new Integer(7));
m.put("b", new Integer(5));
sqlMap.queryForObject("Account.maxOutProcedure", m);
// m.get("c") should be 7 now.
```

Stored procedures can also return multiple rows of data, as mentioned earlier in this chapter. This capability can be used to dramatically improve the performance of complex queries over large data sets that cannot be optimized using traditional SQL optimization techniques. Some examples of more difficult operations to optimize are outer joins and filters requiring calculations. If you are planning on using stored procedures for this purpose in your application, you should make sure that you have a good understanding of the real bottlenecks, or you may end up wasting time instead of saving it.

5.6 Summary

In this chapter, we looked at nearly all of the options for modifying data in a database using iBATIS. After reading chapter 4 and this chapter, you should have all of the information you need to create an application that maintains data using the iBATIS framework.

In chapter 6, we continue to expand on what you have learned. We examine more advanced query techniques to help you better leverage the investment you have made in your database skills and platform.

6 Using advanced query techniques

This chapter covers

- Using XML
- Declaring relationships
- N+1 solutions

Beyond the simple database operations we have looked at in the last two chapters, iBATIS can be used to perform much more advanced tasks. In this chapter, we will examine techniques that you can use to reduce the amount of code you need to write, and you will learn ways to improve performance and minimize the footprint of your application.

6.1 Using XML with iBATIS

Sometimes, you may need to work with XML-based data. The iBATIS framework will allow you to use XML when passing parameters into a query, and also for returning results from them. In both cases, it probably does not add much value to use XML where you do not need to—using a plain old Java object (POJO) instead is much more efficient in most cases.

In addition, it is possible that this feature will be dropped in the next major release for a couple of reasons. One of those reasons will become apparent as we look at the functionality. The other reason is that it just doesn't fit with the philosophy of the iBATIS framework, which is to make mapping queries to objects easier.

We will take a look at this feature, in case you have a system where you have to use it; but we will also show you some ways to transition away from it so that if it does disappear, you won't be left hanging high and dry looking for a way to make your application work.

6.1.1 XML parameters

Using XML to pass parameters into a mapped statement can be accomplished with either a String value or a DOM object, both of which use the exact same structure.

The structure of parameters is not exactly XML, but it is a well-formed XML fragment. In this structure, a parameter element wraps the values to be passed in and the values themselves are wrapped in elements, which provide the names. For example:

```
<parameter><accountId>3</accountId></parameter>
```

Here, the mapped statement would get a single parameter named `accountId`, with a value of 3. The following example uses an XML string to pass a parameter into a mapped statement:

```
<select id="getByXmlId" resultClass="Account" parameterClass="xml">
  select
    accountId,
    username,
    password,
```

```
    firstName,
    lastName,
    address1,
    address2,
    city,
    state,
    postalCode,
    country
  from Account
  where accountId = #accountId#
</select>

String parameter = "<parameter><accountId>3</accountId></parameter>";
Account account = (Account) sqlMapClient.queryForObject(
    "Account.getByXmlId",
    parameter);
```

Similarly, a DOM object can be passed into iBATIS to achieve the same results:

```
<select id="getByDomId" resultClass="Account" parameterClass="dom">
  select
    accountId,
    username,
    password,
    firstName,
    lastName,
    address1,
    address2,
    city,
    state,
    postalCode,
    country
  from Account
  where accountId = #accountId#
</select>

Document parameterDocument = DocumentBuilderFactory.newInstance()
    .newDocumentBuilder().newDocument();
Element paramElement = parameterDocument
    .createElement("parameterDocument");
Element accountIdElement = parameterDocument
    .createElement("accountId");
accountIdElement.setTextContent("3");
paramElement.appendChild(accountIdElement);
parameterDocument.appendChild(paramElement);
Account account = (Account) sqlMapClient.queryForObject(
    "Account.getByXmlId", parameterDocument);
```

As we mentioned earlier, that is a lot of code just to make your parameters into XML. However, if you are working with a tool like Cocoon, or writing web services in a framework that does not transform XML into objects for you, it can be useful.

Depending on the structure of the XML that you are starting with, it could be easier to use XSL to transform it into the structure required by iBATIS than to process the XML and turn it into a Java object, which is your alternative in those cases.

6.1.2 XML results

The iBATIS framework also allows you to create XML results from mapped statements. When running a mapped statement that returns XML, you get a complete XML document for each returned object.

To use this feature, you create a mapped statement that has a result class of `xml`. Here is a simple example:

```
<select id="getByIdValueXml" resultClass="xml"
        xmlResultName="account">
  select
    accountId,
    username,
    password
  from Account
  where accountId = #value#
</select>

String xmlData = (String) sqlMap.queryForObject(
                             "Account.getByIdValueXml",
                             new Integer(1));
```

The results returned in this case will look like this (well, not exactly; we added some whitespace and line feeds to make it more readable):

```
<?xml version="1.0" encoding="UTF-8"?>
<account>
  <accountid>1</accountid>
  <username>lmeadors</username>
  <password>blah</password>
</account>
```

Getting that data back is real handy if you have a single record that you want to get as an XML document. If you want to get multiple objects, you can do that as well:

```
<select id="getAllXml" resultClass="xml" xmlResultName="account">
  select
    accountId,
    username,
    password,
    firstName,
    lastName,
    address1,
    address2,
    city,
```

```
      state,
      postalCode,
      country
    from Account
  </select>

  List xmlList = sqlMap.queryForList("Account.getAllXml", null);
```

The resulting list in this case is a list of XML documents. Just what you wanted, right? Well, in some cases, maybe—but in most cases, no. Instead of a single XML document with multiple account elements in it, you get a list of strings like our previous result, which means that you have to manipulate the strings if you want to concatenate them all together into a single document. This is not exactly optimal.

The workaround is to not use iBATIS to get the XML results. A simple approach is to use a normal iBATIS mapped statement that returns a collection and creates the XML from that. One way to do that (if you are using a bean for your results) is to create a method like the following to help create the XML:

```
public String toXml(){
  StringBuffer returnValue = new StringBuffer("");
  returnValue.append("<account>");
  returnValue.append("<accountid>" + getAccountId() +"</accountid>");
  returnValue.append("<username>" + getUsername() + "</username>");
  returnValue.append("<password>" + getPassword() + "</password>");
  returnValue.append("</account>");
  return returnValue.toString();
}
```

Another approach to this issue is to create a class that uses reflection to convert a bean to XML. This is a fairly simple exercise. Here is a small utility that will get you started on this. Although this code is abbreviated to save some space, it demonstrates the technique.

```
public class XmlReflector {
  private Class sourceClass;
  private BeanInfo beanInfo;
  private String name;

  XmlReflector(Class sourceClass, String name) throws Exception {
    this.sourceClass = sourceClass;
    this.name = name;
    beanInfo = Introspector.getBeanInfo(sourceClass);
  }

  public String convertToXml(Object o) throws Exception {
    StringBuffer returnValue = new StringBuffer("");
    if (o.getClass().isAssignableFrom(sourceClass)) {
      PropertyDescriptor[] pd = beanInfo.getPropertyDescriptors();
```

```
      if (pd.length > 0){
        returnValue.append("<" + name + ">");
        for (int i = 0; i < pd.length; i++) {
          returnValue.append(getProp(o, pd[i]));
        }
        returnValue.append("</" + name + ">");
      } else {
        returnValue.append("<" + name + "/>");
      }
    } else {
      throw new ClassCastException("Class " + o.getClass().getName() +
          " is not compatible with " + sourceClass.getName());
    }
    return returnValue.toString();
  }

  private String getProp(Object o, PropertyDescriptor pd)
                                              throws Exception {
    StringBuffer propValue = new StringBuffer("");
    Method m = pd.getReadMethod();
    Object ret = m.invoke(o);
    if(null == ret){
      propValue.append("<" + pd.getName() + "/>");
    }else{
      propValue.append("<" + pd.getName() + ">");
      propValue.append(ret.toString());
      propValue.append("</" + pd.getName() + ">");
    }
    return propValue.toString();
  }
}
```

This sample class can be used to easily take a bean and convert it to an XML fragment instead of an XML document. Here is an example:

```
XmlReflector xr = new XmlReflector(Account.class, "account");
xmlList = sqlMap.queryForList("Account.getAll", null);
StringBuffer sb = new StringBuffer(
    "<?xml version=\"1.0\" encoding=\"UTF-8\" ?><accounts>");
for (int i = 0; i < xmlList.size(); i++) {
  sb.append(xr.convertToXml(xmlList.get(i)));
}
sb.append("</accounts>");
```

Using this technique to process a large set of records would be very expensive in terms of memory—there would be a list of objects in memory, as well as the string buffer used to build the XML document. In section 6.3, we revisit this example as we look at more effective ways to manage larger results.

6.2 Relating objects with mapped statements

The iBATIS framework also offers various means by which you can relate complex objects, such as an order and its order lines (and their products, customers, etc.). Each method has its own advantages and disadvantages, and as with most things, no single solution is the right one. Depending on your needs, one of them may do what you need.

NOTE For brevity's sake, in the rest of the examples in this chapter, we are leaving out attributes of the data that are not required to show what we are doing. For example, when we get a customer, we are not going to get *all* of the fields of the customer, but only the primary and foreign keys.

6.2.1 Complex collections

In chapter 4, you learned how to get data out of your database using `SELECT` statements. In those examples, we only worked with a single object type in the results, even when joining multiple tables. If you have more complex objects, you can also use iBATIS to load them.

This capability is useful if you like to have your application's model look like your data model. It is possible to use iBATIS to define your data model in terms of related objects, and have iBATIS load them all at once. For example, if you have a database in which `Account` records have related `Order` records that have related `OrderItem` records, those relationships can be set up so that when you request an `Account`, you also get all of the `Order` objects and all of the `OrderItem` objects as well. Listing 6.1 shows how you would define your SQL map to make this work.

Listing 6.1 Mapping a complex collection

```
<?xml version="1.0" encoding="UTF-8" ?>
<!DOCTYPE sqlMap
    PUBLIC "-//ibatis.apache.org//DTD SQL Map 2.0//EN"
    "http://ibatis.apache.org/dtd/sql-map-2.dtd">
<sqlMap namespace="Ch7">

  <resultMap id="ResultAccountInfoMap"                    <-- 1
    class="org.apache.mapper2.examples.bean.AccountInfo">
    <result property="account.accountId"
            column="accountId" />
    <result property="orderList"
            select="Ch6.getOrderInfoList"
            column="accountId" />
  </resultMap>

  <resultMap id="ResultOrderInfoMap"  <-- 2
```

```
    class="org.apache.mapper2.examples.bean.OrderInfo">
    <result property="order.orderId" column="orderId" />
    <result property="orderItemList" column="orderId"
      select="Ch6.getOrderItemList" />
  </resultMap>

  <resultMap id="ResultOrderItemMap"                        ⊲── ❸
    class="org.apache.mapper2.examples.bean.OrderItem">
    <result property="orderId" column="orderId" />
    <result property="orderItemId" column="orderItemId" />
  </resultMap>

  <select id="getAccountInfoList"             ⊲── ❹
          resultMap="ResultAccountInfoMap" >
    select accountId
    from Account
  </select>

  <select id="getOrderInfoList"          ⊲── ❺
          resultMap="ResultOrderInfoMap">
    select orderId
    from orders
    where accountId = #value#
  </select>

  <select id="getOrderItemList"          ⊲── ❻
          resultMap="ResultOrderItemMap">
    select
      orderId,
      orderItemId
    from orderItem
    where orderid = #value#
  </select>
</sqlMap>
```

If you look at the result maps (`ResultAccountInfoMap` ❶, `ResultOrderInfoMap` ❷, and `ResultOrderItemMap` ❸), you will see that the first two use the `select` attribute for one of the mapped properties. The presence of that attribute tells iBATIS that the property is to be set using the results of another mapped statement, which is named by its value. For example, when we run the `getAccountInfoList` mapped statement ❹, the `ResultAccountInfoMap` result map has `<result property="orderList" select="Ch6.getOrderInfoList" column="accountId" />`. That tells iBATIS to get the value for the `orderList` property by running the `"Ch6.getOrderInfoList"` mapped statement ❺, passing it the value of the `accountId` column, and then putting the returned data into `orderList`. Similarly, the `getOrderItemList` ❻ mapped statement is executed to get the value of the `orderItemList` property in the result map `ResultOrderInfoMap` ❷.

In spite of the convenience this functionality offers, two issues can arise. First, the creation of lists with many objects in them can turn into a massive memory consumer. Second, this approach can cause major database I/O problems very quickly due to a phenomenon known as the "N+1 Selects" problem, which we will talk about in a moment. The iBATIS framework provides solutions to each of those problems, but nothing can solve both at once.

Database I/O

Database I/O is one measure of how your database is being used, and is one of the major bottlenecks in database performance. When reading or writing to a database, the data has to be transferred from disk to memory or from memory to disk, which are expensive operations in terms of time. Avoiding database I/O with caching will make your application faster, but this strategy can be problematic if not used with caution. For more information on when and how to use the caching mechanisms that iBATIS provides, see chapter 10.

To illustrate the database I/O problems you can encounter when using related data, imagine a case where you have 1,000 `Accounts`, each related to 1,000 `Orders` that have 25 `OrderItems` each. If you try to load all of that into memory, it would result in the execution of over 1,000,000 SQL statements (one for the accounts, 1,000 for the orders, and 1,000,000 for the order items) and the creation of around 25 million Java objects—doing this will certainly get you a slap on the wrist from your system administrators!

Looking at the N+1 Selects problem

The N+1 Selects problem is caused by trying to load child records that are related to a list of parent records. So, if you run one query to get the parent records, and there are some number, *N*, of them, then you have to run *N* more queries to get the child records for the parent records, resulting in "N+1 Selects."

Solutions to these problems

Lazy loading (which we cover in more detail in section 6.2.2) can mitigate some of the memory problem by breaking the loading process into smaller, more manageable pieces. However, it still leaves the database I/O problem, because in the worst case it will still hit your database just as hard as the non-lazy version did since it still uses the N+1 Selects approach (which we'll solve in section 6.2.3) as it loads the data. When we solve the N+1 Selects problem to reduce the database I/O, however, we can do it with a single database query, but we get all 25,000,000 rows in one big chunk.

To decide whether to use complex properties, you need to understand your database and how your application will use it. If you use the techniques described in this section, you can save yourself a good deal of programming effort, but if you misuse it, you can create a big mess. In the next two sections, we look at how to decide which strategy to use, depending on your goals.

Let's start by asking this question: is the example of relating accounts to orders to order items a good example of when to relate your data this way? Actually, no—the order-to-order item relationship is solid, but the account-to-order relationship is not a requirement.

Our reasoning is that the order items are not complete objects without the order that owns them, while the account is. Think about it in terms of how you would use them. Generally, you would not be able to do much with an order without its order items, and conversely, the order items without the order are somewhat meaningless. An account, on the other hand, is something that could be thought of as a complete object.

For the purposes of our example, however, the relationship shows the technique well using concepts that are familiar and recognizable (`Accounts` have `Orders`, `Orders` have `Order Items`), and that is what we are trying to accomplish here, so we will stick with it for a while longer.

6.2.2 Lazy loading

The first of the options we will look at is *lazy loading*. Lazy loading is useful if all of the related data will not be needed immediately. For example, if our application called for a web page to show all accounts, then a sales representative (our user) could click on an account to view all of the orders for that account, and then click on an order to view all of the details for that order. All we need in this case is a single list at any time. This is a reasonable use of lazy loading.

To use lazy loading, we need to edit the `SqlMapConfig.xml` file to enable it by changing the `lazyLoadingEnabled` attribute to `true` in the `<setting>` element. If you want to use the cglib enhanced version of lazy loading, you will want to download it, add it to your application's classpath, and change the `enhancementEnabled` attribute of the `<setting>` element to `true` as well. One thing to note is that this is a global setting, so all of the mapped statements in the SQL map will use lazy loading if these properties are enabled.

Once we have enabled lazy loading, we can get to more reasonable numbers for object creation and database I/O. For one user to get down to the order detail level, we have three queries (one for the accounts, one for the orders, and one for the order details), and the application would only create 2,025 objects (1,000 accounts, 1,000 orders, and 25 order details). This is all done without any changes to the application code and only minor changes to the XML configuration of iBATIS.

In one totally nonscientific test that we performed, using a non-lazy loading relationship to load the data took over three times as long to get the first list than the lazy version. However, to get all of the data, the lazy version took about 20 percent longer than the non-lazy loader. Obviously, this will depend greatly on the amount of data being loaded, and as with most things, your mileage may vary. Experience is the best guide.

There are times when you do not want to defer the loading of all the data but want it all loaded when the data is first requested. In those cases, you can use the technique described in the next section, which will do just that, and do it all in one single query instead of several. This next approach avoids the N+1 Selects problem.

6.2.3 Avoiding the N+1 Selects problem

There are two ways to avoid the "N+1 Selects" problem that we will consider. One is by using the `groupBy` attribute in iBATIS, and the other is by using a custom component called a `RowHandler`.

Using the `groupBy` attribute is similar to the previous technique. In short, you define the relationships using result maps, and then associate the top-level result map with the mapped statement. The following example builds the same structure as the lazy loading example earlier, but with only one SQL statement run on the database server.

Three result maps are involved: one for the accounts, one for the orders, and one for the order items.

The result map for the accounts has three functions:

- It maps the properties for the account objects.
- It tells iBATIS what property indicates that a new account needs to be created.
- It tells iBATIS how to map the next set of related objects, which in this case is the related set of order objects for the account.

One very important thing to note here is that the `groupBy` attribute is referring to a property name, not a column name.

The result map for the orders has the same three functions:

- It maps the order data to the order objects.
- It tells iBATIS what property indicates a new order.
- It tells iBATIS what result map is to be used for any child records.

Finally, the order item result map is a normal result map that is only responsible for mapping the order items to objects. Listing 6.2 shows the mapping for this example.

Listing 6.2 Using the N+1 Selects solution

```
<resultMap id="ResultAccountInfoNMap"           <-- 1 Declares the result map for account data
           class="AccountInfo"
           groupBy="account.accountId" >
  <result property="account.accountId"
          column="accountId" />
  <result property="orderList"
          resultMap="Ch6.ResultOrderInfoNMap" />
</resultMap>

<resultMap id="ResultOrderInfoNMap"             <-- 2 Declares the result map for the order data
           class="OrderInfo"
           groupBy="order.orderId" >
  <result property="order.orderId" column="orderId" />
  <result property="orderItemList"
          resultMap="Ch6.ResultOrderItemNMap" />
</resultMap>

<resultMap id="ResultOrderItemNMap"             <-- 3 Declares the result map for the order item
           class="OrderItem">
  <result property="orderId"
          column="orderId" />
  <result property="orderItemId"
          column="orderItemId"  />
</resultMap>

<select id="getAccountInfoListN"                <-- 4 Ties the result map to the <select> element
      resultMap="ResultAccountInfoNMap">
  select
    account.accountId as accountid,
    orders.orderid as orderid,
    orderitem.orderitemid as orderitemid
  from account
  join orders on account.accountId = orders.accountId
  join orderitem on orders.orderId = orderitem.orderId
  order by accountId, orderid, orderitemid
</select>
```

By calling the `getAccountInfoListN` mapped statement ❹, we get the same data back that we did with the previous two examples (a list of accounts, each with a list of orders that have their associated order items as a list property on them), but because we are running only one SQL statement it is much faster. The `getAccountInfoListN` mapped statement ❹ is run, and the results are mapped using the `resultAccountInfoNMap` result map ❶, which uses the `groupBy` attribute. That attribute tells iBATIS that it only needs to create a new `AccountInfo` instance when the `account.accountId` property changes. Further, because the `orderList` property is mapped to the `ResultOrderInfoNMap` result map ❷, that list is populated as rows from the query are processed. Since the `ResultOrderInfoNMap` result map also uses the `groupBy` attribute, the process is repeated for the `orderItemList` using the `ResultOrderItemNMap` result map ❸ for the `orderItemList` property.

Using our totally nonscientific measurement from earlier, we receive a performance improvement of about 7 to 1 with a small set of data. We suspect that with the example we started with (25 million records), both cases would still be showstoppers.

It is important to remember that in spite of the performance increase, the memory consumption is still the same as the non-lazy version. All rows are in memory at one time, so even though it gets the list faster, memory utilization may still be a problem.

The bottom line here is that, depending on your needs, one of these techniques may help you out. How do you decide? Table 6.1 provides a guide.

Table 6.1 Differences between lazy loading and the N+1 select solution

Lazy loading	N+1 Select solution
Good for cases when you are getting a larger data set that may not all be used.	Good for a smaller data set or a data set where you know you will use all of the data.
Performance up front is a priority and you are willing to pay for it later.	Overall performance is the priority.

So, that is about all there is to mapping complex results. Next, let's see some other uses of iBATIS.

6.3 Inheritance

Inheritance is a fundamental concept in object-oriented programming. Inheritance allows us to extend classes, effectively inheriting fields and methods from a base class—or even a hierarchy of many base classes. The new class can override the existing methods to enhance or replace the functionality. Inheritance features of an object-oriented language such as Java yields many benefits, including:

- *Code reuse*—An abstract base class can be built that contains a lot of common logic, but by itself is incomplete. The subclasses that extend the base class can complete the functionality while reusing the common features of the base class. The result is that you can have a number of implementations of a feature without rewriting or duplicating the common aspects.
- *Enhancement and specialization*—Sometimes you might decide to extend a class to add more useful features. This is a common reason to extend collection classes. For example, one might decide to extend the ArrayList class to only support Strings called StringArray. New features could then be added, such as features for searching based on a regular expression.
- *Common interface*—Although using an actual interface instead of an abstract class might be a better choice here, it is possible to use a base class as a common interface in a framework or some other sort of pluggable system.

There are other benefits of inheritance, but there are also many risks. Inheritance is notoriously inflexible for modeling business domains. Business is often too complex to commit to a single hierarchy. This is especially true in a language such as Java, where you can only extend from a single superclass (single inheritance). Even if your programming language of choice supports multiple inheritance, it still may not be the best choice.

Many patterns and best practices that have emerged over the years have suggested favoring alternatives to inheritance. These alternatives include:

- *Favor composition over inheritance*—A good example of this is roles that people play. A generally poor design would have a Manager class extending from Employee, which extends from Person. That is to say that a Manager "is an" Employee and an Employee "is a" Person. This may indeed be true, but what happens when that same person is a Customer? For example, a Manager decides to shop at his own store. Where does a person who is both a Customer and an Employee fit in that hierarchy? Certainly a Customer is not necessarily an Employee, nor is an Employee necessarily a customer. Instead of modeling this using inheritance, you might want to consider using composition. Change the "is a" relationship to a "has a" relationship by keeping a collection of Roles on the Person class. That way a person can have any combination of the roles described.
- *Favor interfaces over abstract classes*—In cases in which your intent is to have a common interface to describe a certain set of functionality, you're better off

using an actual interface type instead of an abstract class directly. A good approach to achieve both code reuse and a separation between interface and implementation is a tripartite design. In a tripartite design you still use an abstract class to achieve some level of code reuse, but you design the abstract class to implement an interface, and then expose only the interface to the public application programming interface (API). Finally, the specialized (or concrete) classes extend from the base class and inherently implement the interface.

6.3.1 Mapping Inheritance

iBATIS supports inheritance hierarchies by using a special mapping called a discriminator. Using a discriminator you can determine the type of class to be instantiated based on a value in the database. The discriminator is a part of the Result Map and works much like a switch statement. For example:

```
<resultMap id="document" class="testdomain.Document">
 <result property="id" column="DOCUMENT_ID"/>
 <result property="title" column="TITLE"/>
 <result property="type" column="TYPE"/>
 <discriminator column="TYPE" javaType="string" >
  <subMap value="Book" resultMap="book"/>
  <subMap value="Newspaper" resultMap="news"/>
 </discriminator>
</resultMap>
```

The discriminator above can be read this way:

> If the column “TYPE” contains the value “Book,” then use the result map called “book,” otherwise if the column TYPE contains the value “Newspaper,” then use the result map called “news.”

The sub maps are just normal result maps referenced by name (see below). If the discriminator can’t find a value to match one of the sub maps, then the parent result map is applied. If an appropriate value is found, then only the sub map is applied—the parent’s defined result mappings are not applied unless the sub maps explicitly extend the parent map, as you can see in the following example.

```
<resultMap id="book" class="testdomain.Book" extends="document">
 <result property="pages" column="DOCUMENT_PAGENUMBER"/>
</resultMap>
```

The `extends` attribute of the result map effectively copies all of the result mappings from the referenced result map. However, it does not imply anything about the class hierarchy. Remember, iBATIS is not an object/relational mapping framework per se. It is a SQL Mapper. The difference is that iBATIS does not know or care about the mappings between classes and database tables. Therefore there is no requirement that the sub maps use a class that extends from the class referenced in the parent result map. In other words, you're free to use discriminators however you like, for whatever purpose seems natural. Of course, inheritance is an obvious application, but you may find other situations where discriminators come in handy.

6.4 Other miscellaneous uses

The iBATIS framework is designed to be flexible. The `<statement>` mapped statement type is another way to open more doors for uses that may not be possible using the other mapped statement types.

6.4.1 Using the statement type and DDL

The `<statement>` type is a bit of an oddball in that unlike all of the other types (`<insert>`, `<update>`, `<delete>`, and `<select>`) it has no corresponding method to call it with. That is a hint: the use of `<statement>` is not encouraged, and it should be employed only as a last resort.

Data Definition Language (DDL) is a subset of SQL statements that are used to define the structure of a database schema. You would use DDL to define tables and indexes, and to perform other operations that do not change the data, but change the data structure instead.

Although using DDL is officially unsupported, your database may allow you to execute DDL statements via iBATIS using the `<statement>` type. The PostgreSQL database, for example, allows using the `<statement>` type to create and drop database tables:

```
<statement id="dropTable">
  DROP TABLE Account CASCADE;
</statement>

sqlMap.update("Account.dropTable", null);
```

There are no guarantees that your database will support running DDL statements this way, but if so, it can be useful for writing routines that create or modify database structures.

In the next section, we look at one of the features of iBATIS that makes it very flexible but that is often overlooked: row handlers.

6.4.2 Processing extremely large data sets

Occasionally you may find that requirements for an application seem to make the use of large data sets look like the right choice. In most cases, those requirements can be met in other ways, and in those cases, some probing questions can uncover the real need.

For instance, suppose you are handed a requirement document dictating that the entire contents of a 30,000-row data table be output as HTML for users to browse. The first question to ask is, "Do you really need *all* of that data?" It's our experience that there is no "Yes" answer from a logical and defensible position. While we do not doubt that the users do need to see all of that data, we do question whether they need to see all of that data *at one time*. In almost every case, a filter that limits what is returned will work better for your users than a "fire hose" report that just dumps the output of a "select * from table" type of query onto a screen.

If the results are not required for output but are required for processing, you should seriously consider whether a stored procedure would work better for it than Java code. Although stored procedures are often viewed as the anathema of the "Write once, run anywhere" goal of Java, we have seen cases where an application that took 10–15 minutes to run as pure Java ran in under 10 seconds with a stored procedure. The users of that system do not care about the purity of the application; they care about being able to use it to get their job done.

No more dodging the question...

So, now that we have tried to avoid the issue of dealing with massive data sets, and decided that we really do have to deal with them, let's look at what iBATIS provides to handle them: the `RowHandler` interface was created just for these cases.

The `RowHandler` interface is a simple one that allows you to insert behavior into the processing of a mapped statement's result set. The interface has only one method:

```
public interface RowHandler {
  void handleRow(Object valueObject);
}
```

The `handleRow` method is called once for each row that is in the result set of a mapped statement. Using this interface, you are able to handle very large amounts of data without loading it all into memory at one time. Only one row of the data is loaded into memory, your code is called, that object is discarded, and the process repeats until the results have all been processed.

RowHandler objects can help speed up the processing of large sets of data if needed. This is a last resort for dealing with large data sets, but it is also the Swiss army knife of iBATIS. You can do almost anything with a RowHandler.

In section 6.1.2, we looked at the XML result-generation capabilities in iBATIS, and found them to be lacking in some ways—notably in the case where you want to get a single XML document for a list of objects or for a complex object. In that section we promised to show you how to get XML data using less memory than getting an entire list or object graph and iterating through it. Using a RowHandler, we still iterate through the objects, but only one element of that list is in memory at one time. Here is a row handler that builds a single XML document with multiple <account> elements in it:

```
public class AccountXmlRowHandler implements RowHandler {
  private StringBuffer xmlDocument = new StringBuffer("<AccountList>");
  private String returnValue = null;

  public void handleRow(Object valueObject) {
    Account account = (Account) valueObject;
    xmlDocument.append("<account>");

    xmlDocument.append("<accountId>");
    xmlDocument.append(account.getAccountId());
    xmlDocument.append("</accountId>");

    xmlDocument.append("<username>");
    xmlDocument.append(account.getUsername());
    xmlDocument.append("</username>");

    xmlDocument.append("<password>");
    xmlDocument.append(account.getPassword());
    xmlDocument.append("</password>");

    xmlDocument.append("</account>");
  }

  public String getAccountListXml(){
    if (null == returnValue){
      xmlDocument.append("</AccountList>");
      returnValue = xmlDocument.toString();
    }
    return returnValue;
  }
}
```

The code to use this with an existing mapped statement that returns a list of Account objects is remarkably simple. The basic design is that you create an instance of a RowHandler and call the queryWithRowHandler method, passing in the mapped statement to run, the parameters required by the mapped statement, and the row handler instance. The following example creates an XML document with all of the accounts returned by a mapped statement encoded as XML:

```
AccountXmlRowHandler rh = new AccountXmlRowHandler();
sqlMapClient.queryWithRowHandler("Account.getAll", null, rh);
String xmlData = rh.getAccountListXml();
```

If XML is not your cup of tea, maybe this next example will help you see how useful row handlers can be.

Another more interesting RowHandler example

Another example of how to use a row handler is to handle several aspects of multiple table relationships. For example, in our sample database, we have accounts (or customers), who can have multiple orders, which can have multiple order items, which have a product, and each product has a manufacturer. Figure 6.1 shows the data model for the relationships.

Let's imagine a requirement where we need to provide a list of products that were ordered and a list of the accounts that had ordered that product. We also want a list of accounts, and we want each of those accounts to have a list of manufacturers that they had ordered from. It might also be nice to have these as a Map object (by ID) that we could use to quickly find an account or product.

Although we could do that using the existing `groupBy` attribute and the `queryForMap` method, using four mapped statements, this approach would require four separate select statements (meaning more database I/O) and would potentially give us multiple copies of each object. The customer objects returned by the first

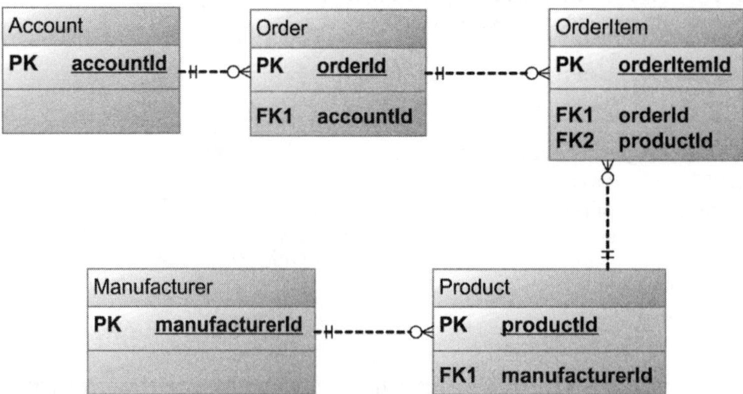

Figure 6.1 Entity relationship diagram for examples

mapped statement would not be the same objects as those returned by the second mapped statement (meaning more memory use). We can do better than that!

Using a RowHandler, we can meet this requirement with a single SQL statement. That way, we have to process the results only once to get both of the main lists with the related lists, the Maps, and all of that without any duplicate objects. Using this approach requires a bit more coding but uses less processing time, less database I/O, and less memory.

To make this happen, we join the data, then as we look at each row, we add new items to the lists (of products and accounts) and to the maps. That sounds simple enough, so let's look at the code.

First, we create the mapped statement. It will join the tables, retrieve the relevant data, and map it into three distinct objects in a composite that has all three things that we care about:

```
<resultMap id="AmpRHExample"
class="org.apache.mapper2.examples.chapter6.AccountManufacturerProduct">
  <result property="account.accountId" column="accountId" />
  <result property="manufacturer.manufacturerId"
          column="manufacturerId" />
  <result property="product.productId" column="productId" />
</resultMap>

<select id="AMPRowHandlerExample" resultMap="AmpRHExample">
  select distinct
    p.productId as productId,
    o.accountId as accountId,
    m.manufacturerId as manufacturerId
  from product p
  join manufacturer m
    on p.manufacturerId = m.manufacturerId
  join orderitem oi
    on oi.productId = p.productId
  join orders o
    on oi.orderId = o.orderId
  order by 1,2,3
</select>
```

The AccountManufacturerProduct class is simply a class with three properties: account, manufacturer, and product. The result map populates the properties, just as we would do if we were going to create a regular flattened view of the data.

Next, the row handler takes these objects as it encounters them, and categorizes them by productId, accountId, and manufacturerId into maps. The first time it encounters a particular account or product, it also adds that object to the account List or product List, respectively. If the selected objects have already been loaded, the existing one (from the maps) replaces the one that was just loaded from the database.

Finally, after it has gotten the single instance of a particular account, manufacturer, or product, it adds them to the appropriate objects, as shown in listing 6.3.

Listing 6.3 A very powerful row handler

```
public class AMPRowHandler implements RowHandler {
  private Map<Integer, AccountManufacturers> accountMap
      = new HashMap<Integer, AccountManufacturers>();
  private Map<Integer, Manufacturer> manufacturerMap
      = new HashMap<Integer, Manufacturer>();
  private Map<Integer, ProductAccounts> productMap
      = new HashMap<Integer, ProductAccounts>();
  private List<ProductAccounts> productAccountList
      = new ArrayList<ProductAccounts>();
  private List<AccountManufacturers> accountManufacturerList
      = new ArrayList<AccountManufacturers>();

  public void handleRow(Object valueObject) {      <-- 1 Contains only required method
    AccountManufacturerProduct amp;
    amp = (AccountManufacturerProduct)valueObject;
    Account currentAccount = amp.getAccount();
    Manufacturer currentMfgr = amp.getManufacturer();
    AccountManufacturers am;
    ProductAccounts pa;                              Checks for duplicate accounts 2
    Product currentProduct = amp.getProduct();
    if (null == accountMap.get(currentAccount.getAccountId())) {   <--
      // this is the first time we have seen this account
      am = new AccountManufacturers();
      am.setAccount(currentAccount);
      accountMap.put(currentAccount.getAccountId(), am);
      accountManufacturerList.add(am);
    } else {
      // Use the accoutn from the account map
      am = accountMap.get(currentAccount.getAccountId());
      currentAccount = am.getAccount();
    }
    // am is now the current account / manufacturerlist

    if (null ==
        manufacturerMap.get(currentMfgr.getManufacturerId())) {   <--
     // we have not seen this manufacturer yet
      manufacturerMap.put(                           Checks for duplicate manufacturers 3
          currentMfgr.getManufacturerId(),
          currentMfgr);
    } else {
      //  we already have this manufacturer loaded, reuse it
      currentMfgr = manufacturerMap.get(
```

```
            currentMfgr.getManufacturerId());
      }
      am.getManufacturerList().add(currentMfgr);                Checks for ❹
                                                          duplicate products
      if (null == productMap.get(currentProduct.getProductId())) {  <-
        // this is a new product
        pa = new ProductAccounts();
        pa.setProduct(currentProduct);
        productMap.put(currentProduct.getProductId(), pa);
        productAccountList.add(pa);
      } else {
        // this prodcut has been loaded already
        pa = productMap.get(currentProduct.getProductId());
      }
      // pa is now the current product's product / account list
      pa.getAccountList().add(currentAccount);
      am.getManufacturerList().add(currentMfgr);
    }                                                   Gets list of ❺
                                                 ProductAccount beans
    public List<ProductAccounts> getProductAccountList() {  <-
      return productAccountList;
    }                                                      Gets list of ❻
                                                AccountManufacturer beans
    public List<AccountManufacturers> getAccountManufacturerList() {  <-
      return accountManufacturerList;
    }                                              Gets product map ❼

    public Map<Integer, ProductAccounts> getProductMap() {  <-
      return productMap;
    }                                                  Gets account map ❽

    public Map<Integer, AccountManufacturers> getAccountMap() {  <-
      return accountMap;
    }
  }
```

Although the code here looks pretty complex, keep in mind that what it is doing is also quite complex. We start with the one and only required method ❶, and in it we process the returned data to build the exact lists and maps that we want by keeping only unique account objects ❷, manufacturer objects ❸, and product objects ❹, which we then expose to the caller using the getters (❺, ❻, ❼, and ❽) on the row handler. In addition, we provide object identity, so the account, product, and manufacturer instances in all cases are the same objects. In other words, the account with an ID value of 1 is the same instance of the account class in all of the data structures—therefore, a change to it will be reflected in all other places that it occurs.

6.5 Summary

In this chapter, you learned how to map XML data into iBATIS as well as how to use iBATIS to generate XML for your results. We also discussed relating multiple tables using multiple SQL statements, or one statement to bring all of the related data together.

In chapters 4 through 6, you have seen almost everything that iBATIS can do when mapping statements—from the simple to the exotic. In the next chapter, you'll learn how to use iBATIS in a more transaction-oriented environment.

7 Transactions

This chapter covers

- Introduction to transactions
- Automatic, local, and global transactions
- Custom transactions
- Transaction demarcation

Transactions are one of the most important concepts to understand when working with a relational database. Few decisions you make will have a greater impact on stability, performance, and data integrity. Knowing how to identify and demarcate the transactions in the system you are building is imperative. In this chapter, we'll discuss what transactions are and how to work with them.

7.1 What is a transaction?

In the simplest terms, a *transaction* is a unit of work, usually involving a number of steps that must succeed or fail as a group. Should any step in the transaction fail, all steps are rolled back so that the data is left in a consistent state. The easiest way to explain a transaction is with an example.

7.1.1 A simple banking example

A common example of why transactions are important is a bank funds transfer. Consider two bank accounts owned by Alice and Bob, as shown in table 7.1.

Table 7.1 Starting balances

Alice's account		Bob's account	
Balance	$5,000.00	Balance	$10,000.00

Now consider a transfer of $1,000.00 from Alice to Bob (table 7.2).

Table 7.2 Desired transaction

Alice's account		Bob's account	
Balance	$5,000.00	Balance	$10,000.00
Withdrawal	$1,000.00		
		Deposit	$1,000.00
Balance	$4,000.00	Balance	$11,000.00

The withdrawal from Alice's account and the deposit into Bob's account must be completed within a single transaction. Otherwise, if the deposit failed, Alice's account balance would be $4,000.00, but Bob's would still only be $10,000.00 (table 7.3). The $1,000.00 would be lost in limbo.

Table 7.3 Failed deposit

Alice's account		Bob's account	
Balance	$5,000.00	Balance	$10,000.00
Withdrawal	$1,000.00		
		Deposit (FAILS)	**~~$1,000.00~~**
Balance	$4,000.00	Balance	$10,000.00

Table 7.4 Failed deposit

Alice's account		TX	Bob's account	
Balance	$5,000.00		Balance	$10,000.00
Withdrawal (Rollback)	**~~$1,000.00~~**	TX1		
		TX1	**Deposit (FAILS)**	**~~$1,000.00~~**
Balance	$5,000.00		Balance	$10,000.00

This is quite a simple example. As you can imagine, a true-life transfer of funds within a banking system would be much more complex. For that reason, there are various types of transactions that allow transactions to encompass a much broader scope.

Transactions can be very small and basic, perhaps consisting of only a couple of SQL statements that change data in a single table of a single database. However, transactions can also become very large and complex. A business-to-business transaction could even leave the realm of computers and require physical interaction with human beings (e.g., a signature). The topic of transactions could easily fill a book of its own, so we'll only consider four scopes of transactions that iBATIS supports:

- *Automatic*—For simple, single statements that don't require an explicitly demarcated transaction.
- *Local*—A simple, narrowly scoped transaction involving many statements but only a single database.

- *Global*—A complex, broadly scoped transaction involving many statements and many databases or potentially other transaction capable resources such as JMS (Java Messaging Service) queues or JCA (J2EE Connector Architecture) connections.
- *Custom*—iBATIS supports user-provided connections for which you can manage the transactions however you like.

We've dedicated a section of this chapter to each of these scopes. Before we discuss them in more detail, let's first talk about the properties of transactions.

7.1.2 Understanding transaction properties

Certain properties, or features, are required for a system to be able to honestly claim it is capable of performing transaction processing. Nearly all modern relational databases support transactions, and any that don't should not be considered for enterprise solutions. The properties are known as the ACID (atomicity, consistency, isolation, and durability) properties.

Atomicity

The feature that guarantees that all steps in a transaction either succeed or fail as a group is called *atomicity*. Without this, it's possible that the database could be left in an inaccurate state because one step of the transaction failed. This can be illustrated very simply by thinking of mathematical addition. Let's add up some numbers and consider each addition as a step in the transaction (table 7.5).

Table 7.5 Desired transaction

Transaction state	Operation
Initial State	10
Step 1	+ 30
Step 2	+ 45
Step 3	+ 15
End State	= 100

Now let's say one of those additions failed, say step 3 (table 7.6).

Table 7.6 Nonatomic transaction

Transaction state	Operation
Failed Step 3	~~+ 15~~
End State	= 85

The data is incorrect because one of the steps in the transaction failed (table 7.7).

Initial State	10
Step 1	+ 30
Step 2	+ 45
Failed Step 3	+ 15
Rolled Back Initial State	= 10

In a system that guarantees atomicity, none of the operations would be performed, and the data in the database would not be impacted.

Consistency

Many good database schemas define constraints to ensure integrity and consistency. The ACID feature called *consistency* requires that at both the beginning and the end of a transaction the database must be in a consistent state. A consistent state is defined as one whereby all constraints—including integrity constraints, foreign keys, and uniqueness—are met.

Isolation

Databases are often centralized resources shared by a number of users. It doesn't matter how many users you have; if there's more than one user, it becomes very important to keep transactions from conflicting with each other. The ACID feature

isolation

transaction (table 7.8)?

Table 7.8 Isolated transaction

User 1	Operation	User 2
Initial State	10	
Step 1	+ 30	
Step 2	+ 45	
Intermediate State	= 85	<< Read
Step 3	+ 15	
End State	= 100	

There is no simple answer, as there are various isolation levels that a database *may* support. The trade-off for the level of isolation is performance. The more isolated a transaction needs to be, the slower it will be—especially concurrent access performance. The isolation levels are as follows:

- *Read uncommitted*—This is the lowest level of isolation, and is really no isolation at all. It will read data from a table, even if it is the result of an incomplete transaction. Hence, in our example, this isolation level would result in 85 being returned.
- *Read committed*—This level of isolation prevents uncommitted data from being returned. However, within a transaction, if rows are selected there is nothing stopping those rows from being modified by another user, even before the transaction is complete. This means that if the same rows are queried once at the beginning of the transaction and once at the end, they aren't guaranteed to be the same.
- *Repeatable read*—This level ensures that only committed data will be read, and in addition will acquire read-locks on queried rows to prevent them from being modified by another user before the end of the transaction. However, this level of protection depends completely on the type of query used. If the query contains a range clause (e.g., `BETWEEN`), a range lock will not be acquired, and therefore the rows may be changed by another user

and again cause different results when the same ranged query is run twice within the same transaction (known as *phantom reads*).

- *Serializable*—This is the highest level of isolation possible. Essentially it executes all transactions in order, one after the other, so that there is no conflict among any one of them. Obviously this imposes a significant performance penalty for highly concurrent systems, because everyone ends up standing in line to complete their work.

Durability

A database that doesn't persist data in a durable way is like a bridge that doesn't support the cars that drive on it. The ACID feature of *durability* requires that once the database has reported a transaction as ending successfully, the results are safe. Even if a system failure occurs *after* the transaction, the data should be safe.

Now that you're familiar with the basics of transactions and the qualities that make them what they are, let's discuss how you work with various types of transactions in iBATIS.

7.2 Automatic transactions

iBATIS only deals in transactions; it has no concept of ever working outside of a transaction scope. So although JDBC has a concept of "autocommit" mode, iBATIS does not support it directly. Instead, iBATIS supports automatic transactions. This allows you to run a simple update statement or query with a single method call, and without worrying about demarcating the transaction. The statement will still be run inside a transaction, but you do not have to explicitly start, commit, or end it.

There's nothing special you need to do to run a statement within an automatic transaction—you simply execute your statement. The configuration is the same as for local transactions, which we discuss in the next section. Listing 7.1 shows how this is done. Note that each statement is a separate transaction, including the calls to `queryForObject` and `update()`.

Listing 7.1 Automatic transaction

```
public void runStatementsUsingAutomaticTransactions()
{
     SqlMapClient sqlMapClient =
       SqlMapClientConfig.getSqlMapClient();
      Person p = (Person)
         sqlMapClient.queryForObject("getPerson",
                                     new Integer(9));
```

```
        p.setLastName("Smith");
        sqlMapClient.update("updatePerson", p);
}
```

Where is the transaction? Well, since it's automatic, it just happens behind the scenes, but it does happen. Many times that is adequate, but sometimes you need to have finer control, and in those cases, you'll need to use more explicit local or global transactions.

7.3 Local transactions

Local transactions are the most common type of transaction, and are really the minimum you should use on any project involving a relational database. Even automatic transactions, as discussed in the previous section, are a less verbose form of local transaction. A local transaction is one that is contained within a single application and involves a resource, such as a relational database, that is capable of only a single transaction. Figure 7.1 depicts this.

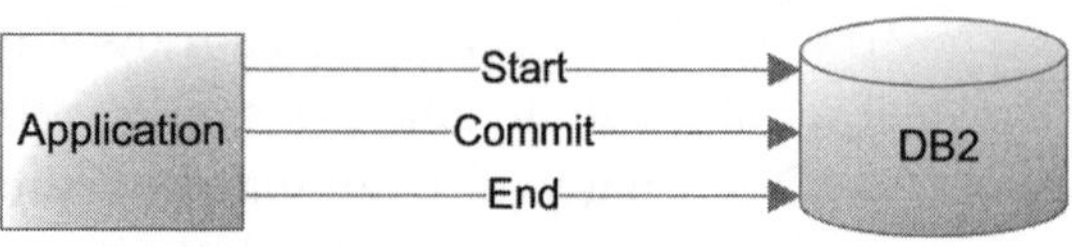

Figure 7.1 Local transaction scope

Local transactions are configured in the iBATIS SQL Map configuration XML file as a JDBC transaction manager. Listing 7.2 shows how the transaction manager configuration might read.

Listing 7.2 Local transaction manager configuration

```
<transactionManager type="JDBC">
      <dataSource type="SIMPLE">
            <property …/>
            <property …/>
            <property …/>
      </dataSource>
</transactionManager>
```

The `type="JDBC"` attribute tells iBATIS to use the standard JDBC Connection API for managing transactions. Using the SqlMapClient API to demarcate transactions is very easy. Listing 7.3 shows the typical pattern for transaction demarcation.

Listing 7.3 Local transaction

```
public void runStatementsUsingLocalTransactions() {
  SqlMapClient sqlMapClient =
    SqlMapClientConfig.getSqlMapClient();
  try {
      sqlMapClient.startTransaction();
      Person p =
       (Person)sqlMapClient.queryForObject
                      ("getPerson", new Integer(9));
      p.setLastName("Smith");
      sqlMapClient.update("updatePerson", p);

      Department d =
       (Department)sqlMapClient.queryForObject
                      ("getDept", new Integer(3));
      p.setDepartment(d);
      sqlMapClient.update("updatePersonDept", p);
      sqlMapClient.commitTransaction();
  } finally {
        sqlMapClient.endTransaction();
  }
}
```

The two update statements in listing 7.3 will be run within the same transaction, and therefore if either one fails, both will fail.

It's very important to note the `try/finally` block that surrounds the transaction demarcation methods. This pattern ensures that the transaction will be properly ended, even in the event of an error. Using a `try/finally` block is simpler and more effective than using a `try/catch` block, because it doesn't require you to catch an exception that you probably can't do anything with anyway.

7.4 Global transactions

Global transactions define a much wider transaction scope than local transactions do. They can involve other databases, message queues, and even other applications. Figure 7.2 shows such systems and illustrates just how complicated global transactions can become.

Luckily, as far as iBATIS goes, using a global transaction isn't any harder than using a local one. But, there are some things to be aware of, as well as some choices to make, some of which are best discovered through trial and error.

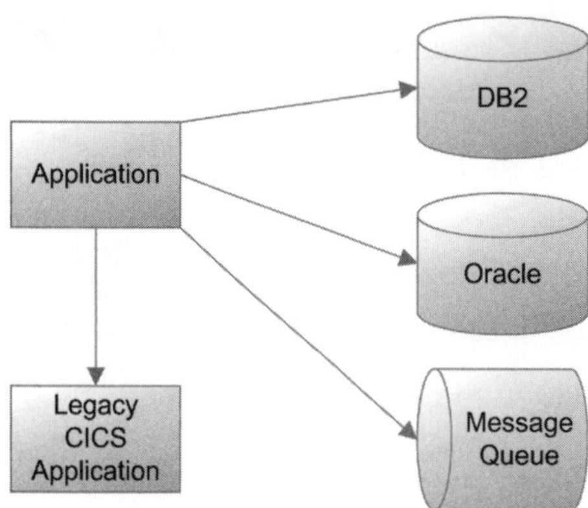

Figure 7.2
Example of global transaction scope

7.4.1 Using active or passive transactions

iBATIS can participate in a global transaction in one of two ways: actively or passively. When configured to actively participate, iBATIS will look for the global transaction context and attempt to manage it appropriately. This means that iBATIS can check the state of an existing transaction or start one if necessary. It will also be able to set the state to "rollback-only" in the event of an error, which will notify other participating resources that the transaction should not be committed.

When configured to passively participate in a global transaction, iBATIS will simply ignore all instructions to start, commit, and end transactions. It will throw exceptions in the case of an error, which iBATIS assumes will cause the transaction to be rolled back.

Deciding which to use is sometimes a matter of just trying it. Different application servers and different architectures will work better one way or the other. The good thing is, it's very easy to switch back and forth. Listing 7.4 shows the configuration for both active participation and passive participation.

Listing 7.4 Global transaction manager configuration options

```
<transactionManager type="JTA">
      <property name="UserTransaction"
      value="java:/ctx/con/someUserTransaction"/>
      <dataSource type="JNDI">
            <property name="DataSource"
      value="java:comp/env/jdbc/someDataSource"/>
      </dataSource>
</transactionManager>
```

Active participation

```
<transactionManager type="EXTERNAL">
      <dataSource type="JNDI">
```

Passive participation

```
        <property name="DataSource"
      value="java:comp/env/jdbc/someDataSource"/>
     </dataSource>
</transactionManager>
```

Passive participation

Notice how in both cases the DataSource is retrieved from a JNDI context. This is a practical requirement, since the connections you will need must be managed within a global transaction manager scope. In the case of JTA, a UserTransaction instance is also required from a JNDI context, so that it can actively participate. In the case of the EXTERNAL transaction manager, it does not need the UserTransaction instance, as it assumes that some external system is managing the transaction participation.

7.4.2 Starting, committing, and ending the transaction

Coding for a global transaction is exactly the same as coding for automatic or local transactions. So you should still start, commit, and end the "inner transaction scope." You might ask why, considering the transaction is globally defined. There are two reasons. First, it helps iBATIS manage other resources such as connections to the database so that you don't unnecessarily keep requesting and returning connections from the data source. Second, it allows you to switch back and forth between local and global transactions without any code changes. Listing 7.5 shows the same transaction as in the local example; and as you can see, it doesn't make a difference to iBATIS whether you're using local or global transactions.

Listing 7.5 Global transaction

```
public void runStatementsUsingGlobalTransactions() {
  SqlMapClient sqlMapClient =
    SqlMapClientConfig.getSqlMapClient();
  try {
      sqlMapClient.startTransaction();
      Person p =
       (Person)sqlMapClient.queryForObject
                      ("getPerson", new Integer(9));
      p.setLastName("Smith");
      sqlMapClient.update("updatePerson", p);

      Department d =
       (Department)sqlMapClient.queryForObject
                      ("getDept", new Integer(3));
      p.setDepartment(d);
      sqlMapClient.update("updatePersonDept", p);
      sqlMapClient.commitTransaction();
```

```
    } finally {
        sqlMapClient.endTransaction();
    }
}
```

So, now that you know how to carry out either local or global transactions, how do you decide which to use? Read on for help making that decision.

7.4.3 Do I need a global transaction?

The answer to this question is: "probably not." In general, there is a great deal of overhead involved with global transactions. This is mostly due to the fact that they are distributed and that they typically require more network traffic and state management than local transactions. If there were no cost, we probably would just use global transactions for everything. In addition to the lost performance, global transactions are harder to set up. They need more infrastructure, more software, and more resources. So even if you're using container-managed transactions, ensure that you're only using global transactions if you're absolutely certain you need them. Most good application servers have very simple configuration options to enable or disable distributed transactions.

If none of the options we have looked at will meet your needs, more options are available.

7.5 Custom transactions

As you've already seen, iBATIS allows you to manage transactions in various ways. If none of the provided transaction management approaches works for you, then there are a couple of options for managing transactions yourself. The first is by writing your own transaction manager using the iBATIS interfaces and then plugging it into the SQL Map configuration file. This approach is discussed in chapter 12. The second approach is to simply pass iBATIS a JDBC `Connection` instance to work with, thereby allowing you full control over the connection and transaction. There are two ways to pass a `Connection` instance to a `SqlMapClient`. The first is `setUserConnection(Connection)`, which is shown in listing 7.6.

Listing 7.6 Custom transaction control with setUserTransaction()

```
public void runStatementsUsingSetUserConnection() {
  SqlMapClient sqlMapClient =
    SqlMapClientConfig.getSqlMapClient();
  Connection conn = null;
```

```
  try {
    conn = dataSource.getConnection();
    conn.setAutoCommit(false);
    sqlMapClient.setUserConnection(conn);
    Person p =
      (Person)sqlMapClient.queryForObject
                       ("getPerson", new Integer(9));
    p.setLastName("Smith");
    sqlMapClient.update("updatePerson", p);

    Department d =
      (Department)sqlMapClient.queryForObject
                     ("getDept", new Integer(3));
      p.setDepartment(d);
      sqlMapClient.update("updatePersonDept", p);
      conn.commit();
  } finally {
      sqlMapClient.setUserConnection(null);
      if (conn != null) conn.close();
  }
}
```

The second way is to use openSession (Connection). This is the preferred approach, because iBATIS can do a better job of resource management. Listing 7.7 shows how this is done with openSession().

Listing 7.7 Custom transaction control with openSession()

```
public void runStatementsUsingSetUserConnection() {
  SqlMapClient sqlMapClient =
  SqlMapClientConfig.getSqlMapClient();
  Connection conn = null;
  SqlMapSession session = null;
  try {
    conn = dataSource.getConnection();
    conn.setAutoCommit(false);
    session = sqlMapClient.openSession(conn);
    Person p =
      (Person)session.queryForObject("getPerson",
                                  new Integer(9));
      p.setLastName("Smith");
      session.update("updatePerson", p);

      Department d =
       (Department)session.queryForObject
                     ("getDept", new Integer(3));
      p.setDepartment(d);
      session.update("updatePersonDept", p);
```

```
        conn.commit();
    } finally {
        if (session != null) session.close();
        if (conn != null) conn.close();
    }
}
```

The code isn't as elegant this way, which is sometimes a good reason to write your own transaction manager. Furthermore, you should still define a transaction manager of type EXTERNAL and also provide at least a SIMPLE `DataSource`; otherwise certain features such as lazy loading will not work properly.

Avoid using this approach if possible, and always consider writing your own transaction manager.

7.6 Demarcating transactions

Now that you know how to start and end transactions in various ways, you might be asking yourself, "Where should I start and end my transaction?" As it turns out, this question of *where* can be harder to answer than the question of *how*. As with most difficult questions, the answer is: "It depends." You'll find a lot of different answers depending on whom you ask.

Where you demarcate your transaction will determine how long the transaction remains open, as well as how much work is included within the scope of the transaction. Knowing this, it is obvious that performance will suffer with longer-lived, wider-scoped transactions. However, these larger transactions are also somewhat safer in that they ensure the integrity of what is probably a group of related work (otherwise, why would it all be taking place within a single request?). Because it can be difficult to make the decision, here is a simple rule of thumb:

> *The scope of a transaction should be as wide as possible, but should not extend beyond the scope of a single user action.*

For example, in a web application, when a user clicks a button to submit a form, the transaction scope should begin immediately, but by the time the response page is rendered in the user's browser, the transaction should be complete. In a rich client application, the rule is generally the same. A transaction should include all of the work involved in a single user operation—which is generally represented by a single button click. Another way to think about it is this: a user should never be able to walk away from their computer and leave a transaction open, or incomplete.

So where do we stop and start transactions then? Ideally, you would start the transaction nowhere. In other words, you'd let the container do it. So declaratively you would configure your application such that the transactions were demarcated by the container. Whether you're using an application server with stateless session beans, or a lightweight container like the Spring Framework, you can configure transactions declaratively. The container will ensure that the transactions are started, committed, and ended appropriately. iBATIS has a unified programming model for transactions, meaning you can and should still use `startTransaction()`, `commitTransaction()`, and `endTransaction()` within your code, even if the container itself will demarcate the real transaction. This allows you to port your persistence code outside of a container and still have a relatively clean transaction story. When configured for EXTERNAL transaction management, iBATIS will let the container handle the transactions.

If you're not in a position to allow for container-managed transactions, you can manage them yourself. With a layered architecture, you have a number of options for starting and ending your transactions. Regardless of what you choose, it's important that you remain consistent. Referring to figure 7.3, which shows a diagram of a layered architecture, you could conceivably demarcate your transactions at the presentation layer, the business logic layer, or the persistence layer.

Let's take a close look at how you would demarcate transactions in each of these three layers.

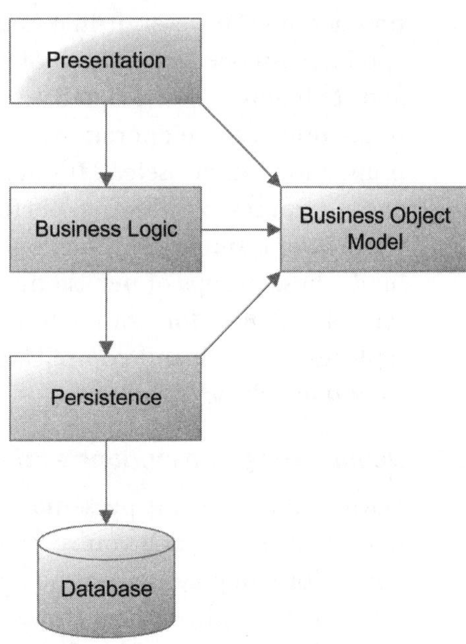

Figure 7.3 Layered architecture

7.6.1 Demarcating transactions at the presentation layer

Demarcating transactions at the presentation layer will create very large, wide-scoped, long-lived transactions. However, such transactions are also very safe, provide the best data integrity, and are easy to implement. You can use a Servlet filter or a plug-in for your presentation framework to start, commit, and end your transactions. The disadvantage of this approach is that performance may suffer with such long-lived transactions. The presentation layer is also generally unaware of exactly why the transaction is being started, as it is quite far from the persistence layer. As a result, many transactions can end up being unnecessarily long-lived. The other disadvantage is that if you have multiple user interfaces for your application, such as a website, a web services API, and a rich client, then you must reimplement the transaction scopes for each UI, which can create some inconsistencies.

Since the presentation tier is too far away from the persistence layer to be a logical place to demarcate transactions, why not go straight to the persistence layer?

7.6.2 Demarcating transactions at the persistence layer

The persistence layer is where most people would naturally think to demarcate transactions. However, it makes a surprisingly poor choice. The reason is that a good persistence layer is built of rather narrowly scoped methods, loosely coupled and yet highly cohesive database operations. It's actually rare that one would use a single one of these operations alone within a transaction, as that would make the transaction rather useless. It's more common that a group of these database operations requires execution to perform some useful business function. So the persistence layer is simply too fine grained. It's possible to build an additional layer that binds these groups of persistence operations together, and therefore makes for a sensible choice for transaction demarcation. However, that's creating more unnecessary work and complicates the design, all for the sake of something that should ideally be transparent.

7.6.3 Demarcating transactions at the business logic layer

Having eliminated the presentation and persistence layers, we are left with the business logic layer, which you've probably guessed is the right choice. Well, as we've said before, depending on the application requirements, any one of these layers could be the right choice. However, experience has shown that the business logic layer often makes a good choice for demarcating transactions. This is a common and familiar approach to both EJB developers and Spring framework developers alike. Stateless session beans are a business logic component, and often transaction requirements are declared as part of their configuration. In a similar way, Spring allows transactions to be declared for almost any method, and often the business logic components are chosen over the DAOs, simply because it's common for a single business operation to require more than one DAO.

On another technical note, demarcating your transactions at the business logic layer also allows you to have multiple interfaces to your application while maintaining a single, consistent transaction model.

So what do you think? Does demarcating transactions at the business logic layer feel natural? Well, it should. Architects, database administrators, and developers often think of transactions as a technical concept. After all, a transaction is "something that a database does." But we should think of transactions at a higher level. A transaction scope should encompass a business operation or a business function. It shouldn't just be thought of as a database feature. Furthermore, databases are not the only infrastructural elements that support transactions. Our business operation may include calls through a connector to a mainframe or publishing messages to a message queue, or it may even involve human intervention (think workflow) as part of the transaction—all of which may indeed support transactions.

The business layer is a perfect place to demarcate transactions, both logically and technically speaking.

7.7 Summary

In this chapter we discussed transactions, what they are, and how to use them within iBATIS. We discussed the ACID properties that are imperative for proper transaction management. Atomicity ensures that all transaction steps succeed or fail as a group. Consistency ensures that all database constraints are met both at the beginning and at the end of a transaction. Isolation ensures that concurrent transactions do not unexpectedly conflict with each other. Durability ensures that the data is safe once the transaction has successfully completed.

We discussed the various transaction scopes, including automatic transactions, local transactions, global transactions, and custom transactions. Automatic transactions are the narrowest-scoped transactions, involving only a single statement, but within a transaction nevertheless. Local transactions are wider-scoped transactions involving multiple update statements, but still only a single application with a single database. Global transactions are much more complicated and allow for transactions to span multiple databases, resources, and applications. Custom transactions provide a means for developers to gain full control over the connection, and therefore the transaction, used by iBATIS.

Local transaction scope, including automatic transactions, is the narrowest scope that should be used for any application involving a relational database. Global transactions should be used whenever multiple resources are involved. Custom transactions (user-provided connections) should be used judiciously and, if possible, avoided by writing a custom transaction manager implementation.

Choosing where to demarcate your transactions can be difficult sometimes, but for the most part you should think of transactions as encompassing a business function. Therefore, the business logic layer often makes the best choice.

8 Using Dynamic SQL

This chapter covers

- Introduction to Dynamic SQL
- Simple Dynamic SQL example
- Advanced Dynamic SQL
- Future directions

In chapter 4 we discussed how to write simple static SQL. Static SQL only requires that values be assigned via the property (`#...#`) or literal (`$...$`) syntax. Although most of the SQL you will write in iBATIS will likely be static, there are several occasions where it will not remain that simple. For example, you will quickly run into more involved scenarios where you need to iterate over a list of values for an `IN` statement, provide users with the ability to determine which columns will be displayed, or simply have a changing `WHERE` criterion based on your parameter object's state. iBATIS provides a set of dynamic SQL tags that can be used within mapped statements to enhance the reusability and flexibility of the SQL.

In this chapter we'll provide you with an understanding of what Dynamic SQL is, its usefulness, and when best to use it. We'll also give you some comparative context regarding other solutions you may use for dealing with Dynamic SQL requirements. In the end you should have a strong understanding of how to add Dynamic SQL to your arsenal of problem-solving techniques.

Before we examine dynamic tags in detail, let's demonstrate their value by jumping right into an example of one of the most common situations where you will need Dynamic SQL: the `WHERE` clause.

8.1 Dealing with Dynamic WHERE clause criteria

In the following example we are querying a table named Category from our shopping cart application. The table column `parentCategoryId` is a self-referencing column. In other words, `parentCategoryId` references `categoryId` in the same Category table, as shown in figure 8.1.

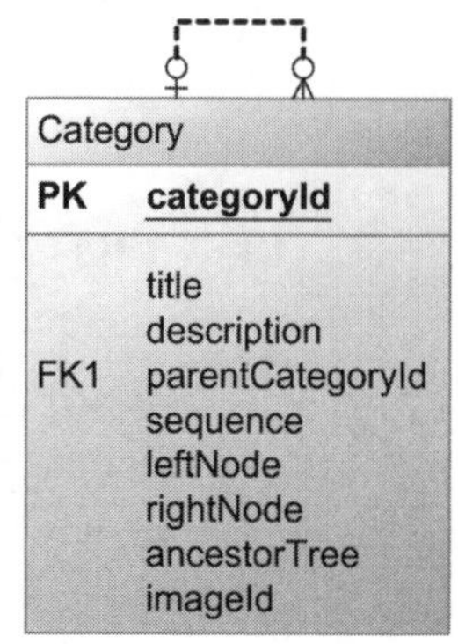

Figure 8.1 Category table diagram

The requirements are simple. If the `parentCategoryId` property of the passed-in `Category` object is null, then it means that we want to query all top-level categories. If the `parentCategoryId` property has a non-null numeric value, then that means that we want to query for all child `Category` objects of the parent `Category`. The parent `Category` is indicated by the `parentCategoryId` value.

In SQL, an equal sign (=) cannot be used to compare null equalities. The `IS` keyword is needed to successfully test for equality with a NULL. Since we want to use the same SQL statement to handle both NULL and non-NULL comparisons, we will use Dynamic SQL to accomplish this with one mapped statement. We will use this mapped statement to examine the anatomy of Dynamic SQL (listing 8.1).

Listing 8.1 Example of Dynamic WHERE clause

```
...
<select id="getChildCategories" parameterClass="Category"
        resultClass="Category">
SELECT *
FROM category
<dynamic prepend="WHERE ">
  <isNull property="parentCategoryId">
    parentCategoryId IS NULL
  </isNull>
  <isNotNull property="parentCategoryId">
    parentCategoryId=#parentCategoryId#
  </isNotNull>
</dynamic>
</select>
...
```

The anatomy of Dynamic SQL always begins with a parent tag. A parent tag can be any of the Dynamic SQL tags. In this case we are using the `<dynamic>` tag as the parent. The `<dynamic>` tag does not evaluate any values or state like the other Dynamic SQL tags do. It will generally use only the `prepend` attribute, which will prefix the attribute's value to the resulting body content of the `<dynamic>` tag. In our example, the value `WHERE` will be prefixed to any resulting SQL produced by the processing of the nested Dynamic SQL tags.

The body of the parent tag may contain either simple SQL syntax or other Dynamic SQL tags. You can see in the example that we have `<isNull>` and `<isNotNull>` tags nested in the body of the `<dynamic>` tag. Our concern here is that the appropriate SQL be part of the `WHERE` criteria depending on the null state of the `parentCategoryId` property of the `Category` parameter class (`parameterClass="Category"`).

At this point it is important to note how the `prepend` attribute is evaluated for prefixing. If the body content were to result in no text being produced, then the `prepend` value would be ignored. In order for the `prepend` attribute to be prefixed, there needs to be resulting SQL to prepend to. In our scenario there will always be resulting SQL. In other cases where the body resulted in no content being produced, the `WHERE` value in the `prepend` attribute would simply be ignored.

One of the benefits of Dynamic SQL is that it enhances the reusability of your SQL code. Had we not used Dynamic SQL in this example, we would have found ourselves writing two select statements to accommodate the scenario. We would also be required to push the examination of our category object's `parentCategoryId` property into the DAO layer (see chapter 10) and call the appropriate select statement based on the parentCategoryId's null state. Although handling this simple example without Dynamic SQL would not have inconvenienced us that much, the real value of Dynamic SQL becomes evident when several different combinations of properties result in an exponential growth of statement possibilities. By using Dynamic SQL, we increase mapped statement reuse and avoid having to write multiple static SQL statements.

Now that we have gained a good context for the usage and power of Dynamic SQL, let's delve deeper into exploring all the tags and their attributes.

8.2 Getting familiar with the dynamic tags

iBATIS addresses the need for Dynamic SQL through a robust set of tags which are used to evaluate various conditions surrounding the parameter object that you pass into your mapped statement. It is important to know the full range of tags that exist and the various roles they play in producing correct SQL output. The following sections break the tags into five categories: `<dynamic>`, binary, unary, parameter, and `<iterate>`. Each grouping contains one or more related tags that share common traits. Before we examine each of these groupings, let's take a moment to note some common attributes and behaviors shared by all Dynamic SQL tags.

All of the dynamic tags share the `prepend`, `open`, and `close` attributes. The `open` and `close` attributes function the same in each of the tags. They unconditionally place their values on either the beginning or the end of the resulting content of a tag. The `prepend` attribute functions the same in all of the tags except the `<dynamic>` tag. The `<dynamic>` tag will always prefix the `prepend` value when the processing of its body results in content. There is no way to prevent the value from being prefixed with the `<dynamic>` tag. Listing 8.2 shows some of the Dynamic SQL tags in action.

Listing 8.2 Mock removeFirstPrepend example

```
...
<dynamic prepend="WHERE ">          <-- 1 Opening <dynamic> tag
...
  <isNotEmpty property="y">         2 Simple isNotEmpty tag
    y=#y#
  </isNotEmpty>

  <isNotNull property="x" removeFirstPrepend="true"      3 More complex
             prepend="AND" open="(" close=")">              isNotEmpty tag
```

```
    <isNotEmpty property="x.a" prepend="OR">
      a=#x.a#
    </isNotEmpty>
                                                   ❹ Nested dynamic tag
    <isNotEmpty property="x.b" prepend="OR">
      a=#x.b#
    </isNotEmpty>

    <isNotEmpty property="x.c" prepend="OR">
            a=#x.c#
    </isNotEmpty>

  </isNotNull>
...
</dynamic>
...
```

At ❶, the opening <dynamic> tag implicitly enforces the remove first prepend functionality on child tags. If this <isNotEmpty> tag proves true ❷, then the implicit removeFirstPrepend will be met for the <dynamic> tag. Any following tags on the same level will have their prepend values prepended. This <isNotNull> tag ❸ specifies the removeFirstPrepend attribute. The open and close attribute values will wrap the content produced in its body. At ❹, the first nested content-producing <isNotEmpty> tag will satisfy the removeFirstPrepend requirement. The first content-producing <isNotEmpty> tag will not have its OR prepend value prepended. This will produce correct SQL wrapped in the parentheses.

The *remove first prepend* functionality is supported implicitly or explicitly in all of the tags. The <dynamic> tag supports it implicitly. All other tags support it explicitly with the removeFirstPrepend attribute. The remove first prepend functionality removes the first prepend of a child tag that produces content. If the first content-producing child does not specify a prepend attribute, it will still count and all following content-producing child tags will have their prepend attribute prefixed to their content.

The final piece of shared functionality to note is that all tags can be used independently of each other. This means that you do not have to nest all of your Dynamic SQL tags inside the <dynamic> tag. You could start with an <iterate> tag and nest <isNull> tags inside as easily as you could wrap them both with a <dynamic> tag. This functionality is provided because it is only necessary to use a <dynamic> tag when you want to use its open, close, or prepend value on its resulting content.

Let's now analyze each tag category.

8.2.1 The <dynamic> tag

The `<dynamic>` tag is a top-level only tag; this means that it cannot be nested. It is used to demarcate a section of Dynamic SQL. The tag is meant to provide a means for prefixing a common `prepend`, `open`, or `close` value to the resulting content of its body. The `<dynamic>` tag attributes are shown in table 8.1.

Table 8.1 <dynamic> tag attributes

`prepend` (optional)	This value is used to prepend to the tag's resulting body content. The `prepend` value will not be prepended when the tag's resulting body content is empty.
`open` (optional)	This value is used to prefix to the tag's resulting body content. The `open` value will not be prefixed if the tag's resulting body content is empty. The `open` value is prefixed before the `prepend` attribute's value is prefixed. For example, if `prepend="WHEN"` and `open="("`, then the resulting combined prefix would be `"WHEN ("`.
`close` (optional)	This value is used to append to the tag's resulting body content. The `append` value will not be `appended` if the tag's resulting body content is empty.

Now that you have a reference for the attributes that can be used in the tag, listing 8.3 illustrates how to use the `<dynamic>` tag.

Listing 8.3 <dynamic> tag example

```
...
<select id="getChildCategories" parameterClass="Category"
        resultClass="Category">
SELECT *
FROM category
<dynamic prepend="WHERE ">
  <isNull property="parentCategoryId">
    parentCategoryId IS NULL
  </isNull>
  <isNotNull property="parentCategoryId">
    parentCategoryId=#parentCategoryId#
  </isNotNull>
</dynamic>
</select>
...
```

In listing 8.3, we use Dynamic SQL to build a `WHERE` clause for our select statement that looks at the `parentCategoryId` property and builds the SQL based on it.

8.2.2 Binary tags

Binary tags compare the value of a parameter property to another value or parameter property. The body content is included if the result of the comparison is true. All binary tags share the property `compareProperty` as well as `compareValue` attributes. The `property` attribute serves as the primary value to be compared against, while compareProperty and `compareValue` serve as the secondary compare values. The `compareProperty` attribute specifies a property of the parameter object that will contain a value used to compare against the primary value. `compareValue` specifies a static value that will be used to compare against the primary value. The name of the tag indicates how the values should be compared. The tag attributes are shown in table 8.2.

Table 8.2 Binary tag attributes

`property` (required)	The property of the parameter used to compare against the `compareValue` or `compareProperty`.
`prepend` (optional)	This value is used to prepend to the tag's resulting body content. The `prepend` value will not be prepended (a) when the tag's resulting body content is empty; (b) if the tag is the first to produce body content and is nested in a tag with the `removeFirstPrepend` attribute set to true; or (c) if the tag is the first to produce body content following a `<dynamic>` tag with a `prepend` attribute value that is not empty.
`open` (optional)	This value is used to prefix to the tag's resulting body content. The `open` value will not be prefixed if the tag's resulting body content is empty. The `open` value is prefixed before the `prepend` attribute's value is prefixed. For example, if `prepend="OR "` and `open="("` then the resulting combined prefix would be `"OR ("`.
`close` (optional)	The `close` value is used to append to the tag's resulting body content. The `append` value will not be appended if the tag's resulting body content is empty.
`removeFirstPrepend` (optional)	This value defines whether the first nested content-producing tag will have its `prepend` value removed (optional).
`compareProperty` (required if `compareValue` is not specified)	This value names a property on the parameter object to compare against the property named by the `property` attribute.
`compareValue` (required if `compareProperty` is not specified)	This static comparison value is compared against the property named by the `property` attribute.

All of the binary dynamic tags share those attributes, and the tags themselves are listed in table 8.3.

Table 8.3 iBATIS binary dynamic tags

`<isEqual>`	Compares the `property` attribute with `compareProperty` or `compareValue` to determine if they are equal
`<isNotEqual>`	Compares the `property` attribute with `compareProperty` or `compareValue` to determine if they are equal
`<isGreaterThan>`	Determines whether the `property` attribute is greater than `compareProperty` or `compareValue`
`<isGreaterEqual>`	Determines whether the `property` attribute is greater than or equal to `compareProperty` or `compareValue`
`<isLessThan>`	Determines whether the `property` attribute is less than `compareProperty` or `compareValue`
`<isLessEqual>`	Determines whether the `property` attribute is less than or equal to `compareProperty` or `compareValue`

Tables are good references but provide lousy examples, so listing 8.4 shows how to put these tags together.

Listing 8.4 Binary tag example

```
…
<select id="getShippingType" parameterClass="Cart"
        resultClass="Shipping">
  SELECT * FROM Shipping
  <dynamic prepend="WHERE ">
    <isGreaterEqual property="weight" compareValue="100">
      shippingType='FREIGHT'
    </isEqual>
    <isLessThan property="weight" compareValue="100">
      shippingType='STANDARD'
    </isLessThan>
  </dynamic>
</select>
…
```

In listing 8.4, we create a select statement, and then examine the `weight` property to determine which shipping type to use for it—less than 100 means standard shipping, and greater than or equal to 100 means freight.

8.2.3 Unary tags

Unary tags examine the state of a bean property and do not perform comparisons against any other values. The body content is included if the result of the state is true. All unary tags share the `property` attribute. The `property` attribute is used to specify the property on the parameter object that will be used to examine the state. The name of the tag indicates the type of state that is being examined. The unary tag attributes are shown in table 8.4.

Table 8.4 Unary tag attributes

`property` (required)	The property of the parameter used for state comparison.
`prepend` (optional)	This value is used to prepend to the tag's resulting body content. The `prepend` value will not be prepended (a) when the tag's resulting body content is empty; (b) if the tag is the first to produce body content and is nested in a tag with the `removeFirstPrepend` attribute set to true; or (c) if the tag is the first to produce body content following a `<dynamic>` tag with a `prepend` attribute value that is not empty.
`open` (optional)	This value is used to prefix to the tag's resulting body content. The `open` value will not be prefixed if the tag's resulting body content is empty. The `open` value is prefixed before the `prepend` attribute's value is prefixed. For example, if `prepend="OR "` and `open="("`, then the resulting combined prefix would be `"OR ("`.
`close` (optional)	This value is used to append to the tag's resulting body content. The `append` value will not be appended if the tag's resulting body content is empty.
`removeFirst-Prepend` (optional)	This attribute value defines whether the first nested content-producing tag will have its `prepend` value removed.

All of the attributes in table 8.4 are available in the unary dynamic SQL tags listed in table 8.5.

Table 8.5 Unary tags

`<isProperty-Available>`	Determines whether the specified property exists in the parameter. With a bean, it looks for a property. With a map, it looks for a key.
`<isNotProperty-Available>`	Checks whether the specified property does not exist in the parameter. With a bean, it looks for a property. With a map, it looks for a key.
`<isNull>`	Determines whether the specified property is null. With a bean, it looks at the value of the property getter. With a map, it looks for a key. If the key does not exist, it will return true.
`<isNotNull>`	Determines whether the specified property is anything other than null. With a bean, it looks at the value of the property getter. With a map, it looks for a key. If the key does not exist, it will return false.

Table 8.5 Unary tags *(continued)*

<isEmpty>	Determines whether the specified property is a null or empty `String`, `Collection`, or `String.valueOf()`.
<isNotEmpty>	Determines whether the specified property is not a null or empty `String`, `Collection`, or `String.valueOf()`.

Listing 8.5 shows how to use the unary dynamic SQL tags.

Listing 8.5 Unary tag example

```
...
<select id="getProducts" parameterClass="Product"
        resultClass="Product">
  SELECT * FROM Products
  <dynamic prepend="WHERE ">
    <isNotEmpty property="productType">
      productType=#productType#
    </isNotEmpty>
  </dynamic>
</select>
...
```

In listing 8.5, we create a simple select mapped statement, then use a dynamic SQL tag to optionally filter the results based on the `productType` property.

8.2.4 Parameter tags

It is possible to define a mapped statement without a parameter. The parameter tags were created to check whether a parameter has been passed in to the mapped statement. The tag attributes are shown in table 8.6.

Table 8.6 Parameter tag attributes

`prepend` (optional)	This value is used to prepend to the tag's resulting body content. The `prepend` value will not be prepended (a) when the tag's resulting body content is empty; (b) if the tag is the first to produce body content and is nested in a tag with the `removeFirstPrepend` attribute set to true; or (c) if the tag is the first to produce body content following a `<dynamic>` tag with a `prepend` attribute value that is not empty.
`open` (optional)	This value is used to prefix to the tag's resulting body content. The `open` value will not be prefixed if the tag's resulting body content is empty. The `open` value is prefixed before the `prepend` attribute's value is prefixed. For example, if `prepend="OR "` and `open="("`, then the resulting combined prefix would be `"OR ("`.

Table 8.6 Parameter tag attributes *(continued)*

`close` (optional)	This value is used to append to the tag's resulting body content. The `append` value will not be appended if the tag's resulting body content is empty.
`removeFirst-Prepend` (optional)	This attribute value defines whether the first nested content-producing tag will have its `prepend` value removed.

All of the attributes in table 8.6 are available in the tags listed in table 8.7.

Table 8.7 Parameter tags

<isParameterPresent>	Determines whether a parameter object is present
<isNotParameterPresent>	Determines whether the parameter does not exist

Listing 8.6 shows how to use a parameter tag in a select statement.

Listing 8.6 Parameter tag example

```
...
<select id="getProducts" resultClass="Product">
  SELECT * FROM Products
  <isParameterPresent prepend="WHERE ">
    <isNotEmpty property="productType">
      productType=#productType#
    </isNotEmpty>
  </ isParameterPresent >
</select>
...
```

In this example, we create a simple select statement again, and this time we optionally create the `WHERE` for filtering the results based on the `productType` parameter.

8.2.5 The <iterate> tag

The `<iterate>` tag takes a property that is a `Collection` or array to produce repetitive portions of SQL from a set of values. The list is rendered by rendering the values of the list to a SQL fragment separated by the `conjunction` attribute's value. The `open` attribute value is what is prefixed to the beginning of the rendered value list. The `close` attribute is what is appended to the rendered value list. The tag attributes are shown in table 8.8.

Table 8.8 <iterate> tag attributes

`property` (required)	The property of the parameter containing the list.
`prepend` (optional)	This value is used to prepend to the tag's resulting body content. The `prepend` value will not be prepended (a) when the tag's resulting body content is empty; (b) if the tag is the first to produce body content and is nested in a tag with the `removeFirstPrepend` attribute set to true; or (c) if the tag is the first to produce body content following a `<dynamic>` tag with a `prepend` attribute value that is not empty.
`open` (optional)	This value is used to prefix to the tag's resulting body content. The `open` value will not be prefixed if the tag's resulting body content is empty. The `open` value is prefixed before the `prepend` attribute's value is prefixed. For example, if `prepend="OR "` and `open="("`, then the resulting combined prefix would be `"OR ("`.
`close` (optional)	The `close` value is used to append to the tag's resulting body content. The `append` value will not be appended if the tag's resulting body content is empty.
`conjunction` (optional)	This is the value used in between the rendering of the list values to the SQL statement.
`removeFirstPrepend` (optional)	The `removeFirstPrepend` attribute value defines whether the first nested content-producing tag will have its `prepend` value removed.

Listing 8.7 shows how to use the iterate tag to build a more complex `WHERE` condition for our SQL statement.

Listing 8.7 <iterate> tag example

```
...
<select id="getProducts" parameterClass="Product"
        resultClass="Product">
  SELECT * FROM Products
  <dynamic prepend="WHERE productType IN ">
    <iterate property="productTypes"
             open="(" close=")"
             conjunction=",">
      productType=#productType#
    </iterate>
  </dynamic>
</select>
...
```

In this example, we create a select statement, then iterate over a list of product types to create a more complex filter for it.

8.3 A complete simple example

Now that you have a basic knowledge of Dynamic SQL, let's implement a simple search that is used throughout an application. For this example we'll use the JGameStore application (see figure 8.2), to which you'll be more formally introduced in chapter 14. While we build our example, we will be applying a simple approach to help you conceptualize and assemble your Dynamic SQL.

Before we move into our example, let's examine the process we'll use. The process itself is quite simple and the steps involved may be applied in a different order and with varying degrees of effort as your application matures. Everything starts out with a little more work up front because you have to build the foundation. Once the foundation is laid, it becomes less complex to build upon.

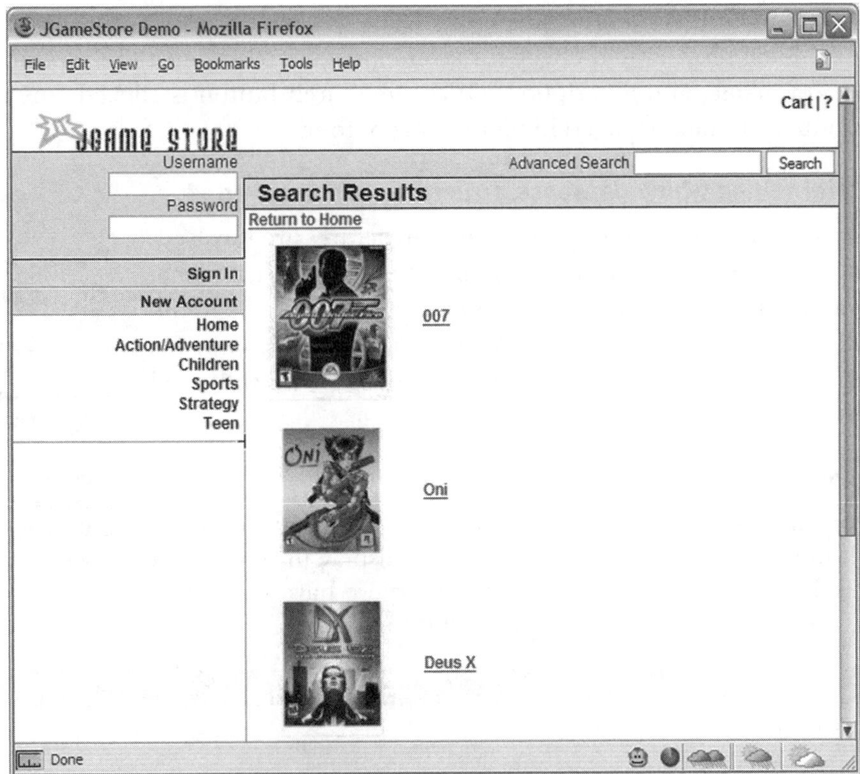

Figure 8.2 Search results screen from JGameStore

The process consists of a few basic steps:

1 Describe how the data will be retrieved and displayed.
2 Determine which database structures are involved.
3 Write out the SQL in static form.
4 Apply Dynamic SQL tags to static SQL.

This is a pretty simple page but, as you know, there is always more behind it than meets the eye. So in the following sections, we'll look at the code to make this work.

8.3.1 Defining how to retrieve and display data

On each page of the JGameStore application we want to implement a simple search field with a search button. The search field will tokenize terms by spaces. For example, if we enter **Adventure Deus** the two terms will be `Adventure` and `Deus`. Each term should check for an inclusive match against the product's `categoryId`, name, and description. Once the search button is clicked, any resulting products should be paged in increments of four.

8.3.2 Determining which database structures are involved

Let's move on to defining which table structures are involved. Since we are only searching against the `categoryId`, name, and description, we will require only the Product table to fulfill our requirements (figure 8.3). The Product table contains all of the individual product information that we will need for search and display.

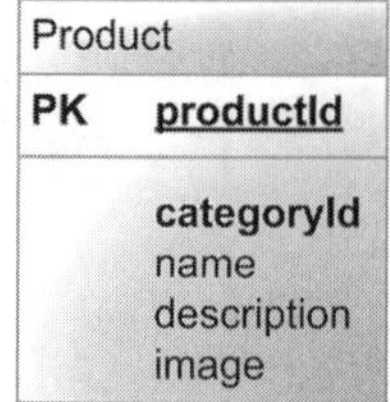

Figure 8.3 Diagram of the table involved in the simple product query

8.3.3 Writing the SQL in static format

For starters we will construct some static SQL that will select all the necessary fields we will need to display in our search results. Listing 8.8 shows the static query we have assembled to accomplish the display of product information.

Listing 8.8 Static SQL mock-up

```
SELECT
  PRODUCTID,
  NAME,
  DESCRIPTION,
  IMAGE,
  CATEGORYID
FROM PRODUCT
```

```
WHERE
  lower(name) like 'adventure%' OR
  lower(categoryid) like 'adventure%' OR
  lower(description) like 'adventure%' OR
  lower(name) like 'Deus%' OR
  lower(categoryid) like 'deus%' OR
  lower(description) like 'deus%'
```

We have now defined our input, output, and table, and it is time to mock up our SQL statement. Once you have the previous information it is quite simple to construct your SQL. The `SELECT` statement will fulfill our need to return a list of products. The `WHERE` clause provides the needed criteria for querying based on the supplied terms again the name, `categoryId`, and description.

8.3.4 Applying Dynamic SQL tags to static SQL

Let's examine our mocked-up SQL statement so we can dissect it and determine where we need to introduce dynamic tags. Since the `SELECT` clause is static, we will not need to make any dynamic alterations to it. The `WHERE` clause is where we will have to make dynamic adjustments. Listing 8.9 shows the SQL that we will be looking at.

Listing 8.9 Dynamic SQL

```
<select id="searchProductList" resultClass="product" >
  SELECT
    PRODUCTID,
    NAME,
    DESCRIPTION,
    IMAGE,
    CATEGORYID
  FROM PRODUCT
  <dynamic prepend="WHERE">
    <iterate property="keywordList" conjunction="OR">
      lower(name) like lower(#keywordList[]#) OR
      lower(categoryid) like lower(#keywordList[]#) OR
      lower(description) like lower(#keywordList[]#)
    </iterate>
  </dynamic>
</select>
```

Since the dynamic tags utilize the parameter that is passed into the mapped statement, we need to consider what it is here and how we will use the dynamic tags with it. The parameter that will be provided to the mapped statement is a List of

Strings. Since we are using a simple List directly, we will use the iterate tag. The iterate tag will traverse through the List of Strings while its body creates the criteria that looks for the provided term in the categoryId, name, and description. We need to be sure to add the conjunction attribute with a value of OR. The conjunction will join each set of term criteria together. Note that it is smart to name your mapped statements in such a way that it adequately describes the function of the SQL contained within it. In this case, we named our mapped statement searchProductList. When you read the name of the mapped statement, the statement's purpose becomes immediately clear.

```
sqlMap.queryForPaginatedList(
  "searchProducts", parameterObject, PAGE_SIZE);
```

As a final requirement, we need to make sure that we return only four records at a time. To accomplish this, we will call our statement using the queryForPaginatedList() method, which takes a pageSize parameter. This will allow us to control how many records are returned.

We have now stepped through a simple example and learned how to plan and develop our Dynamic SQL. It is important to remember that Dynamic SQL should be used with a single purpose that requires multiple options; avoid using it to accomplish multiple purposes. In our example, the purpose was to address how a user can select products. Bear in mind that Dynamic SQL was invented to make the complex simpler and not the simple more complex. Next, let's move on to a more advanced usage of Dynamic SQL.

8.4 Advanced Dynamic SQL techniques

In this example, we will use a shopping cart application that needs to provide a way for customers to search for products using more detail. We'll build on some of the structures involved in our previous examples and step up the complexity. Again we'll apply the analysis approach that you learned about in the previous example.

8.4.1 Defining the resulting data

Let's define our output in generic terms. Our shopping cart application requires that a list of products be displayed when a set of criteria are searched on by a user (see figure 8.4). The output is determined based on specific selected criteria involving the categories, products, and manufacturers. The products must be displayed in increments of four products per page. Our Dynamic SQL must be able to produce the paged product list and handle the complex variations of values the user may enter.

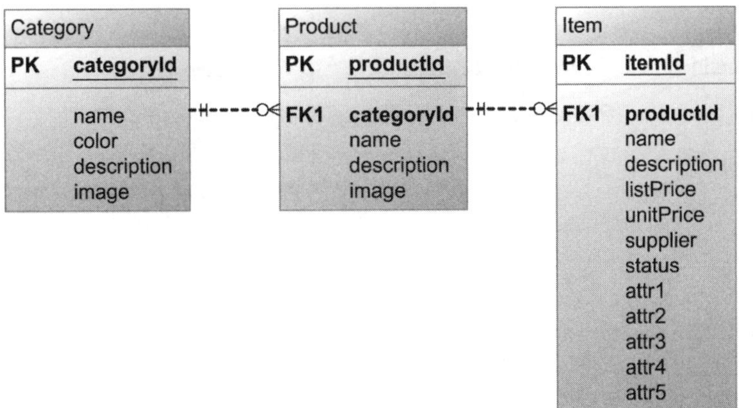

Figure 8.4
Our search form

So, how does the search page work with the database? Listing 8.10 shows part of the answer.

Listing 8.10 SearchCriteria.java parameter class

```
public class ProductSearchCriteria {

  private String[] categoryIds;
  private String   productName;
  private String   productDescription;
  private String   itemName;
  private String   itemDescription;
  …
  // setters and getters
}
```

Essentially, each field on the search page is mapped to a property on the search criteria class, which is a simple JavaBean.

8.4.2 Defining the required input

We are going to break from the form we used in our previous example by determining the input requirements before we identify the database structures involved. The user will perform searches based on five criteria. The list of criteria will contain the categories, product name, product description, item name, and item description. The product name and product description will allow for wildcard searches using the standard database percent (%) syntax. There will be a multiselect drop-down list that will allow users to narrow the search to a list of categories. With these complex input requirements, we will need to understand

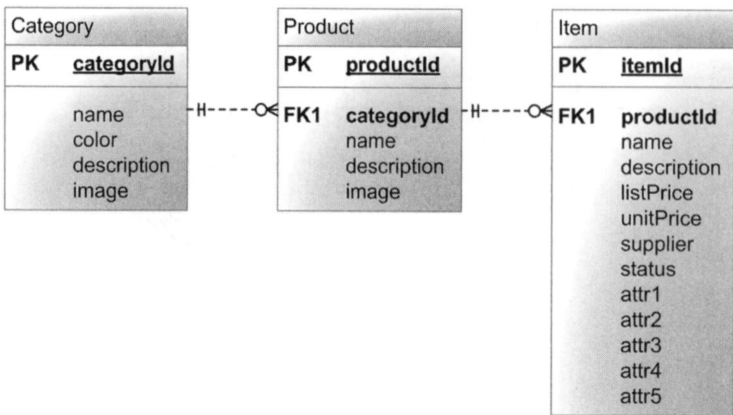

Figure 8.5 The relationships between the various tables involved in searching for a list of products

which database structures are involved with accomplishing this. Figure 8.5 shows the tables that we will be working with in our examination of Dynamic SQL.

Now let's define which table structures are involved. Three database tables are involved in fulfilling our requirements (figure 8.5). We are using the Product table from our previous example. The two new tables introduced in this example are named Category and Item. Category is a simple table that defines the category that the product belongs in. The Item table defines the various product permutations.

8.4.3 Writing the SQL in static format

Now that we have defined the inputs and outputs, we can write the SQL using simple static SQL that we can run in a query tool. Listing 8.11 shows a static SQL statement that we will start with and make into a dynamic statement.

Listing 8.11 Static SQL mock-up

```
SELECT
    p.PRODUCTID AS PRODUCTID,
    p.NAME AS NAME,
    p.DESCRIPTION AS DESCRIPTION,
    p.IMAGE AS IMAGE,
    p.CATEGORYID AS CATEGORYID
  FROM Product p
  INNER JOIN Category c ON
    c.categoryId=p.categoryId
  INNER JOIN Item i ON
    i.productId = p.productId
```

```
WHERE
  c.categoryId IN ('ACTADV')
  AND
  p.name LIKE '007'
  AND
  p.description LIKE '007'
  AND
  i.name LIKE 'PS2'
  AND
  i.description LIKE 'PS2'
```

Now that we know our input needs and what tables are involved, we can mock up a static SQL query. In our static example (listing 8.11), you may have noticed that the WHERE criteria has been expanded to include the largest possible combination of criteria. It is important to make your static SQL as complex as possible in order to provide a good sense of what the dynamic needs will be. Let's move on to assembling the Dynamic SQL.

8.4.4 Applying Dynamic SQL tags to static SQL

Now that we have constructed our static SQL mock-up, let's apply the dynamic tags. As you can see in listing 8.12, the Dynamic SQL has become a bit more complex. Note the use of <isEqual> as a top-level tag. It's not necessary to use the <dynamic> parent because there's no need for any prepend, open, or close values. We simply want to either display the content, or not. The same <isEqual> tag is used to determine the inclusion of a LEFT JOIN.

Listing 8.12 Dynamic SQL for advanced search

```
<select id="searchProductsWithProductSearch"
       parameterClass="productSearch"
       resultClass="product" >
 SELECT DISTINCT
   p.PRODUCTID,
   p.NAME,
   p.DESCRIPTION,
   p.IMAGE,
   p.CATEGORYID
 FROM Product p
   <isEqual property="itemProperties" compareValue="true">
   INNER JOIN Item i ON i.productId=p.productId
   </isEqual>
   <dynamic prepend="WHERE">
```

❶ Contains opening select tag

❷ Contains minimal SQL statement

❸ Checks to see if join needed for item criteria

❹ Contains simple opening dynamic tag

```
      <iterate
        property="categoryIds"
        open="p.categoryId IN (" close=")"
        conjunction="," prepend="BOGUS">
        #categoryIds[]#
      </iterate>

      <isNotEmpty property="productName" prepend="AND">
      p.name LIKE #productName#
      </isNotEmpty>

      <isNotEmpty property="productDescription" prepend="AND">
     p.description LIKE #productDescription#
      </isNotEmpty>

      <isNotEmpty property="itemName" prepend="AND">
      i.name LIKE #itemName#
      </isNotEmpty>

      <isNotEmpty property="itemDescription" prepend="AND">
      i.description LIKE #itemDescription#
      </isNotEmpty>
    </dynamic>
  </select>
```

5 Evaluates the categories property

Evaluates productName property

Evaluates product-Description property

Evaluates item-Name property

Evaluates itemDescription property

The opening select tag ❶ use aliases to define our parameter class type as `productSearch` and the result class type as `product`. The SQL fragment ❷ is the most minimal portion of SQL that could be used—for example, in case the user simply wanted to perform a search that returned everything. The `<isEqual>` tag ❸ is used outside of the dynamic fragment to determine if a join is needed. We use the opening dynamic tag ❹, which has a `prepend` value of `WHERE`. If no content results in its body, then the `WHERE` value specified in the `prepend` attribute will be ignored. As a reminder, the dynamic tag also implicitly removes the `prepend` value of the first content-producing tag in its body. The `<iterate>` tag ❺ is the thing to note because it works hand in hand with the dynamic tag ❹ to make available all the necessary SQL components that will provide search constraints around certain categories. The `prepend` attribute is needed on the `<iterate>` tag because of a current issue in iBATIS. Content produced by the first nested tag is not counted as the first `prepend` and will cause the `prepend` of the next tag to be ignored. As a rule, be sure to specify the `prepend` attribute even if the tag will never need it. The `productName`, `productDescription`, `itemName`, and `itemDescription` properties are evaluated with the `<isNotEmpty>` tag to determine if they have a value other than `''` (empty) or NULL.

So, how do we call that monster?

```
queryForPaginatedList(
  "Product.searchProductsWithProductSearch",
  productSearch, PAGE_SIZE);
```

As in the previous example, our final requirement is to make sure that we only return four records at a time. To accomplish this, we call our statement using the `queryForPaginatedList` method, which takes a page size parameter. See the previous example for some pointers on how to use the ranged `queryForPaginatedList`.

You have now seen a complex example and learned how to perform some intense Dynamic SQL. Keeping in mind the advice from the previous example, we had a single purpose for our Dynamic SQL—to provide product listings based on search criteria entered by the user—and we accomplished that. Although this example may have looked a bit complex, it would be significantly more difficult to write this from scratch in Java code. You should now be armed with what you need to build your own dynamic SQL.

It's important to understand how iBATIS Dynamic SQL compares against other solutions for handling dynamic SQL. Let's take a brief look at how Dynamic SQL might be accomplished with a couple of other means.

8.5 Alternative approaches to Dynamic SQL

Dynamic SQL is by no means a new concept. The complex requirements of a conditionally manufactured SQL query have always been a bit of a challenge. In the past we have had to deal with proprietary internal database approaches that use stored procedures to gain efficiency in the execution of Dynamic SQL. In other cases we paid the price of performance by constructing SQL in a more robust programming language and passed the query into our database via a driver. In both cases, the means of constructing that simple SQL string became unwieldy and increasingly complex. If you are already an iBATIS user, this will be a brief jog down memory lane that will remind you of what you are missing. If you are new to iBATIS, this may be a fresh introductory comparison. Regardless of your background, we hope that this section will provide fresh insight into your practices and convince you that iBATIS can reduce much of the complexity you may be experiencing.

We'll share the same SQL statement between the Java code example and the stored procedure example. Listing 8.13 is a mildly complex select statement that should be fairly simple to code. Once we have shown how each approach solves the problem of Dynamic SQL, we will provide a quick summary of how these approaches compare to using iBATIS.

Listing 8.13 Static SQL mock-up

```
SELECT *
FROM Category
WHERE
categoryId IN ('ACTADV','SPORTS','STRATEGY') AND
name LIKE ('N%')
```

8.5.1 Using Java code

Coding in Java is a great thing. But when you mix Java and SQL together, you have to take care to craft your code in such a way that it retains clarity. As requirements grow more complex, it will become easy to lose track of where all the pieces are. Let's take a look at a mildly complex example that uses straight JDBC to assemble a Dynamic SQL statement and pass it to the database. Listing 8.14 shows the search criteria that we will use to build our SQL statement.

Listing 8.14 CategorySearchCriteria.java

```
public class CategorySearchCriteria implements Serializable {

  private String    firstLetter;
  private List      categoryIds;
  …
  // setters and getters
}
```

Our mildly complex SQL statement will receive an unknown quantity of category IDs from the `categoryIds` property of the `CategorySearchCriteria`. This will be used to populate the `IN` statement. The `firstLetter` property containing a single alpha character will be provided to perform the search against the first letter of the category name. In this example, our focus is on the JDBC interactions and comparing Dynamic SQL solutions. So, we will not expound on anything outside of that. Listing 8.15 shows how to build the Dynamic SQL using only Java code.

Listing 8.15 CategorySearchDao.java

```
public class CategorySearchDao {
…
  public List searchCategory(
    CategorySearchCriteria categorySearchCriteria) {

    List retVal = new ArrayList();
```

```
try {

  Connection conn =
    ConnectionPool.getConnection("MyConnectionPool");          Gets JDBC
                                                               resources
  PreparedStatement ps = null;
  ResultSet rs = null;

  List valueList = new ArrayList();

  StringBuffer sql = new StringBuffer("");      Starts building
  sql.append("SELECT * ");                      SQL query
  sql.append("FROM Category ");
                                                               Starts building
  if(categorySearchCriteria.getCategoryIds() != null <-        dynamic part
     && categorySearchCriteria.getCategoryIds().size() > 0) {

    Iterator categoryIdIt =
      categorySearchCriteria.getCategoryIds().iterator();

    sql.append("WHERE ");
    sql.append("categoryId IN (");

    if(categoryIdIt.hasNext()) {
      Object value = categoryIdIt.next();
      valueList.add(value);
      sql.append("?");
    }

    while(categoryIdIt.hasNext()) {
      Object value = categoryIdIt.next();
      valueList.add(value);
      sql.append(",?");
    }

    sql.append(") ");

  }

  if(categorySearchCriteria.getFirstLetter() != null
     &&
  !categorySearchCriteria.getFirstLetter().trim().equals(""))
  {                                    <-  Don't forget
    if(valueList.size() != 0) {            the AND!
      sql.append("AND ");
    }

    sql.append("name LIKE (?)");
    valueList.add(categorySearchCriteria.getFirstLetter()
                               + "%");
```

```
    }
                                                         Prepares statement
    ps = conn.prepareStatement(sql.toString()); <-        and sets parameters

    Iterator valueListIt =
      valueList.iterator();

    int indexCount = 1;

    while(valueListIt.hasNext()) {
      ps.setObject(indexCount,valueListIt.next());
      indexCount++;
    }
                                             Runs the query
    rs = ps.executeQuery(); <-
                                                 Iterates through results and
    while(rs.next()) {                     <-    builds objects to return
      Category category = new Category();
      category.setCategoryId(rs.getInt("categoryId"));
      category.setTitle(rs.getString("title"));
      category.setDescription(rs.getString("description"));
      category.setParentCategoryId(
                              rs.getInt("parentCategoryId"));
      category.setSequence(rs.getInt("sequence"));

      retVal.add(category);
    }
  } catch (SQLException ex) {
      logger.error(ex.getMessage(), ex.fillInStackTrace());
  } finally {
    if (rs != null)         <-----  The joy of resource cleanup
      try { rs.close(); }
      catch (SQLException ex)
      {logger.error(ex.getMessage(), ex.fillInStackTrace());}
    if (ps != null)
      try { ps.close(); }
      catch (SQLException ex)
      {logger.error(ex.getMessage(), ex.fillInStackTrace());}
    if (conn != null)
      try { conn.close(); }
      catch (SQLException ex)
      {logger.error(ex.getMessage(), ex.fillInStackTrace());}
  }

  return retVal;
 }
...
}
```

When using Java code, you are left to handle all the basic repetitious tasks such as connection retrieval, parameter preparation, result set iteration, and object population over and over again. On top of managing the common tasks, in this example we also deal with the minimal complexity introduced by the need to create an `IN` statement. To deal with this, a List of parameters is created and populated. Even after writing all the code we are still left with less functionality than would be desired to handle our scenario properly. You may have noticed that the `PreparedStatement` simply uses `setObject` to assign the parameters. Ideally we would want to have our types specified, but that requirement would have pushed this code to an unreasonable size.

In the end, this code is reminiscent of those activities in children's magazines in which you attempt to find cleverly hidden pictures contained in a larger picture. Here the challenge would be to find the "Hidden SQL." In this example, straight JDBC becomes seriously inhibitive. Let's move on to take a look at using a stored procedure for Dynamic SQL.

8.5.2 Using stored procedures

Stored procedures can be a real lifesaver for many tasks and they should be appreciated for what they can do. When used for Dynamic SQL, they often suffer the same problems as the Java-coded Dynamic SQL. Listing 8.16 shows you how a stored procedure written in Oracle's PL/SQL deals with Dynamic SQL construction.

Listing 8.16 Oracle stored procedure (provided by Sven Boden)

```
create or replace package category_pkg
     as
       type ref_cursor is ref cursor;

       function get_category(
               categoryid varchar default null,
                   name category.name%type default null)
           return ref_cursor;
         end;
         /

     create or replace package body category_pkg
     as
     function get_category(
            categoryid varchar default null,
               name category.name%TYPE default null)
       return ref_cursor
   is
      return_cursor ref_cursor;
```

```
   sqltext    varchar(4000);
   first     char(1) default 'Y';
begin                                                    Starts building
    sqltext :=                                        <-  the SQL
  'select c.categoryid, c.title, c.description, ' ||
         'c.sequence ' ||
     ' from category c ';                                 Adds category
    if ( categoryid is not null ) then <-                 IDs to the SQL
       if ( first = 'Y' ) then
          sqltext := sqltext ||
                    'where c.categoryid in (' ||
                         categoryid || ') ';
         first := 'N';
      end if;
   end if;

   if ( name is not null ) then <-      Adds names to the SQL
       if ( first = 'Y' ) then
          sqltext := sqltext || 'where ';
       else
          sqltext := sqltext || 'and ';
      end if;
        sqltext := sqltext || 'c.name like ''' ||
                name || '%''' ;
       first := 'N';
   end if;

   open return_cursor for sqltext; <-      Executes the SQL

   return return_cursor; <-      Returns results
 end get_category;

 end;
 /
```

Admittedly the example in listing 8.16 breaks a valuable rule of stored procedures: we did not use parameter binding, which would prevent SQL injection and increase performance. Given that, we would not have reduced our complexity but would have increased it. So, is avoiding complexity always the rule by which we live? Of course not! But in the case of Dynamic SQL we would be hard pressed to arrive at a reason for performing this in a stored procedure.

Two of the major reasons why we use stored procedures are security and performance, neither of which is applicable when it comes to Dynamic SQL. Using parameterized SQL on either the Java side or the stored procedure side will provide an equivalent level of performance and security. When we shift our attention to legibility and maintainability, we may become a bit discouraged. This procedure is more legible than our Java example, and likely this is due to the fact that it is not secured with parameterized SQL. As far as maintainability goes, things become a bit more complex. With a stored procedure, we are left to depend on the database administrator to deploy our DDL scripts when we deploy our application. With the Java example, our SQL stays with the developer and can be deployed with the rest of our code base.

Stored procedures can have varying mileage depending on the database you are using and how well its internal language is suited for complex tasks. When using stored procedures for Dynamic SQL, you end up with the same complexity of the Java example—no security gain, no performance gain, and a more complicated deployment. The other thing to note is that we didn't even include the Java code it takes to call the stored procedure in the first place. If we were drawing up an evaluation, it might be hard to choose between straight Java or a stored procedure. This is where iBATIS comes in.

8.5.3 Comparing to iBATIS

After examining straight Java and stored procedures for Dynamic SQL, we are left wanting something that can give us performance, security, and productivity. Listing 8.17 shows the same Dynamic SQL from listings 8.15 and 8.16 but uses the iBATIS `SqlMaps` framework for Dynamic SQL.

Listing 8.17 iBATIS Dynamic SQL

```
<select id="getCategories" parameterClass="SearchClass"
  resultClass="CategorySearchCriteria">
  SELECT *
  FROM Category
  <dynamic prepend="WHERE">
    <iterate prepend=" categoryId IN"
      open="(" close=")" conjunction=",">
      #categoryIds[]#
    </iterate>
    <isNotEmpty property="categoryName" prepend="AND">
      name LIKE ( #categoryName# || '%')
    </isNotEmpty>
  </dynamic>
</select>
```

So, that is what the mapped statement looks like, and here is how you would call it:

```
queryForList("getCategories",searchObject);
```

You can see that in approximately 14 lines of code we have accomplished what took us several times that to accomplish with Java code or a stored procedure. Since iBATIS uses `PreparedStatements` internally, we were able to gain security against SQL injection and gain the performance of the parameterized SQL. By keeping the SQL in a simple XML file that resides with our Java source code, we are also able to more easily maintain our SQL and deploy it with our application. If iBATIS were in the analysis against straight Java or a stored procedure, there would be no question as to which would be the logical winner.

8.6 The future of Dynamic SQL

iBATIS is already looking into the future and making moves to improve Dynamic SQL. Nearly everything you we have learned in this chapter will continue to be relevant in the future of Dynamic SQL. That aside, it is important that you know the direction iBATIS is heading with its Dynamic SQL.

The initial idea of the Dynamic SQL tag set was developed in iBATIS version 1.*x*. The Dynamic SQL tag set was based largely on concepts borrowed from the Struts taglibs (see Ted Husted's *Struts in Action* [Manning, 2002] for more details). As standards have improved in the Java community, iBATIS has sought once again to borrow concepts from more standard Java concepts and incorporate them into iBATIS. Two areas in need of improvement have emerged: a simplified and more robust tag set, and a simple expression language that can be used in conjunction with the tags. Let's take a moment and look at where iBATIS will be making improvements in Dynamic SQL.

8.6.1 Simplified conditional tags

Currently iBATIS boasts a healthy 16 tags that are used to accomplish Dynamic SQL. These tags are all very specific. In an effort to provide for more general-purpose conditional tags, the iBATIS team plans to introduce a simplified tag set alongside the existing. The goal is that the new-generation Dynamic SQL tags will eventually phase out the old. The new-generation Dynamic SQL will be modeled after JSTL (Java Standard Tag Library). This would reduce our now 16 tags to a mere 6 tags. As of this writing, the proposed new tags are `<choose>`, `<when>`, `<otherwise>`, `<if>`, `<foreach>`, and `<while>`. For the most part, these tags will function in an identical way to their JSTL sister tags, with the exception that they will contain the additional `prepend`, `open`, `close`, and `removeFirstPrepend` attributes.

8.6.2 Expression language

Because the new Dynamic SQL tag set will be more general purpose, a simple expression language is needed. The iBATIS team has decided to model the expression language after Java's J2EE Expression Language (EL). This will provide better support for multiple conditional analyses in a single evaluation. The current dynamic SQL tag set does not support boolean operations such as "and" and "or." With the combination of general-purpose tags and a powerful EL, it will be easier to fulfill complex Dynamic SQL requirements.

8.7 Summary

Dynamic SQL in iBATIS is a powerful tool to have in your arsenal. Taking care to understand its place in developing your database interaction is important. Remember to make simplicity your goal.

In this chapter, you saw how to write simple and more complex Dynamic SQL using Java and PL/SQL code, and also how to accomplish the same thing in iBATIS. While there are times when Dynamic SQL in iBATIS may not do exactly what you want, given the alternatives it is a good way to perform the other 90 percent of your queries.

Part 3

iBATIS in the real world

The iBATIS framework uses a layered architecture that makes it easy to use only the pieces you need without dealing with any features you don't need. However, sometimes you will require a bit more than the basics. Part 3 takes iBATIS to the next level and shows you how to leverage its advanced features. You'll learn about Dynamic SQL and data layer abstraction, and we'll tell you how to extend iBATIS when all else fails.

9 Improving performance with caching

This chapter covers

- Cache philosophy
- Cache configuration
- Caching strategies

Caching in general has broad meaning. For example, in a traditional web application that contains presentation, service, and data access layers, it could make sense to cache on any or all of those layers. The iBATIS cache focuses on caching results within the persistence layer. As such, it is independent of the service or presentation layers, and is not based on object identity.

In this chapter, we will look at how to configure, optimize, and even extend the iBATIS caching implementations.

9.1 A simple iBATIS caching example

IBATIS's robust and simple caching mechanism is completely configuration based and removes the burden of managing the cache directly. Before we get into when, why, and how to use iBATIS caching, let's walk through a quick introduction. Listing 9.1 shows a simple cache configuration and a single mapped statement that uses it.

Listing 9.1 Basic caching example

```
<cacheModel id="categoryCache" type="MEMORY">
  <flushOnExecute statement="insert"/>
  <flushOnExecute statement="update"/>
  <flushOnExecute statement="delete"/>
  <property name="reference-type" value="WEAK"/>
</cacheModel>

<select
  id="getCategory" parameterClass="Category"
  resultClass="Category" cacheModel="categoryCache">
  SELECT *
  FROM Category
  WHERE categoryId=#categoryId#
</select>
```

In the example in listing 9.1, you can see the two major components: the cache model and the mapped statement (`select`). The cache model defines how the cache will store fresh results and clear stale data from the cache. Mapped statements that want to use the cache just need to reference it using the `cacheModel` attributes of the `<select>` and `<procedure>` tags.

In listing 9.1 the cache model specifies a cache type of MEMORY. This is a built-in iBATIS caching that stores results into memory. This is usually the most-used means of caching in iBATIS. Within the body of the cache model are a couple of tags. `<flushOnExecute>` specifies that stored results will be flushed when a particular cache is accessed. It's important to note that all of the cache contents are cleared. This means that if you have several mapped statements that use the same cache model, then all of the results of those mapped statements will be flushed. The final tag to notice is named `<property>`. Each type of cache model has properties that can be specified for custom configuration of the cache model. The `name` attribute is the name of the property that will be set. The `value`, of course, provides the assigned value to the defined property.

As you can see, the iBATIS cache is quite simple. The most work you will experience is discovering the properties that are available for each of the cache model types. We will take time in this chapter to explain what cache models are available and provide some direction on when and how to use them after we take a quick look at the iBATIS caching philosophy.

9.2 iBATIS's caching philosophy

Most caching that developers incorporate into their apps is for long-term, seemingly unchanging data. This is the type of data you usually see in drop-down or selection lists. Data like states, cities, and countries are prime candidates for this type of caching. But caching can reach beyond long-term read-only data and can be used to cache objects that are read/write as well.

The difficulties at this point often have to do with the manual process of checking to see whether the data exists in the cache and then storing it into the cache yourself. Another difficulty with a cache is figuring out how to know whether the data contained within is either stale or fresh. It's easy enough to write simple rules like timed cache flushes, but it is not so easy when the execution of several processes should invalidate a cache's contents. Once dependencies between executing code become important to maintaining the integrity of your cached objects, things begin to get difficult. Often when caching reaches this point of complexity, the *performance-to-effort* ratio can become less than convincing or at minimum be seen as a very annoying task. This is why iBATIS has focused itself on providing caching implementations and strategies for the data access layer only. This focus on the data access layer enables the framework to manage the cache in accordance with an easy-to-manage configuration.

Consider the philosophy of the iBATIS caching framework and how it differs from other persistence solutions. This can often be a sore point for some who are used to how traditional O/RM solutions perform caching. IBATIS is built on the idea of mapping *SQL* to objects, not mapping *database tables* to objects. This is an important distinction to make. Traditional O/RM tools primarily focus on mapping database tables to objects, which influences their caching. Traditional O/RM caching maintains object identification (OID) just as the database would manage the uniqueness of a row in a table. This further means that if two different results return the same object, the object will be cached only once. This is not the case with iBATIS. Because iBATIS is a data-centric framework that is focused on SQL results, we do not cache objects based on their uniqueness. IBATIS caches the full returned result regardless of whether an identical object (value-wise) exists elsewhere in a cache.

Let's take some time to look at the cache model and discuss more in depth what it is and what its common components are. We will see how they can help avoid the mundane manual management of caching results and their dependencies.

9.3 Understanding the cache model

The simplest description of the cache model is that it is a cache configuration. More specifically, it is the base from which all iBATIS cache implementations are defined. The cache model configuration is defined within a SQL Map configuration and can be utilized by one or more query mapped statements.

The cache configuration is defined by the `<cacheModel>` tag, which contains the attributes in table 9.1.

Table 9.1 <cacheModel> tag attributes

`id` (required)	This value specifies the unique ID that will be referenced by query mapped statements that want to use the cache model's configured cache.
`type` (required)	This is the type of cache that the cache model will be configuring. Valid values include MEMORY, LRU, FIFO, and OSCACHE. This attribute can also contain the fully qualified class name of a custom `CacheController` implementation.
`readOnly` (optional)	When set to true, this denotes that the cache will be used solely as a read-only cache. Objects retrieved from a read-only cache should not have their properties changed.
`serialize` (optional)	This attribute specifies whether the cache contents should be "deep copied" upon retrieval.

The `id` attribute is used to identify the cache so that we can tell iBATIS which mapped statements to store in it. Let's take a closer look at the other attributes.

9.3.1 Type

iBATIS provides four default cache implementations that the cache model can take advantage of out of the box. The four types are shown in table 9.2.

Table 9.2 Built-in cache model types

Cache model type	Description
MEMORY	This model simply stores the cached data in memory until the garbage collector removes it.
FIFO	This is a fixed size model that uses a "first in, first out" algorithm to remove items from memory.
LRU	This is another fixed-size model that uses a "least recently used" algorithm to remove items from memory.
OSCACHE	This model uses the OpenSymphony (or OS) cache.

The caching implementation used is specified by adding its default keyword (`MEMORY`, `LRU`, `FIFO`, and `OSCACHE`) to the type attribute of the `<cacheModel>` tag. Section 9.5 will discuss the four default cache implementations in detail.

It is also possible to provide your own caching by writing an implementation of the `CacheController` interface and specifying its fully qualified class name in the type attribute (see chapter 12).

9.3.2 *The readOnly attribute*

The `<cacheModel>` tag provides a `readOnly` attribute. This attribute is simply an indicator that provides instruction to the cache model, telling it how it should retrieve and store the cached object. Setting this attribute to true does not prevent retrieved objects from having their contents altered. When specifying a cache as read only, you tell the cache model that it is allowed to pass back a reference to the object that exists in the cache because it is not going to be altered by the application that is requesting it. If the `readOnly` attribute is set to false, this ensures that more than one user does not retrieve the same instance of a cached reference. The `readOnly` attribute works in conjunction with the `serialize` attribute. It is important to understand how these two attributes work together.

9.3.3 *The serialize attribute*

The `serialize` attribute is used to instruct how cached objects are returned. When `serialize` is set to true, each object requested from the cache is returned as a deep copy. This means that the object you retrieve from the cache will have an identical value but will not be the same instance. This ensures that the actual version that is stored in the cache is never returned. It is important to call attention to the fact that this is not serialization as most would think of it. The objects do not get serialized to disk. This is memory-based serialization that creates deep copies of the cached objects that are in memory.

9.3.4 Combining readOnly and serialize

Now that you understand each of these attributes, it may appear that they overlap functionality to some degree. The truth is that they simply work very tightly together. It's important to understand what happens under the hood when you have different combinations of these attributes. We'll look at all four possible combinations and analyze what their benefit is (or lack thereof) in table 9.3.

Table 9.3 Summary of readOnly and serialize attribute combinations

`readOnly`	`serialize`	**Result**	**Reason**
True	False	**Good**	Fastest retrieval of cached objects. Returns a shared instance of the cached objects, which can be problematic if misused.
False	True	**Good**	Fast retrieval of cached objects. Retrieves a deep copy of the cached objects.
False	False	**Caution!**	Cache is only relevant for the life of the calling thread's session and cannot be utilized by other threads.
True	True	**Bad**	This combination would work the same as `readOnly=false` and `serialize=true`, except that it would not make any sense semantically.

The default combination of these two attributes is `readOnly=true` and `serialize=false`. This combination instructs the cache to pass back the same reference that is contained within the cache. When using this combination, it is possible to actually alter the cached object. This can be problematic because the object is shared globally. All users who access the cached object through the query mapped statement using the same parameters could possibly retrieve objects that were inappropriately altered by another session.

When dealing with cached objects that you do want to alter, you should mark `readOnly` as false. This will force the cache to return an instance that is specific to the session. When using this in combination with `serialize` set to true, you are able to get a deep copy of the cached object. This isolates the changes of the retrieved object to the calling session.

Another combination that can be used is to set `readOnly` as false and `serialize` as false. This can be a useful approach, but it's a rare case where it is appropriate. Setting the two attributes to false requires the cache to produce unique instances of the requested objects for the calling thread. Since `serialize` is set to false, it does not use the deep copy strategy. Instead, the cache is created to be used only for the life of the session. This means that if you called the same query mapped statement several times in the same session, then you would get the benefit of the caching. However, each time a session calls a cached query mapped statement for the first time, the database will be hit.

The final combination of these attributes is `readOnly=true` and `serialize=true`. This combination is functionally identical to setting `readOnly` as false and `serialize` as true. The problem here is the semantic that it expresses. It does not make any sense to create a `readOnly` result that you would want to serialize. The intention of `serialize` is that you expect or plan for the objects contained in the cache to be serialized. So, to serialize a read-only cache is quite absurd.

Now that you have a philosophical understanding of the cache, let's dig into setting it up and using it.

9.4 Using tags inside the cache model

Before we examine the different types of cache model implementations that are available, you should become familiar with the common tags that are used within the body of the `<cacheModel>` tag. These tags are used to define common behaviors for flushing caches as well as specifying property values relevant only to the particular cache model implementation.

9.4.1 Cache flushing

Each cache implementation shares a common set of tags for flushing their contents. When thinking through your caching, determine how and when you want objects to be removed from the cache. By default, each cache model type has a means of managing the cached data on a granular level. They can remove individual objects based on memory, recent access, or age. Beyond each cache model's inherent behavior you can further give them instruction on when to the flush their entire contents. The flush tags are made available to provide such functionality.

There are two flush tags, as shown in table 9.4.

Table 9.4 Flush tags, which define rules for clearing items from the cache

Tag name	Purpose
`<flushOnExecute>`	Defines query mapped statements whose execution should flush the associated cache
`<flushInterval>`	Defines a recurring timed flush of the cache

Let's look at each of these flush tags in more depth.

<flushOnExecute>

The <flushOnExecute> tag has a single attribute, statement, and allows for a cache flush to be triggered upon the execution of a particular mapped statement. This is useful when you have results that should be updated when a change is made to the underlying database. For example, if you have a cache containing a list of Categories, you could use <flushOnExecute> to flush the cache whenever a new Category is inserted.

As stated earlier, the cache will be entirely flushed, and therefore you should take care to avoid creating mapped statement flushing dependencies with constantly changing data. This could effectively render your cache useless because of the high rate of flushing and populating the cache. Listing 9.2 defines a cache model and shows an example of how to use the <flushOnExecute> tag to invalidate the cache when new data is added to the database.

Listing 9.2 flushOnExecute caching example

```
<sqlMap namespace="Category">
…
<cacheModel id="categoryCache" type="MEMORY">
  …
  <flushOnExecute statement="Category.insert"/>
  …
</cacheModel>
…
<select
  id="getCategory" parameterClass="Category"
  resultClass="Category" cacheModel="categoryCache">
  SELECT *
  FROM Category
  WHERE parentCategoryId=#categoryId#
</select>
…
<insert id="insert" parameterClass="Category" >
  INSERT INTO Category
  (title,description,sequence)
  VALUES
  (#title#,#description#,#sequence#)
</insert>
…
</sqlMap>
```

To use the <flushOnExecute> tag, you need to specify the statement name, using the statement attribute, which should trigger the cache flush. If the statement is contained within a sqlMap that uses a namespace attribute, you must specify the full namespace in the `statement` attribute. The full namespace notation is required even if the `statement` attribute is referencing a mapped statement within the confines of the same `sqlMap` configuration. When specifying mapped statements that exist in another `sqlMap` configuration, you must also make sure that the dependent `sqlMaps` have been loaded prior to the `statement` attribute referencing it.

<flushInterval>

The other flush tag used to manage the contents of the cache is `<flushinterval>`. The `<flushInterval>` tag is a bit simpler than `<flushOnExecute>` since it does not have any configuration dependencies other than time itself. The `<flushInterval>` tag will flush the cache on a recurring interval. This interval is started at the time the cache is created during the configuration loading and continues until the application is shut down. The `<flushInterval>` tag allows you to specify hours, minutes, seconds, or milliseconds, as shown in table 9.5.

Table 9.5 <flushInterval> tag attributes

Attribute	Represents
`hours` (optional)	The number of hours that should pass before the cache is flushed
`minutes` (optional)	The number of minutes that should pass before the cache is flushed
`seconds` (optional)	The number of seconds that should pass before the cache is flushed
`milliseconds` (optional)	The number of milliseconds that should pass before the cache is flushed

To remove any potential confusion, `<flushInterval>` does not allow you to specify particular times to flush the cache. It is purely interval based. Listing 9.3 shows an example that uses the `<flushInterval>` tag to limit the lifespan of cached objects to 12 hours.

Listing 9.3 <flushInterval> caching example

```
<sqlMap namespace="Category">
…
<cacheModel id="categoryCache" type="MEMORY">
  …
  <flushInterval hours= "12" />
  …
</cacheModel>
```

```
...
<select
  id="getCategory" parameterClass="Category"
  resultClass="Category" cacheModel="categoryCache">
  SELECT *
  FROM Category
  WHERE parentCategoryId=#categoryId#
</select>
...
</sqlMap>
```

Something to keep in mind when using `<flushInterval>` is that only one attribute is allowed. So if you want to flush a cache every 12 hours, 10 minutes, 10 seconds, and 5 milliseconds, you have to calculate that as milliseconds, and enter the value as such.

9.4.2 Setting cache model implementation properties

Because cache models are components that can be plugged into the framework, there must be a way to supply arbitrary values to the component. The `<property>` tag is used to do just that. This tag's attributes appear in table 9.6.

Table 9.6 <property> tag attributes

`name` (required)	The name of the property being set
`value` (required)	The value of the property being set

Both the `name` and `value` attributes are required, and are used to build a `Properties` object that is passed to the cache model component to initialize it.

So, in general, configuration of the cache is not completely independent of the type of cache you use. Therefore, an understanding of the types available, and the options specific to each of them, is required.

9.5 Cache model types

As mentioned in section 9.3.1, four cache model types that come with iBATIS for use in your application:

- MEMORY
- LRU

- FIFO
- OSCACHE

We look at each of these types in the next four sections.

9.5.1 MEMORY

The MEMORY cache is a reference-based cache (see the `java.lang.ref` JavaDocs). Each object in the cache is given a reference type. The reference type provides hints to the garbage collector that let it know how to handle the object. Like the `java.lang.ref` package, the MEMORY cache provides WEAK and SOFT references. Additionally, when specifying the reference type as WEAK or SOFT, the garbage collector determines what stays and what goes, based on memory constraints and/or current access to the cached objects. When you use a STRONG reference type, the cache is guaranteed to retain the object no matter what until a flush interval is called.

The MEMORY cache model is ideal for applications that are more interested in memory management than in object access strategies. Because of the STRONG, SOFT, and WEAK reference types, you can determine which results should persist longer than others. Table 9.7 provides a quick view of how each reference type functions and how the different types determine the length of time the object is cached in memory.

Table 9.7 MEMORY cache reference types

WEAK	The WEAK reference type discards cached objects quickly. This reference type does not prevent the object from being collected by the garbage collector. It merely provides a way to access an object in the cache that will be removed with the first pass of the garbage collector. This is the default reference type and works great for keeping your cache occupied with objects that are accessed on a very consistent basis. Because of the faster rate of discard, your cache is guaranteed to not exceed memory limits. It is more likely that you will get a higher rate of database hits with this reference type.
SOFT	The SOFT reference type is also good for objects that may need to be released when memory constraints are important. This reference type retains the cached object as long as memory constraints allow. The garbage collector will not collect this object unless it is determined that more memory is needed. The SOFT reference is also guaranteed to not exceed memory limits and will likely have fewer database hits than the WEAK reference type.
STRONG	The STRONG reference type holds onto cached objects regardless of memory constraints. Objects stored as STRONG are not discarded until the specified flush interval. The STRONG cache should be reserved for static, small, regularly accessed objects. This reference type will increase performance by reducing database hits and runs the risk of running out of memory if the cache grows too large.

The MEMORY cache type has only one property: `reference-type`, which specifies the unique ID that will be referenced by query mapped statements that want to use the cache model's configured cache.

Listing 9.4 shows a simple MEMORY cache model that uses weak references to hold cached data for no more than 24 hours, and is flushed whenever the insert, update, or delete mapped statement is executed.

Listing 9.4 Sample MEMORY cacheModel

```
<cacheModel id="categoryCache" type="MEMORY">
  <flushInterval hours="24"/>
  <flushOnExecute statement="insert"/>
  <flushOnExecute statement="update"/>
  <flushOnExecute statement="delete"/>
  <property name="reference-type" value="WEAK"/>
</cacheModel>
```

The MEMORY cache type is a simple but effective way to cache the data in your application.

9.5.2 LRU

The LRU cache model type uses a *least recently used* strategy to manage the cache. The internals to this cache determine which objects are accessed least recently and discard them when size limits are exceeded. The discarding of cache objects only occurs when the cache exceeds the size-limit constraint. The size limit defines the number of objects that can be contained within the cache. Avoid placing large memory objects into this type of cache and thus running out of memory.

The LRU cache is a great fit for managing a cache based on popular access to particular objects. Often this kind of caching strategy is used in applications that need to cache objects used for paged results or keyed search results.

The only property that can be specified for the LRU cache type when using the `<property>` tag is `size`, which specifies the maximum number of objects that can be stored in the cache.

Listing 9.5 shows a simple LRU cache model that keeps the last 200 cached objects in memory for up to 24 hours and also flushes the cache whenever the insert, update, or delete mapped statement is called.

Listing 9.5 Sample LRU cacheModel

```
<cacheModel id="categoryCache" type="LRU">
  <flushInterval hours="24"/>
  <flushOnExecute statement="insert"/>
```

```
    <flushOnExecute statement="update"/>
    <flushOnExecute statement="delete"/>
    <property name="size" value="200"/>
</cacheModel>
```

The LRU cache is quite useful for applications where different subsets of data are used for periods of time.

9.5.3 FIFO

The FIFO cache model uses a *first in, first out* strategy. The FIFO is an age-based strategy and removes the oldest cached objects first. The discarding of cache objects occurs only when the cache exceeds the size-limit constraint. The size limit defines the number of objects that can be contained within the cache. Again, avoid placing large memory-consuming objects into this type of cache and thus running out of memory.

Since the FIFO is age based, it is good for caching objects that are more relevant when initially placed into the cache. Over time the results may become less relevant yet still be accessed. A time-based reporting application may find this type of caching useful. If you were reporting stock prices, most inquiries would be relevant in the beginning and yet decline in importance as time went on.

The only property that can be specified for the FIFO cache type when using the `<property>` tag is `size`, which specifies the maximum number of objects that can be stored in the cache.

Listing 9.6 shows a simple FIFO cache model that keeps the last 1,000 cached objects in memory for up to 24 hours, and also flushes the cache whenever the insert, update, or delete mapped statement is called.

Listing 9.6 Sample FIFO cacheModel

```
<cacheModel id="categoryCache" type="FIFO">
    <flushInterval hours="24"/>
    <flushOnExecute statement="insert"/>
    <flushOnExecute statement="update"/>
    <flushOnExecute statement="delete"/>
    <property name="size" value="1000"/>
</cacheModel>
```

The FIFO cache is useful for applications where rolling subsets of data are used for periods of time, like a shopping cart.

9.5.4 OSCACHE

The OSCACHE cache model uses the OSCache 2.0 product from OpenSymphony (www.opensymphony.com/oscache/). OSCache is a robust caching framework that is able to perform many of the same type of caching strategies that iBATIS provides in its other cache models. When using the OSCACHE model, you create a dependency on the OSCache JARs. You will need to include the OSCache JAR in your project when you use this setting. This cache is configured in the same manner as a standard OSCache install. This means that you will need to have an `oscache.properties` file available on the root of your classpath for OSCache to read. For more information on how to install and configure OSCache, access the documentation online at www.opensymphony.com/oscache/documentation.action. Listing 9.7 shows an example of what the OSCACHE cache model may look like.

Listing 9.7 Sample OSCACHE cacheModel

```
<cacheModel id="categoryCache" type="OSCACHE">
  <flushInterval hours="24"/>
  <flushOnExecute statement="insert"/>
  <flushOnExecute statement="update"/>
  <flushOnExecute statement="delete"/>
</cacheModel>
```

9.5.5 Your cache model here

Earlier, we mentioned that the cache model was a pluggable component in the framework. You may be wondering how you create your own cache model, or maybe you're just curious about how you would do it.

There are only two things to remember. First, the four cache model types that come with iBATIS are implementations of the `com.ibatis.sqlmap.engine.cache.CacheController` interface. Second, the names are type aliases that map to the fully qualified names of those implementations.

Moving right along, now that you have a cache model, let's look at some ways to make it work for you.

9.6 Determining a caching strategy

When you're making a determination about caching strategies, you first have to clarify your requirements. IBATIS provides the previously mentioned set of caching strategies for the data access layer. These caching strategies can—and likely will—play into your overall caching strategy, but they probably won't be the sum total of your application's overall caching. If you are exploring an overall caching strategy, there is a lot to consider and the discussion reaches beyond the scope of this book. However, it is important to determine what part iBATIS caching can play in your overall caching strategy.

When caching data on the data access layer, you will be working with either a dedicated or a shared database. With a dedicated database, all access to that database will take place through the application you are developing. With a shared database, multiple applications will access the database and be capable of making alterations to the data.

If your application connects to a database that has a variety of other applications accessing it and altering its data, you will likely want to avoid caching much of it. Using `<flushOnExecute>` will not be an effective strategy if the underlying data has long since expired because another application has made changes to your database. You can still take advantage of caching the more static read-only data that will not impact your read/write data. Examples include time-based report data that does not change, shopping cart page data, or static drop-down list data.

On the other hand, if you are caching for a database that is accessed only through a single application, you can be much more aggressive about your use of iBATIS caching. In a dedicated application, `<flushOnExecute>` becomes much more valuable. You know that the execution of certain mapped statements will force cached data to be invalid and therefore can affect your flush strategies.

Suppose you want more granular control over when certain items are released from the cache, or you want a clustered cache. IBATIS by itself provides no means of caching in this manner, but it can be combined with the OSCACHE cache type (section 9.5.4) to provide this type of robust functionality. However, the same rules apply here as stated earlier. You can be much more aggressive about your use of caching when you know that access to your database is limited to one application. But exercise caution when your application is not the dedicated access to the database.

In the next few sections, we look at some case studies of cache use, as well as some code snippets that illustrate how to get started implementing them.

9.6.1 Caching read-only, long-term data

Often read-only, long-term data is what we cache. It is easy to cache because it doesn't change often. We can place such data into the cache and forget about it until an interval expires for flushing or a mapped statement is executed that triggers a flush. Let's revisit our shopping cart application and step through setting up a read-only cache.

We looked at the shopping cart category in the previous chapter, so we will use it again here. When visitors to the shopping cart select a category, it usually has related subcategories that are also displayed. These categories are accessed quite a bit, and do not change often; consequently, they are prime candidates for long-term, read-only caching.

When thinking through how to set up category caching, consider how the results will be queried and the caching strategy that best fits the pattern of access to that data. In the case of caching subcategory lists, users will typically query for a list of child categories based on their related parent category. Expressing this in SQL terms would mean that the `WHERE` criteria will be based on equality of the `parentCategoryId` with a passed-in parameter. Another consideration is how often this cache should be flushed and which caching strategy should be used. Often users interact with some categories more than others. So, surveying the options we may want to go with a LRU strategy (listing 9.8). Using this approach will keep items around that are accessed more recently while discarding those that have been in the cache longer.

Listing 9.8 Sample LRU cacheModel

```
<cacheModel id="categoryCache" type="LRU">
  <flushInterval hours="24"/>
  <flushOnExecute statement="insert"/>
  <flushOnExecute statement="update"/>
  <flushOnExecute statement="delete"/>
  <property name="size" value="50"/>
</cacheModel>
```

In listing 9.8 we start by setting up the cache model. We specify the type attribute as `LRU`. The `id` attribute provides us with a unique identifier to reference when setting up query mapped statements that will use the cache. By using the `<flush-Interval>` tag, we ensure that the cache is never older than 24 hours. `<flush-Interval>` will clear any cached results that are stored in the identified `categoryCache`. Using `<flushInterval>` we specify that calling the identified insert, update, or delete mapped statement will also trigger a flush of any results stored in the identified `categoryCache`. Finally, we set the limit for how many items will be stored in the cache by using the `<property>` tag and the `<size>` property. Once the cache exceeds 50 stored results, it will begin to remove the least recently used items.

In listing 9.9, the query mapped statement `getChildCategories` takes advantage of `categoryCache` via the `cacheModel` attribute, which identifies `categoryCache` as its associated cache. As users peruse the categories of the shopping cart application, the `getChildCategories` query mapped statement is called. This causes any child results to be cached. As the cache reaches its size of 50, it begins to remove any aged results from the cache. This causes constantly accessed lists of child categories to remain in the cache longer and provides better performance for the users. If an administrator performs an insert, update, or delete on the categories, a flush is triggered and the buildup of the cached results begins all over. This combination of flushing and culling keeps the child categories fresh and up to date while reducing the constant burden of unnecessary database hits.

Listing 9.9 Query mapped statement that uses the categoryCache

```
<select id="getChildCategories" parameterClass="Category"
  resultClass="Category" cacheModel="categoryCache">
  SELECT *
  FROM category
  <dynamic prepend="WHERE ">
    <isNull property="categoryId">
    parentCategoryId IS NULL
    </isNull>
    <isNotNull property="categoryId">
    parentCategoryId=#categoryId:INTEGER:0#
    </isNotNull>
  </dynamic>
  ORDER BY sequence, title
</select>
```

The removing process of the LRU cache can be fine-tuned by adjusting the `size` property up or down to allow for more or fewer categories to be cached. Remember that the goal of the LRU is to cache only items that are accessed constantly. Don't set the size too high. If you do, you effectively make your LRU cache into a STRONG memory cache—which would defeat the whole purpose of the LRU cache.

Now that we've discussed an effective means of caching long-term, read-only data, let's consider another situation that you will often face when asking the "to cache or not to cache" question: caching read-write data.

9.6.2 Caching read-write data

Suppose you want to cache objects that are of a changing nature. You must do this with caution; if you have a high-transaction environment, you may find that your cache is overburdened and effectively useless. The reason for this is that an attempt to keep high-transaction data cached would require that you flush the cache often. Flushing the cache too often could create a twofold burden. First, your application would constantly be in a state of checking the cache, clearing the cache, and repopulating the cache on every request to the database. Consequently, if the cache is constantly being cleared, this means that the database is also being hit to retrieve fresh results. You'll come to a point where it is simply better for performance if you use database techniques such as indexing and table pinning and avoid application-based caching.

Even though you need to be careful when caching data that may change, it also makes sense to do so when the data is of a less volatile state. In the JGameStore application, we find a good example of this with caching products. With many storefronts, there is a need for administrators to enter new products, update existing ones, mark others as sale items, and similar tasks. These kinds of activities will produce a mild level of volatility. Since this is not a high-transaction environment, caching can play a role in improving overall application performance. As long as the cache has time to build up and provide users with improved performance over a span of time, you will avoid the sinkhole described previously.

When examining the nature of the data that you want to cache, consider several factors:

- The number of products will likely be significant.
- The products data is of a changing nature.
- The products that are most often accessed will change throughout the day depending on consumer habits.

In our example, we decide to use the WEAK memory cache because it is a less restrictive means of caching. Unlike LRU, which requires a certain level of predictability for determining the number of results that should be cached, the WEAK memory cache allows us to decide which items to retain and discard before a predetermined artificial limit is met. Since the cache uses the `java.lang.ref.Reference` implementations to store data in the cache, it can remove or retain results based on internal analytics. When using the WEAK reference type with the MEMORY cache, the results are wrapped with a `WeakReference` (`java.lang.ref.WeakReference`) and stored in the cache. Then, the garbage collector is able to handle the wrapped results at its discretion.

Now let's move on to configuring the `<cacheModel>` tag. As expected, the `cacheModel` type attribute is specified as `MEMORY`. Note that we are setting the readOnly attribute on the <cacheModel> tag to true in an environment that is a read-write environment. Additionally, we set serialize to false to eliminate the burden of the deep copy. That means that objects that are retrieved from the cache may be altered. This is a safe approach for several reasons. First, only the person managing the cart will be altering product objects. The users who are actually shopping will never change the product object through their actions. Second, whenever a product update occurs, the cache is flushed. Finally, specifying the reference-type property as WEAK will not allow products to hang around very long because it discards them at the discretion of the garbage collector. Listing 9.10 shows an example of our cache model configuration.

Listing 9.10 Cache model for productCache

```
<cacheModel id="productCache" type="MEMORY"
  readOnly="true" serialize="false">
  <flushOnExecute statement="Product.add" />
  <flushOnExecute statement="Product.edit" />
  <flushOnExecute statement="Product.remove" />
  <property name="reference-type" value="WEAK" />
</cacheModel>
```

We can now use the defined <cacheModel> from a query mapped statement. We tell the getProductById query mapped statement to use productCache by specifying it in the cacheModel. Whenever the getProductById select is called from the application, the cached product object will be retrieved according to the specifications of the productCache cache model. Listing 9.11 shows a simple example of how a <select> statement can take advantage of the defined <cacheModel>.

Listing 9.11 Query mapped statement that uses productCache

```
<select id="getProductById" resultClass="Product"
  parameterClass="Product" cacheModel="productCache">
  SELECT * FROM Product WHERE productId=#productId#
</select>
```

9.6.3 Caching aging static data

This final case study is a somewhat unusual situation, but it's a fun test case nonetheless. Situations arise where you need to deal with smaller static portions of data that become less relevant as time goes on. Often this type of caching is associated with time-based analytics. Examples of time-based analytics include performance statistics in a call center application, or a stock ticker that provides statistics from previous hours/days/months. To summarize the attributes of the data, we could say that it becomes less relevant as time goes on. It is not a large set of data; it is accessed with high frequency early on and with less frequency as time goes by. The data does not change, or in other words it is "static."

Our JGameStore application does not have this type of requirement, but we will continue with the shopping cart analogy. Let's say that we need to collect statistics on the top five products that guests are purchasing every hour. We'll then use this data on the home page of the cart to tell shoppers what the hot items are on an hourly basis. Let's also say that we provide a drop-down list that allows users to choose previous hours to see previous hot-product purchases. Once product purchases take place, they do not change. If five copies of the newest 3D blockbuster are purchased in the last hour, then that will remain true into the future. With these simple requirements, let's see how we might use iBATIS caching to ensure enhanced performance.

Due to the fact that this data becomes less relevant over time and is of an aging nature, FIFO comes to mind as a prime candidate cache. Our description of the FIFO cache mentioned that it is an "aging" cache. Any data that is placed into it will "age out" as the size limits are exceeded. So, as the hours tick away and items are added to the cache, the product listings that are not the most current will be accessed less and less. Those items will eventually be discarded as newer product lists are cached each hour. If we set the FIFO cache size to 24, then our list will only retain the last 24 hours' worth of items; anything past that will be discarded. Let's move on and see how the other requirements fit with the FIFO cache.

Since the product purchases will remain the same over time, we can safely assume they are static. Storing static data in the FIFO cache works well. The static data will eventually age out and does not require the use of constant flushing to subvert the aging process. The only time we would need to flush the cache is when there are updates to products. Since this is not a constant occurrence, we can simply allow processes to flow as needed and push the items on through the FIFO cache.

The five products we will be storing each hour should have a small memory footprint. Since FIFO only discards when the specified size is exceeded, it is undesirable to place large memory-consuming objects into it. The FIFO cache will not discard items if memory restrictions become strained, which could ultimately result in an out-of-memory exception. In the case of our product listings, we should be perfectly safe.

High-frequency access and low-frequency access are part of the game when it comes to caching. It doesn't matter which you experience as long as there is a true benefit from the fact that it is or may be accessed more than once. Fine-tuning the size is the only thing we need to be concerned with. Depending on the number of people who are accessing the current popular purchases or past popular purchases, we can set our cache size to accommodate.

Now that we have looked at the list of requirements and how the FIFO cache fits with them, let's move on to configuring the cache model. Our cache model is quite simple. As shown in listing 9.12, we want to display correct product information for purchased products. This requires that we first set up the appropriate `<flushOnExcecute>` tags to flush `hotProductsCache` when product data changes. We only need to specify `Product.update` or `Product.delete` to flush the cache. We do not include `insert` here because we don't care about products that don't exist. If a product is added and then becomes a popular purchase, we will have no problem adding it to `hotProductCache`. It is only when the product is updated or deleted that we need to worry at all about a flush. We would not want to display a cached product that is no longer for sale (i.e., deleted). We would also not want to display an old pricing on a product that has had a pricing update.

Listing 9.12 Cache model and mapped statement for hotProductsCache

```
<cacheModel id="hotProductCache" type="FIFO">
  <flushOnExecute statement="Product.update"/>
  <flushOnExecute statement="Product.delete"/>
  <property name="size" value="12"/>
</cacheModel>

<select
  id="getPopularProductsByPurchaseDate"
  parameterClass="Product"
  resultClass="Product" cacheModel="hotProductsCache">
  SELECT count(productId) countNum, productId
  FROM productPurchase
  WHERE
  purchaseDate
    BETWEEN
      #startDate#
    AND
      #endDate#
  GROUP BY productId
  ORDER BY countNum DESC
  LIMIT 5
</select>
```

With the cache flush configuration behind us, let's move on to setting up the FIFO cache size property. Setting the `size` property to 12 allows us to hold a maximum of 12 results in the cache (see listing 9.12). Once 12 results occupy the cache, the oldest item is discarded and the newest item is added to the beginning of the cache. Since the SQL we use will only provide our cache with a new result every hour or more, our cache should hold up just fine to aging the data appropriately. The newer results will always occupy the "front" of the cache while the older results are discarded.

9.7 Summary

iBATIS provides a good selection of persistence layer cache options. Making the appropriate choice requires that you exercise thought and care. It's important to remember that iBATIS caching is value based (versus OID) and intended to handle caching specifically on the persistence layer.

If the default iBATIS cache options do not meet your needs, you can look into extending iBATIS (chapter 12) to provide a cache that does. The examples in this chapter can help you get started; experience will be the best guide. Spend time getting to know the various types of caches and their options. Become familiar with each type's particular strengths and weaknesses. This knowledge will help you determine which option will meet your particular needs.

10 iBATIS data access objects

This chapter covers

- DAO rationale
- Configuration
- A SQL Map DAO example

Applications often need to access data from multiple data sources: relational databases, file systems, directory services, web services, and other providers. Each of these data stores has a different API to access the underlying storage mechanism, along with a whole set of idiosyncrasies.

The Data Access Object (DAO) pattern is used to hide the unique implementation quirks of these APIs. It provides a simple and common API for application developers so that the consumers of the data can be free of the complexities of the data access APIs.

The iBATIS Data Access Objects subproject is a simple implementation of the core J2EE pattern of the same name.

10.1 Hiding implementation details

One of the key principles of object-oriented programming is encapsulation—the separation of an implementation and its public interface. The DAO pattern is one more tool that allows you to do that in your applications. Before we go too far into the DAO pattern, let's look at figure 10.1, to see what one looks like.

If you are thinking that figure 10.1 looks more like JDBC than a DAO, then you are only half right. It is JDBC, but the JDBC API in Java is a good example of the DAO pattern in action.

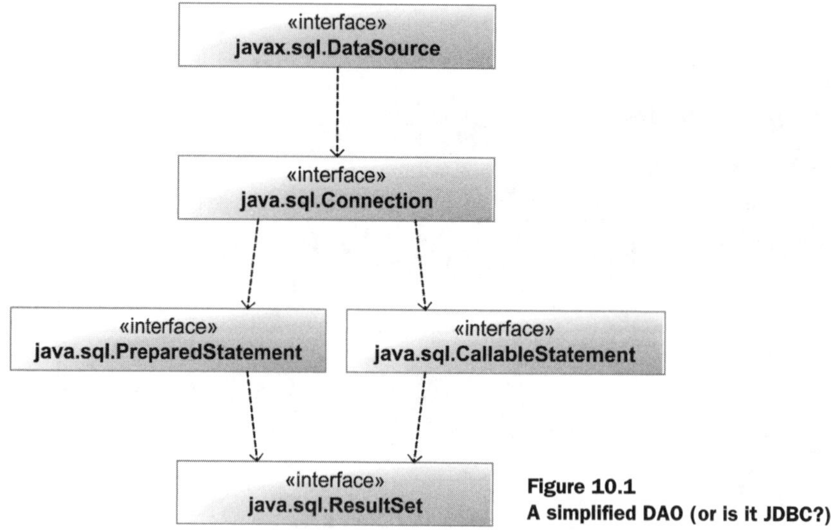

Figure 10.1
A simplified DAO (or is it JDBC?)

You have a factory on the top (the `DataSource` interface), which creates instances of objects that implement the `Connection` interface. Once you have the `Connection`, you can get `PreparedStatement` or `CallableStatement` objects, which in turn provide you with `ResultSet` objects. You do not need to know how the `DataSource` creates the connection, or how the connection creates the `PreparedStatement`, how the `PreparedStatement` binds the parameters to the query, or even how the `ResultSet` is constructed. All of the details are irrelevant as long as you know that when you call the `Connection`'s `prepareStatement()` method you get a `PreparedStatement` back.

10.1.1 Why the separation?

By separating the data access implementation from the data access interface, we are able to provide a homogenous set of interfaces to heterogeneous data. An application can access data from multiple databases, each with a different underlying data access mechanism using a single consistent data access API.

The JDBC API is just one type of DAO pattern. In that realm, you have a set of interfaces, and database vendors implement them in a way that makes it possible to use them interchangeably—for the most part. In a few cases, where vendors feel that the interfaces do not provide the capability to do things they want to do, they work outside the interface.

To give you an idea of how much the DAO pattern in the JDBC API simplified its use (and yes, we really mean "simplified"), take a look at a JDBC driver implementation some time. For example, one major database vendor's implementation of the five interfaces in figure 10.1 is composed of nine more (vendor-specific) interfaces before getting to the five classes that actually implement them (this is not counting any classes or interfaces that are outside of the lineage of the actual implementing classes). One of the authors did actually build the UML for this, and intended on putting it in here as an example, but this chapter was already too long, and we would have had to add another page. Yes, it was that complex.

This pattern is one reason why tools like iBATIS SQL maps and O/RM tools are possible. Because nearly all database vendors implement the JDBC APIs very accurately, tools can be written that operate against those interfaces instead of the underlying implementations. For the most part, those tools will work with any vendor's implementation, and you only need to refer to the vendor's software when you create the `DataSource`—from there on, you are working with the common API.

This is also one of the goals of the iBATIS DAO: to help you provide a set of interfaces to your applications that hide the underlying implementation of the data access. So, if you have a Hibernate-based application that uses the DAO pattern, you can replace that with a SQL Map–based implementation, or a JDBC-based implementation, without having to rewrite the entire application. Instead, all that needs to be changed is the implementations of the interfaces that the application is using. As long as the DAO interface is implemented correctly, the application will continue to function as expected.

As a rule, the DAO will not expose any interfaces that involve objects from the java.sql or javax.sql packages. This means that the DAO is the layer of your application where the integration with the data sources happens, and that the layers accessing it do not have to be concerned with those low-level details. It also means that in addition to being able to change the data access mechanism (i.e., `SqlMaps`, Hibernate, JDBC, etc.), the DAO pattern allows you to change the data source in a similar fashion. Because the interface is created in a data source–agnostic manner, the application does not need to know if the data is coming from Oracle or PostgreSQL—or even from a non-SQL-based database for that matter. All it has to deal with are JavaBeans. Where those beans originate from is irrelevant as far as the application is concerned.

An added benefit of this sort of separation is that testing becomes much easier, because you are not working with interfaces that are specific to the data access method that the DAO uses—you are working with more common objects like List and Map, as well as beans specific to your application.

10.1.2 A simple example

Let's start with a simple example of how to configure and use the iBATIS DAO. Before we do that, look at figure 10.2, which is the DAO that we will be configuring.

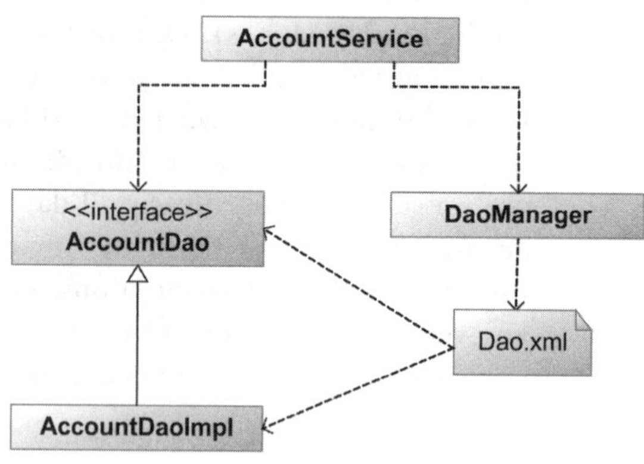

Figure 10.2 An even simpler DAO (really)

This DAO (which is much simpler than the JDBC example) is composed of one interface (`AccountDao`), and its implementation (`AccountDaoImpl`). The other two classes show one use of the interface, and the `DaoManager` class, which is the factory class used by iBATIS to create DAOs. The DaoManager class is configured using the Dao.xml configuration file.

The Dao.xml configuration file

To configure the DaoManager, you start with an XML configuration file, commonly named dao.xml, which contains the information required to tell iBATIS how to put the DAO together. Listing 10.1 contains an example of an XML configuration file for a SQL Map–based DAO layer.

Listing 10.1 A simple dao.xml example

```
<?xml version="1.0" encoding="UTF-8" ?>
<!DOCTYPE daoConfig
    PUBLIC
    "-//ibatis.apache.org//DTD DAO Configuration 2.0//EN"
    "http://ibatis.apache.org/dtd/dao-2.dtd">
<daoConfig>
  <context id="example">                          <-1 The DAO context
    <transactionManager type="SQLMAP">  <-2 The transaction manager
      <property
        name="SqlMapConfigResource"
          value="examples/SqlMapConfig.xml"/>
    </transactionManager>
    <dao                                          <-3 The one and only DAO defined
      interface="examples.dao.AccountDao"
      implementation="examples.dao.impl.AccountDao"/>
  </context>
</daoConfig>
```

Listing 10.1 defines a DAO context named example (1) that will use SQL Maps (2) for managing transactions (which were covered in chapter 7) and contains a single Account DAO (3). In the next section, we'll look more closely at this file's contents, so if you are not totally clear on it, that is OK.

Creating the DaoManager

Next, you need to create a DaoManager instance (which is analogous to JDBC's DataSource as the starting point of our data access layer) from which you can get the DAO. Because building the DAO manager takes time, you will want to create an instance of it and store it in a known location for later use. In section 10.4, we look at some other ways to accomplish this; but for now, let's create a simple DaoService class that will create and store our DaoManager instance for us (see listing 10.2).

Listing 10.2 A simple example of using a DAO

```
package org.apache.mapper2.examples.chapter10.dao;

import com.ibatis.dao.client.DaoManager;
import com.ibatis.dao.client.DaoManagerBuilder;
import com.ibatis.common.resources.Resources;
import java.io.Reader;
import java.io.IOException;

public class DaoService {
  private static DaoManager daoManager;

  public static synchronized DaoManager getDaoManager(){
    String daoXmlResource = "dao.xml";   ❶ Specifies location of config file
    Reader reader;
    if (null == daoManager){
      try {
        reader =
          Resources.getResourceAsReader(daoXmlResource);   ❷ Gets a reader for the builder
        daoManager =
          DaoManagerBuilder.buildDaoManager(reader);   ❸ Builds DAO manager
        return daoManager;
      } catch (IOException e) {
        throw new RuntimeException(
                      "Unable to create DAO manager.", e);
      }
    } else {
      return daoManager;
    }
  }

  public static Dao getDao(Class interfaceClass){
    return getDaoManager().getDao(interfaceClass);
  }
}
```

We will look briefly at this listing, because it does have some bits of code that will prove relevant later. The first in order of importance is the `daoXmlResource` variable ❶, which contains the location of the `dao.xml` file we saw in listing 10.1 earlier. That is important because it is not a path, but rather a resource location on the classpath. For example, if you are working on a web application, it would be in the `WEB-INF/classes` directory. The `Resources` class ❷ searches the classpath for that file, and then we pass it as a `Reader` to the `DaoManagerBuilder` ❸ to get our `DaoManager` instance. Now, for our DAO, we can simply call this:

```
AccountDao accountDao = (AccountDao)
                         DaoService.getDao(AccountDao.class);
```

So, now that you have seen an example of the goodness of using the DAO pattern, you may be wondering just how to use it. First, you have to set up the configuration—which is the next topic we'll discuss.

10.2 Configuring the DAO

The `dao.xml` file is the only configuration file required when using the iBATIS DAO framework. It is a very simple file, and is used to provide the DAO manager with the information required to manage transactions for your DAO classes and tell it how to supply DAO implementations for your interfaces.

First, we look at the configuration elements that are available, and then examine some ways to use them to solve common problems.

10.2.1 The <properties> element

The `<properties>` element is used in the same manner as it is in the `SqlMapConfig.xml` file. It is used to specify a properties file, and any properties listed in it are available for use in the configuration of the DAO layer using the `${name}` syntax.

This approach is very useful in cases where you have separate servers for development and production (and potentially staging and testing servers as well). In these cases, you can configure all of your DAO classes and put just the items that differ by environment into the properties file. Then, when you deploy to each environment, all that has to be changed is the properties file.

10.2.2 The <context> element

A DAO context is a grouping of related configuration information and DAO implementations:

```
<context id="example">
```

Usually a context is associated with a single data source such as a relational database or a flat file. By configuring multiple contexts, you can easily centralize access configuration to multiple databases.

In section 10.3, we look at using contexts to create multiple DAO groups that employ different data access models—one that uses SQL maps (of course!), one that uses Hibernate, and finally, one that uses straight JDBC.

Each context has its own transaction manager and set of DAO implementations. In the next two sections, you will learn how to configure each of those items.

10.2.3 The <transactionManager> element

As the name implies, the transaction manager manages transactions (which were covered in detail in chapter 7) for your DAO classes. The `<transactionManager>` element provides the name of a `DaoTransactionManager` implementation. The iBATIS DAO framework comes with seven different transaction managers that can work with different data access tools, as shown in table 10.1.

Table 10.1 Transaction managers available with the iBATIS DAO framework

Type alias	Transaction manager/properties	Comments
EXTERNAL	`ExternalDaoTransactionManager`	A "do-nothing" transaction that allows you to manage your own transactions outside of the iBATIS DAO framework.
HIBERNATE	`HibernateDaoTransactionManager`	Delegates to the Hibernate transaction management functionality.
JDBC	`JdbcDaoTransactionManager` * `DataSource` * `JDBC.Driver` * `JDBC.ConnectionURL` * `JDBC.Username` * `JDBC.Password` * `JDBC.DefaultAutoCommit`	Uses JDBC to provide connection pooling services via the `DataSource` API. Three `DataSource` implementations are supported: SIMPLE, DBCP, and JNDI. SIMPLE is an implementation of the iBATIS `SimpleDataSource`, which is a stand-alone implementation ideal for minimal overhead and dependencies. DBCP is an implementation that uses the Jakarta DBCP `DataSource`. Finally, JNDI is an implementation that retrieves a `DataSource` reference from a JNDI directory. This is the most common and flexible configuration, as it allows you to centrally configure your application via your application server.
JTA	`JtaDaoTransactionManager` * `DBJndiContext` * `UserTransaction`	Manages transactions using the Java Transaction Architecture (JTA) API. Requires that the `DataSource` implementation be retrieved via JNDI and that `UserTransaction` instances also be accessible via JNDI.
OJB	`OjbBrokerTransactionManager`	Delegates to the OJB transaction management functionality.
SQLMAP	`SqlMapDaoTransactionManager`	Delegates to the SQL map transaction management functionality.
TOPLINK	`ToplinkDaoTransactionManager`	Delegates to the TOPLINK transaction management functionality.

OK, so now that you know what your options are, let's take a closer look to see what makes each one unique.

The EXTERNAL transaction manager

The EXTERNAL transaction manager is the simplest to configure (it has no properties, and any that are passed to it are ignored), but potentially the most difficult to use, because you are 100 percent responsible for all transaction management in your application.

The HIBERNATE transaction manager

The HIBERNATE transaction manager is also very simple to configure. It takes all of the properties that are passed to it, and simply passes them on to the Hibernate session factory. In addition, any properties that are passed in with names that begin with `class.` are assumed to be classes to be managed by Hibernate, and are added to the configuration object that is used to build the session factory. Likewise, any properties passed in that begin with `map.` are assumed to be mapping files, and are also added to the configuration object.

The JDBC transaction manager

The JDBC transaction manager is probably the most difficult one to configure. The `DataSource` property is required for this transaction manager and must be one of the following: SIMPLE, DBCP, or JNDI.

The SIMPLE data source

The SIMPLE data source is an implementation of the iBATIS `SimpleDataSource`, which is a stand-alone implementation ideal for minimal overhead and dependencies. It has five required properties:

- `JDBC.Driver`—This is the fully qualified name of the JDBC driver to be used for managing transactions in this DAO context.
- `JDBC.ConnectionURL`—This is the JDBC URL that is to be used to connect to the database for this DAO context.
- `JDBC.Username`—This is the username that is to be used to connect to the database for this DAO context.
- `JDBC.Password`—This is the password of the user to be used to connect to the database for this DAO context.
- `JDBC.DefaultAutoCommit`—If `true` (or any expression that the Boolean class in Java interprets as true), then the `autoCommit` property of connections returned by this data source will be set to true in this DAO context.

In addition to those required properties, eight optional properties can be used to configure the connection pool:

- `Pool.MaximumActiveConnections`—This is the number of connections that the pool can have active at one time. The default value of this property is 10 connections.
- `Pool.MaximumIdleConnections`—This specifies the number of connections that the pool can have idle at one time. The default value of this property is 5 connections.
- `Pool.MaximumCheckoutTime`—This is the maximum number of milliseconds that a connection is reserved before it can be given to another request. The default value of this property is 20,000 milliseconds, or 20 seconds.
- `Pool.TimeToWait`—This represents the number of milliseconds to wait for a connection if one is not available when requested. The default value of this property is 20,000 milliseconds, or 20 seconds.
- `Pool.PingEnabled`—If `true` (or any expression that the Boolean class in Java interprets as true), then connections will be tested using the query defined in the `Pool.PingQuery` property when they are determined to be at risk for invalidation. The default value for this property is `false`, meaning that connections will never be pinged before use. The next three properties are used to determine the behavior of connection pinging.
- `Pool.PingQuery`—This is the query to be executed if a connection needs to be tested to see if it is still valid. Be sure to make this a statement that will return very quickly. For example, on Oracle, something like `select 0 from dual` would work very well.
- `Pool.PingConnectionsOlderThan`—This represents the age (in milliseconds) at which connections are considered to be at risk for invalidation. The default value for this property is 0, which means that if pinging is enabled, then every time a connection is used it will be checked. In a high-transaction environment, this could have a serious impact on performance.
- `Pool.PingConnectionsNotUsedFor`—This is the number of milliseconds to let a connection sit idle before considering it "at risk" for invalidation.

The DBCP data source

The DBCP data source is a wrapper around the Jakarta Commons Database Connection Pooling (DBCP) project's data source implementation, and is intended to allow you to use a more robust implementation at the expense of an added dependency. The properties for this transaction manager are handled differently, based on what properties are available. The old way of setting up a DBCP transaction manager (which is still supported) was to set these eight properties:

- `JDBC.Driver`—This specifies the JDBC driver to be used by this DAO context.
- `JDBC.ConnectionURL`—This is the JDBC URL to be used for connecting to this DAO context's database.
- `JDBC.Username`—This is the username to be used when connecting to the database.
- `JDBC.Password`—This is the password to be used when connecting to the database.
- `Pool.ValidationQuery`—This is a query to use to validate database connections.
- `Pool.MaximumActiveConnections`—This specifies the maximum number of active connections that are to be in the connection pool.
- `Pool.MaximumIdleConnections`—This specifies the maximum number of idle connections that are to be in the connection pool.
- `Pool.MaximumWait`—This specifies the maximum time (in milliseconds) to wait for a connection before giving up.

The new way of configuring the DBCP data source is much more flexible, because it simply treats it as a bean, so that all properties exposed with get/set methods are available for your use in iBATIS. For example, to set the `driverClassName` for the data source, you would do this:

```
<property
  name="driverClassName"
  value="com.mysql.jdbc.Driver"/>
```

NOTE To learn more about using and configuring the DBCP data source, visit the official website at the Jakarta project: http://jakarta.apache.org/commons/dbcp/.

The JNDI data source

The JNDI data source is intended to allow you to leverage any JNDI context that your applications container may provide. It is also probably the simplest one to set up. It has one required property, `DBJndiContext`, which provides the name of the context that contains the data source.

This data source also allows you to pass other properties to the `InitialContext` constructor by using the prefix `context.` in any contained properties elements. For example, to pass a property named `someProperty`, you would use this syntax:

```
<property name="context.someProperty" value="someValue"/>
```

The JTA transaction manager

The Java Transaction API (JTA) transaction manager allows you to use distributed transactions with multiple databases. This means that you can commit or roll back changes made across multiple databases as easily as you would with a single database.

Only two properties are required to configure this transaction manager, because the bulk of the configuration work is done in JNDI. The first property, `DBJndiContext`, specifies the name of the context that contains the data source to be used for the transaction manager. The other required property, `UserTransaction`, provides the name of the context that contains the user transaction.

The OJB transaction manager

ObJectRelationalBridge (OJB) is another object/relational mapping tool to provide persistence for Java Objects using relational databases. The OJB transaction manager is a wrapper for the transaction management interface provided by OJB.

All of the configuration for OJB transaction management is done just as it would be done without the iBATIS DAO.

NOTE For more information on the OJB tool, and to see how to configure its transaction manager, visit http://db.apache.org/ojb/.

The SQLMAP transaction manager

SQLMAP is probably the most common choice of transaction manager when using the iBATIS DAO. The SQLMAP transaction manager requires either the `SqlMapConfigURL` or the `SqlMapConfigResource` property to be present. It uses the same transaction manager that the SQL Map uses for its transaction manager.

The `SqlMapConfigURL` property is expected to be a string that the `java.net.URL` class can parse and retrieve a resource from, including the `http:` and `file:` protocols. The `SqlMapConfigResource` property is used to refer to a resource that exists on the current classpath.

The TOPLINK transaction manager

Oracle's TopLink product is yet another O/RM tool. The only required property for the TOPLINK transaction manager is `session.name`, which is used to get the session that will be used by this DAO context.

Using your own or another transaction manager

In addition to these transaction manager implementations, the `DaoTransactionManager` is an interface that you can implement and insert into the DAO configuration by providing the fully qualified name of your implementation in the `type` attribute of the transaction manager configuration element. Any properties that are listed in the body of the transaction manager element are passed to the `configure()` method of the transaction manager class:

```
<transactionManager
   type="com.mycompany.MyNiftyTransactionManager">
  <property name="someProp" value="aValue"/>
  <property name="someOtherProp" value="anotherValue"/>
</transactionManager>
```

In the previous example, the iBATIS DAO framework would create an instance of the `MyNiftyTransactionManager` class, and pass it a `Properties` object with entries for `someProp` and `someOtherProp`. We will look at the anatomy of an existing `DaoTransactionManager` implementation in more detail in chapter 11.

10.2.4 The DAO elements

Once the transaction manager has been chosen and configured, the DAO elements can be added to the DAO context to define the DAO interfaces and implementations that your context will make available for your application.

The `<dao>` element only has two properties: `interface` and `implementation`.

NOTE Just because the attribute name `interface` is used to identify the DAO implementation, you do not actually need to use an interface. In our previous example, both of the attributes (`interface` and `implementation`) could have been the fully qualified class name of the implementation. While this may seem like an easy way to reduce some code, it is strongly discouraged, because it essentially eliminates the value added by the DAO layer—that is, the separation of the interface from the implementation. As for the code savings, nearly all IDEs now provide refactoring tools to allow you to extract an interface from an implementation, meaning that you are able to write and test your DAO implementation without creating the interface and then create the interface with a few mouse clicks.

The `interface` property is used to identify the DAO in the DAO map, and is generally used in the following way:

```
<dao interface="com.mycompany.system.dao.AccountDao"
     implementation=
       "com.mycompany.system.dao.impl.AccountDaoImpl"/>
```

Let's look at an example of this. Assume a class relationship like the one described earlier in figure 10.2. In this diagram, there is an `AccountDao` interface and an `AccountDaoImpl` class that implements that interface. To use the `DaoManager` to get the DAO, use the following code:

```
AccountDao accountDao = (AccountDao)
                    daoManager.getDao(AccountDao.class);
```

In this line of code, we declare our `AccountDao` variable, request it from the `DaoManager` instance using the interface name, and then cast it to the `AccountDao` interface, because the DAO manager simply returns `Object`.

In the previous version of the DAO, it was also possible to pass in a String instead of an interface class. In version 2.*x*, that functionality was dropped, because it eliminated a potential point of failure. By forcing the use of a class name for identifying DAO implementations, you ensure that misspellings can be avoided in the Java environment, because if the interface name is misspelled, the code will not compile. Early failure is a good thing.

So, now that you have a solid foundational understanding of what you can do with the iBATIS DAO framework, we can start looking at other more advanced uses of it.

10.3 Configuration tips

Although the DAO configuration looks very simple on the surface, it still offers a great deal of flexibility. By creatively configuring the DAO manager, you can accomplish some pretty sophisticated approaches to common problems. Let's look at a few of them.

10.3.1 Multiple servers

As mentioned earlier, it is not uncommon in most development shops to have different servers for their development, QC testing, UA testing, and production environments.

In these cases, it is very useful to be able to remove the environment-specific information from the `dao.xml` file and put it into an external file. The `properties` element was created to accomplish just that sort of thing. Listing 10.3 is a sample `dao.xml` file that uses this technique to make the JDBC settings external to the `dao.xml` file.

Listing 10.3 A sample dao.xml with JDBC settings inserted with a <properties /> element

```
<?xml version="1.0" encoding="UTF-8" ?>
<!DOCTYPE daoConfig
    PUBLIC
    "-//ibatis.apache.org//DTD DAO Configuration 2.0//EN"
    "http://ibatis.apache.org/dtd/dao-2.dtd">
<daoConfig>
  <properties resource="server.properties"/>
  <context>
    <transactionManager type="JDBC">
      <property name="DataSource" value="SIMPLE"/>
      <property name="JDBC.Driver" value="${jdbcDriver}" />
      <property name="JDBC.ConnectionURL"
                                value="${jdbcUrl}" />
      <property name="JDBC.Username" value="${jdbcUser}" />
      <property name="JDBC.Password"
                           value="${jdbcPassword}" />
      <property name="JDBC.DefaultAutoCommit"
                         value="${jdbcAutoCommit}" />
    </transactionManager>
    <dao interface="..." implementation="..."/>
  </context>
</daoConfig>
```

In this example, all of the property values are stored in a file named `server.properties` that is to be loaded from the root of the classpath.

This is an approach that we like to use, because all of the files can be kept under version control, and the different versions of the properties files can be named in a way that identifies them based on the environment (i.e., `server-production.properties`, `server-user.properties`, etc.) so that the build procedure can automatically copy the correct version to the correct location.

This approach also works well in more sensitive environments, where the configuration settings are considered to be more secure by not having them under version control. In those environments, it makes manual configuration simpler, because the configuration file that changes based on the environment is always the same file.

10.3.2 Multiple database dialects

If you are using the DAO pattern to support database platforms that are different enough to require different code (i.e., using MySQL without stored procedures, and Oracle with stored procedures), you can do something similar to the way we performed earlier with the JDBC settings and make the package name part of the properties file (see listing 10.4).

Listing 10.4 A dao.xml using a <properties /> element to insert implementation information

```
<?xml version="1.0" encoding="UTF-8" ?>
<!DOCTYPE daoConfig
    PUBLIC
    "-//ibatis.apache.org//DTD DAO Configuration 2.0//EN"
    "http://ibatis.apache.org/dtd/dao-2.dtd">
<daoConfig>
  <properties resource="config.properties"/>
  <context>
    <transactionManager type="JDBC">
      <property name="DataSource" value="SIMPLE"/>
      <property name="JDBC.Driver" value="${jdbcDriver}" />
      <property name="JDBC.ConnectionURL"
                                  value="${jdbcUrl}" />
      <property name="JDBC.Username" value="${jdbcUser}" />
      <property name="JDBC.Password"
                             value="${jdbcPassword}" />
      <property name="JDBC.DefaultAutoCommit"
                           value="${jdbcAutoCommit}" />
    </transactionManager>
    <dao interface="com.company.system.dao.AccountDao"
         implementation="${impl}.AccountDaoImpl"/>
  </context>
</daoConfig>
```

In listing 10.4, all of the server settings and the data access implementation are external to the main configuration file.

10.3.3 Runtime configuration changes

As if this were not enough flexibility, the DAO manager can also be built with properties that are determined at runtime and passed in when the DAO manager is created.

A second form of the code we saw in section 10.1.1 to pass in runtime configuration information might provide a method like listing 10.5.

Listing 10.5 Creating a DaoManager with runtime properties

```
public static DaoManager getDaoManager(Properties props)
{
  String daoXml = "/org/apache/mapper2/examples/Dao.xml";
  Reader reader;
  DaoManager localDaoManager;

  try {
```

```
    reader = Resources.getResourceAsReader(daoXml);
    localDaoManager =
        DaoManagerBuilder.buildDaoManager(reader, props);
  } catch (IOException e) {
    throw new RuntimeException(
              "Unable to create DAO manager.", e);
  }

  return localDaoManager;
}
```

The code in listing 10.5 would create a dynamically configured DAO manager whose properties were passed in at runtime, instead of the shared one that would normally be returned. While this would provide much more flexibility, it would also require the user of this DAO manager to keep a copy of it around, instead of creating it every time it was needed.

Next we'll look at how to use the iBATIS DAO framework, and create some DAO classes that it will manage for us.

10.4 A SQL Map DAO implementation example

The DAO pattern is all about hiding the data access implementations behind interfaces, but you still have to build the underlying implementations. In this section, we build a SQL Map implementation of our DAO interface. You'll learn more about how to use the DAO pattern in chapter 11, where we will implement this same interface again using different data access technologies: one with Hibernate, and one with straight JDBC.

Before we build the implementations, let's build our DAO interface (listing 10.6).

Listing 10.6 The interface for our DAO

```
package org.apache.mapper2.examples.chapter10.dao;

import org.apache.mapper2.examples.bean.Account;
import org.apache.mapper2.examples.bean.IdDescription;

import java.util.List;
import java.util.Map;

public interface AccountDao {
  public void insert(Account account);
  public void update(Account account);
  public int delete(Account account);
```

```
  public int delete(Integer accountId);
  public List<Account> getAccountListByExample(
                              Account account);
  public List<Map<String, Object>>
              getMapListByExample(Account account);
  public List<IdDescription>
        getIdDescriptionListByExample(Account account);
  public Account getById(Integer accountId);
  public Account getById(Account account);
}
```

This is a reasonable interface for the account table—we have all the basic CRUD operations, as well as a few more convenience methods to make the API simpler to use. Because we are talking primarily about iBATIS, let's start our DAO implementations with a SQL Map–based version of the interface we defined earlier. First, we will look at the `dao.xml` that is used to describe the configuration for iBATIS.

10.4.1 Configuring the DAO in iBATIS

Listing 10.7 shows a DAO configuration that uses a single SQL Map–based DAO. We define a context named `sqlmap` that will be defined in a `SqlMapConfig.xml` file which is available on the classpath (for example, if this were used in a web application, that file would live in `/WEB-INF/classes/`).

Listing 10.7 Sample iBATIS dao.xml

```
<?xml version="1.0" encoding="UTF-8" ?>
<!DOCTYPE daoConfig
    PUBLIC
    "-//ibatis.apache.org//DTD DAO Configuration 2.0//EN"
    "http://ibatis.apache.org/dtd/dao-2.dtd">
<daoConfig>
  <context id="sqlmap">
    <transactionManager type="SQLMAP">
      <property name="SqlMapConfigResource"
                value="SqlMapConfig.xml"/>
    </transactionManager>
    <dao interface="com.mycompany.system.dao.AccountDao"
         implementation=
         "com.mycompany.system.dao.sqlmap.AccountDaoImpl"/>
  </context>
</daoConfig>
```

The dao.xml file is used by the DaoManagerBuilder to create a DaoManager instance. Let's look at that next.

10.4.2 Creating a DaoManager instance

In order to use the DAO manager we have defined, we need to use a DaoManager-Builder to create an instance of it. Listing 10.8 shows a fragment of code that you can use to create a DaoManager instance.

Listing 10.8 Sample code to build a DaoManager

```
private DaoManager getDaoManager() {
  DaoManager tempDaoManager = null;
  Reader reader;
  try {
    reader = Resources.getResourceAsReader("Dao.xml");
    tempDaoManager =
            DaoManagerBuilder.buildDaoManager(reader);
  } catch (Exception e) {
    e.printStackTrace();
    fail("Cannot load dao.xml file.");
  }
  return tempDaoManager;
}
```

Now that we have some code and configuration elements to look at, let's take a closer look to see what is going on with all this stuff.

This code looks for a resource named Dao.xml, which is located at the root of some location that the classloader will look in. For example, in Tomcat, it might be in your web application's WEB-INF/classes directory or in a JAR file in its WEB-INF/lib directory (as long as it was at the top level of the JAR file).

Once it has the configuration file, it passes the data to the DaoManagerBuilder, and requests that it build a DaoManager instance.

This code is from a JUnit test that we used to build and test the DAO implementations which we are looking at, so the exception handling is pretty weak. In a real production application, this is not how you would want to handle the exception.

10.4.3 Defining the transaction manager

Next, we define a transaction manager that will be based on the transaction manager we defined in our SQL Map configuration file, which we define using the SqlMapConfigResource property nested in the <transactionManager> element. All of the transaction management functionality that was available when using SQL Maps directly is still available in our DAO implementation. Listing 10.9 contains the `SQLMapConfig.xml` we used for this example.

Listing 10.9 Sample SQLMapConfig.xml file

```
<?xml version="1.0" encoding="UTF-8" ?>
<!DOCTYPE sqlMapConfig
    PUBLIC
    "-//ibatis.apache.org//DTD SQL Map Config 2.0//EN"
    "http://ibatis.apache.org/dtd/sql-map-config-2.dtd">
<sqlMapConfig>
  <properties resource="SqlMapConfig.properties" />
  <settings
    errorTracingEnabled="true"
    cacheModelsEnabled="true"
    enhancementEnabled="true"
    lazyLoadingEnabled="true"
    maxRequests="32"
    maxSessions="10"
    maxTransactions="5"
    useStatementNamespaces="true"
  />
  <transactionManager type="JDBC" >
    <dataSource type="SIMPLE">
      <property name="JDBC.Driver" value="${driver}"/>
      <property name="JDBC.ConnectionURL"
                            value="${connectionUrl}"/>
      <property name="JDBC.Username" value="${username}"/>
      <property name="JDBC.Password" value="${password}"/>
    </dataSource>
  </transactionManager>
  <sqlMap
    resource=
       "com/mycompany/system/dao/sqlmap/Account.xml" />
</sqlMapConfig>
```

All of the settings for this file are covered in detail in chapter 4, so we won't rehash them here.

10.4.4 Loading the maps

In addition to defining transaction management, all of the maps defined in our SQL Map configuration file are loaded as well. For this example, that is simply a sample `Account.xml` file that defines all of the mapped statements for our DAO class, as shown in listing 10.10.

Listing 10.10 A sample SQL Map file

```
<?xml version="1.0" encoding="UTF-8" ?>
<!DOCTYPE sqlMap
    PUBLIC "-//ibatis.apache.org//DTD SQL Map 2.0//EN"
    "http://ibatis.apache.org/dtd/sql-map-2.dtd">
<sqlMap namespace="Account">

  <typeAlias alias="Account"
             type="${BeanPackage}.Account" />
  <typeAlias alias="IdDescription"
             type="${BeanPackage}.IdDescription" />

  <insert id="insert" parameterClass="Account">
    <selectKey keyProperty="accountId" resultClass="int">
      SELECT nextVal('account_accountid_seq')
    </selectKey>
    INSERT INTO Account (
      accountId,
      username,
      password,
      firstName,
      lastName,
      address1,
      address2,
      city,
      state,
      postalCode,
      country
    ) VALUES(
      #accountId#,
      #username:varchar#,
      #password:varchar#,
      #firstName:varchar#,
      #lastName:varchar#,
      #address1:varchar#,
      #address2:varchar#,
      #city:varchar#,
      #state:varchar#,
      #postalCode:varchar#,
      #country:varchar#
    )
  </insert>

  <update id="update">
    update Account set
      username  = #username:varchar#,
      password = #password:varchar#,
      firstName = #firstName:varchar#,
      lastName = #lastName:varchar#,
      address1 = #address1:varchar#,
```

```
      address2 = #address2:varchar#,
      city = #city:varchar#,
      state = #state:varchar#,
      postalCode = #postalCode:varchar#,
      country = #country:varchar#
    where accountId = #accountId#
  </update>

  <delete id="delete">
    delete from Account
    where accountId = #accountId#
  </delete>

  <sql id="allFields">                         ❶ SQL fragment for the field list
    accountId as "accountId",
    username,
    password,
    firstName as "firstName",
    lastName as "lastName",
    address1,
    address2,
    city,
    state,
    postalCode as "postalCode",
    country
  </sql>

  <sql id="whereByExample">                    ❷ SQL fragment for the WHERE
    <dynamic prepend=" where ">
      <isNotEmpty property="city">
        city like #city#
      </isNotEmpty>
      <isNotNull property="accountId" prepend=" and ">
        accountId = #accountId#
      </isNotNull>
    </dynamic>
  </sql>

  <sql id="getByExample">                      ❸ Composite SQL fragment
    select
    <include refid="allFields" />
    from Account
    <include refid="whereByExample" />
  </sql>

  <select id="getAccountListByExample"
          resultClass="Account">               ❹ Mapped statement for a bean
    <include refid="getByExample" />
  </select>
```

```
<select id="getMapListByExample" resultClass="hashmap">
  <include refid="getByExample" />    <-- 5 Mapped statement for a map
</select>

<select id="getIdDescriptionListByExample"
        resultClass="IdDescription">
  select
    accountId as id,
    COALESCE(firstname, '(no first name)')
      || ' '
      || COALESCE(lastname, '(no last name)')
                                    as description
  from Account
  <include refid="whereByExample" />    <-- 6 Mapped statement for a name/value list
</select>

<select id="getById" resultClass="Account">
  select
    <include refid="allFields" />
  from Account
  where accountId = #value#
</select>

</sqlMap>
```

In this SQL map, we define a SQL fragment ❶ that list all of our fields. In this case, the driver we are using messes with the case of the columns, so we used explicit column aliases to make sure they were right for our implicit property mapping. Another SQL fragment ❷ is used to define a complex WHERE clause that we will use. A third SQL fragment ❸ is used to pull the other two into a single fragment that we then use in two select statements—one to get a List of beans ❹ and another to get a List of Maps ❺. In the getIdDescriptionListByExample mapped statement ❻, we use the complex WHERE clause again to get a List of a different type of beans.

10.4.5 *Coding the DAO implementation*

Finally, we get to the actual DAO implementation. As we mentioned before, to create a DAO, we provide both an interface and an implementation. In this case, the interface is defined as com.mycompany.system.dao.AccountDao, and the implementation is defined as com.mycompany.system.dao.sqlmap.AccountDaoImpl.

We saw the interface in section 10.3, so we will not repeat it here, but we will take a look at the DAO implementation class (see listing 10.11).

Listing 10.11 Our Account DAO implementation

```
package org.apache.mapper2.examples.chapter10.dao.sqlmap;

import com.ibatis.dao.client.DaoManager;
import com.ibatis.dao.client.template.SqlMapDaoTemplate;
import org.apache.mapper2.examples.bean.Account;
import org.apache.mapper2.examples.bean.IdDescription;
import
      org.apache.mapper2.examples.chapter10.dao.AccountDao;

import java.util.List;
import java.util.Map;

public class AccountDaoImpl extends SqlMapDaoTemplate
             implements AccountDao {
  public AccountDaoImpl(DaoManager daoManager) {
    super(daoManager);
  }

  public Integer insert(Account account) {
    return (Integer) insert("Account.insert", account);
  }

  public int update(Account account) {
    return update("Account.update", account);
  }

  public int delete(Account account) {
    return delete(account.getAccountId());
  }

  public int delete(Integer accountId) {
    return delete("Account.delete", accountId);
  }

  public List<Account> getAccountListByExample(
                             Account account) {
    return queryForList("Account.getAccountListByExample",
                        account);
  }

  public List<Map<String, Object>>
              getMapListByExample(Account account) {
    return queryForList("Account.getMapListByExample",
                        account);
  }

  public List<IdDescription>
             getIdDescriptionListByExample(
                                    Account account) {
```

```
    return
      queryForList("Account.getIdDescriptionListByExample",
                   account);
  }

  public Account getById(Integer accountId) {
    return (Account)queryForObject("Account.getById",
                                   accountId);
  }

  public Account getById(Account account) {
    return getById(account.getAccountId());
  }
}
```

On the surface, it does not look like there is really much there. In the class declaration, we see that the class implements the `AccountDao` interface and extends the `SqlMapDaoTemplate` class.

The `SqlMapDaoTemplate` class does much of the heavy lifting for us by providing all of the components of the SQL Map API in one tidy little package. In addition, it provides local methods that delegate calls to the `SqlMapExecutor` for us, so instead of getting an instance of a `SqlMapClient` or a `SqlMapExecutor`, we can just call their methods as though they were part of our DAO class.

While this may seem like a lot of work just to separate our DAO class from its implementation, subsequent DAO classes only require the creation of the interface, the creation of the implementation, the creation of the SQL Map, and finally a one-line addition to the `Dao.xml` file. In the next chapter, we implement the same DAO interface with Hibernate and JDBC directly. All three implementations use the same API (the `AccountDao` interface), in spite of using radically different underlying technologies for accessing the database.

10.5 Summary

In this chapter, we explained the rationale for using a data access layer in an application, and how to set up the iBATIS DAO framework. We also looked at some of the more advanced ways to configure the iBATIS DAO framework, and you saw how to create a SQL Map–based DAO.

In the next chapter, we will look at how to set up other DAO types, as well as a more advanced use of the iBATIS DAO framework by building a non–SQL DAO implementation. We will also explore other ways to implement a DAO layer in your application using the Spring framework, and look at some things you need to consider when creating your own DAO layer from scratch.

11 Doing more with DAO

This chapter covers

- More sample DAOs
- Using Spring instead of IBATIS
- Creating a DAO layer from scratch

As we saw in the previous chapter, the Data Access Object (DAO) pattern can be used to hide the unique implementation peculiarities of data-related APIs to provide a simple and common API for application developers. This pattern is very powerful, and is not unique to iBATIS, as other projects have created DAO implementations that you can use with iBATIS.

In this chapter, we look at a couple more SQL-based DAO implementations, as well as a couple of DAO implementations for other data sources (LDAP and web services). Then we explore the other options for DAO layers, including the Spring framework's excellent DAO implementation. We also consider the implications of creating your own custom DAO layer.

11.1 Non-SQLMap DAO implementations

In the last chapter, we defined an interface for a DAO, and then built a SQL Map–based implementation of it. In the next two sections, we implement that interface again with both Hibernate and JDBC to show you how the DAO pattern can make it easier to use different database access technologies with iBATIS in your application.

11.1.1 A Hibernate DAO implementation

The Hibernate DAO implementation is very different from the SQL Map version, but because of the DAO interface, it is used in exactly the same manner as far as the application code that uses it is concerned.

Defining the DAO context

Listing 11.1 shows the XML fragment that we need in the `Dao.xml` file to describe the DAO context that will use Hibernate.

Listing 11.1 XML fragment defining a DAO context using Hibernate

```
<context id="hibernate">
  <transactionManager type="HIBERNATE">
    <property name="hibernate.connection.driver_class"
              value="org.postgresql.Driver" />
    <property name="hibernate.connection.url"
              value="jdbc:postgresql:ibatisdemo" />
    <property name="hibernate.connection.username"
              value="ibatis" />
    <property name="hibernate.connection.password"
              value="ibatis" />
    <property name="hibernate.connection.pool_size"
              value="5" />
```

```
    <property name="hibernate.dialect"
          value=
          "net.sf.hibernate.dialect.PostgreSQLDialect" />
    <property name="map.Account"
          value=
          "${DaoHomeRes}/hibernate/Account.hbm.xml" />
  </transactionManager>
  <dao interface="${DaoHome}.AccountDao"
          implementation=
          "${DaoHome}.hibernate.AccountDaoImpl"/>
</context>
```

As was discussed in chapter 10 (section 10.2.2), the HIBERNATE transaction manager simply expects that the properties you would normally put in the `hibernate.properties` file are listed as properties to the `<transactionManager>` element.

Because we wanted to keep our source tree clean, we did not put the Hibernate mapping file for the `Account` bean (`Account.hbm.xml`) in the same package as our `Account` bean, but instead added it to the configuration by using a `map.` property that added it to our Hibernate configuration. Remember, it is all about keeping the implementation of the data access separate from the interface.

Mapping the Account table

The mapping file, shown in listing 11.2, is very simple, because we map directly from the properties files to the columns that have the same names, and there are no related entities.

Listing 11.2 Hibernate mapping file for our Account table

```
<?xml version="1.0"?>
<!DOCTYPE hibernate-mapping
    PUBLIC "-//Hibernate/Hibernate Mapping DTD//EN"
    "http://hibernate.sourceforge.net/hibernate-mapping-2.0.dtd">
<hibernate-mapping>
  <class
    name="org.apache.mapper2.examples.bean.Account"     (1) Mapping table to a class
    table="Account">
   <id name="accountId" type="int" column="accountid">  (2) Hooking up sequence for ID generation
      <generator class="sequence">
        <param
          name="sequence">account_accountid_seq</param>
      </generator>
    </id>
    <property name="username" />
    <property name="password" />
    <property name="firstName" />
```

```
    <property name="lastName" />
    <property name="address1" />
    <property name="address2" />
    <property name="city" />
    <property name="state" />
    <property name="postalCode" />
    <property name="country" />
  </class>
</hibernate-mapping>
```

If you have used Hibernate before, the file in listing 11.2 will be obvious to you—it is a fairly simple table mapping. If you have not used Hibernate before, it may not be so clear. What this configuration file does is map the properties from our `Account` bean to columns in our account table in the database ❶. It also tells Hibernate how we want to generate the `id` property in the bean for newly created database rows ❷.

The actual DAO implementation

The Java source code for the DAO implementation is more verbose, because we are mapping the `Account` table to several different classes of objects. This is a bit more difficult with Hibernate, as listing 11.3 shows.

Listing 11.3 Hibernate implementation of our Account DAO interface

```
public class AccountDaoImpl
    extends HibernateDaoTemplate
    implements AccountDao {

  private static final Log log =
    LogFactory.getLog(AccountDaoImpl.class);

  public AccountDaoImpl(DaoManager daoManager) {
    super(daoManager);
    if(log.isDebugEnabled()){
      log.debug("Creating instance of " + getClass());
    }
  }

  public Integer insert(Account account) {     ❶ Inserts new account
    try {
      getSession().save(account);
    } catch (HibernateException e) {
      log.error(e);
      throw new DaoException(e);
    }
    return account.getAccountId();
```

```
  }

  public int update(Account account) {    ◁── ❷ Updates account
    try {
      getSession().save(account);
    } catch (HibernateException e) {
      log.error(e);
      throw new DaoException(e);
    }
    return 1;
  }

  public int delete(Account account) {    ◁── ❸ Deletes account
    try {
      getSession().delete(account);
    } catch (HibernateException e) {
      log.error(e);
      throw new DaoException(e);
    }
    return 1;
  }

  public int delete(Integer accountId) {    ◁── ❹ Deletes account
    Account account = new Account();
    account.setAccountId(accountId);
    return delete(account);
  }

  public List<Account> getAccountListByExample(    ◁── ❺ Gets list of beans
    Account acct) {
    List accountList;
    Session session = this.getSession();

    Criteria criteria =
      session.createCriteria(Account.class);
    if (!nullOrEmpty(acct.getCity())) {
      criteria.add(
        Expression.like("city", acct.getCity())
      );
    }
    If (!nullOrEmpty(acct.getAccountId())) {
      criteria.add(
        Expression.eq("accountId", acct.getAccountId())
      );
    }

    try {
      accountList = criteria.list();
    } catch (HibernateException e) {
      log.error(
        "Exception getting list: " +
```

```
      e.getLocalizedMessage(), e);
    throw new DaoException(e);
  }
  return (List<Account>)accountList;
}

public List<Map<String, Object>> getMapListByExample(     <-- 6 Gets list of maps
  Account account
)
{
  List<Account> accountList =
    getAccountListByExample(account);
  List<Map<String, Object>> mapList =
    new ArrayList<Map<String, Object>>();
  for (Account acctToAdd : accountList) {
    Map<String, Object> map =
      new HashMap<String, Object>();
    map.put("accountId", acctToAdd.getAccountId());
    map.put("address1", acctToAdd.getAddress1());
    map.put("address2", acctToAdd.getAddress2());
    map.put("city", acctToAdd.getCity());
    map.put("country", acctToAdd.getCountry());
    map.put("firstName", acctToAdd.getFirstName());
    map.put("lastName", acctToAdd.getLastName());
    map.put("password", acctToAdd.getPassword());
    map.put("postalCode", acctToAdd.getPostalCode());
    map.put("state", acctToAdd.getState());
    map.put("username", acctToAdd.getUsername());
    mapList.add(map);
  }
  return mapList;
}

public List<IdDescription> getIdDescriptionListByExample(
  Account exAcct              <-- 7 Gets different list of beans
) {
  List<Account> acctList =
    getAccountListByExample(exAcct);
  List<IdDescription> idDescriptionList =
    new ArrayList<IdDescription>();
  for (Account acct : acctList) {
    idDescriptionList.add(
      new IdDescription(
        acct.getAccountId(),
        acct.getFirstName() + " " + acct.getLastName()
      )
    );
  }
  return idDescriptionList;
}
```

```
  public Account getById(Integer accountId) {   ⟵ ❽ Fetches single account
    Session session = this.getSession();
    try {
      return (Account) session.get(
        Account.class, accountId);
    } catch (HibernateException e) {
      log.error(e);
      throw new DaoException(e);
    }
  }

  public Account getById(Account account) {   ⟵ ❾ Fetches single account
    return getById(account.getAccountId());
  }
}
```

There is a good deal more here than in the SQL Map implementation. In the cases where we are dealing with `Account` objects (❶ through ❺ and ❽ through ❾), it is pretty simple, but things get more interesting when we start looking at returning a List of `Map` objects ❻ or `IdDescription` objects ❼. Because Hibernate is designed to map a database table to a Java class, it becomes more difficult to map the same table to different classes.

In the next example DAO implementation, we will get away from any mapping tool, and use straight JDBC to build our DAO.

11.1.2 A JDBC DAO implementation

The last DAO implementation that we will build under this interface will use straight JDBC. The greatest advantages that a simple JDBC-based implementation provides are minimal configuration and increased flexibility.

Listing 11.4 shows our `dao.xml` configuration file.

Listing 11.4 XML fragment defining a DAO context using JDBC

```
<context id="jdbc">
  <transactionManager type="JDBC">
    <property name="DataSource"
              value="SIMPLE"/>
    <property name="JDBC.Driver"
              value="org.postgresql.Driver" />
    <property name="JDBC.ConnectionURL"
              value="jdbc:postgresql:ibatisdemo" />
    <property name="JDBC.Username"
              value="ibatis" />
    <property name="JDBC.Password"
```

```
                value="ibatis" />
        <property name="JDBC.DefaultAutoCommit"
                value="true" />
    </transactionManager>
    <dao interface="${DaoHome}.AccountDao"
        implementation="${DaoHome}.jdbc.AccountDaoImpl"/>
</context>
```

That is the end of the configuration—everything else is in the code that follows, and it shows. The JDBC implementation of this DAO is over twice as many lines of code as the Hibernate version, and nearly seven times longer than the SQL Map version. If we include configuration files, our "lines of code" statistics look like table 11.1. So, by eliminating configuration, we still end up doubling our total coding effort. We are not saying that developing applications with JDBC is a bad idea; we are simply saying that the trade-off for flexibility and minimal configuration is that much more code needs to be written.

Table 11.1 Lines of code and configuration for DAO implementations

Version	Configuration	Code	Total
iBATIS	118+8=126	53	179
Hibernate	23+20=43	141	184
JDBC	18	370	388

Looking at the JDBC DAO implementation

Because of the size of the JDBC DAO implementation, we will not be looking at the entire class here, but we focus on some of the tricks used to build it.

The first thing that we do is build our DAO by extending the `JdbcDaoTemplate` class provided by iBATIS. By doing that, we get to be a little lazy, because it manages the connection for us—which means we do not have to close it in our code.

While that may seem like a trivial matter, failing to manage connections correctly in a large system will cripple it in a matter of hours (if not minutes). That brings us to our next code-saving tip, which is creating methods to help manage the other resources we need to use:

```
private boolean closeStatement(Statement statement) {
  boolean returnValue = true;
  if(null != statement){
    try {
      statement.close();
```

```
      } catch (SQLException e) {
        log.error("Exception closing statement", e);
        returnValue = false;
      }
    }
    return returnValue;
  }
```

Because closing a `Statement` can throw a `SQLException`, this method closes it and wraps the `SQLException` as a `DaoException`. So instead of the code above, we simply call `closeStatement()` and it logs the original exception and throws the `DaoException`. A similar method is used to close `ResultSet` objects for the same reasons.

The next shortcuts we build are ways to extract our data structures from a `ResultSet` object:

```
private Account extractAccount(ResultSet rs
) throws SQLException {
  Account accountToAdd = new Account();
  accountToAdd.setAccountId(rs.getInt("accountId"));
  accountToAdd.setAddress1(rs.getString("address1"));
  accountToAdd.setAddress2(rs.getString("address2"));
  accountToAdd.setCity(rs.getString("city"));
  accountToAdd.setCountry(rs.getString("country"));
  accountToAdd.setFirstName(rs.getString("firstname"));
  accountToAdd.setLastName(rs.getString("lastname"));
  accountToAdd.setPassword(rs.getString("password"));
  accountToAdd.setPostalCode(rs.getString("postalcode"));
  accountToAdd.setState(rs.getString("state"));
  accountToAdd.setUsername(rs.getString("username"));
  return accountToAdd;
}

private Map<String, Object> accountAsMap(ResultSet rs
) throws SQLException {
  Map<String, Object> acct =
    new HashMap<String, Object>();
  acct.put("accountId", rs.getInt("accountId"));
  acct.put("address1", rs.getString("address1"));
  acct.put("address2", rs.getString("address2"));
  acct.put("city", rs.getString("city"));
  acct.put("country", rs.getString("country"));
  acct.put("firstName", rs.getString("firstname"));
  acct.put("lastName", rs.getString("lastname"));
  acct.put("password", rs.getString("password"));
  acct.put("postalCode", rs.getString("postalcode"));
  acct.put("state", rs.getString("state"));
  acct.put("username", rs.getString("username"));
  return acct;
}
```

```
private IdDescription accountAsIdDesc(ResultSet rs
) throws SQLException {
  return new IdDescription(
      new Integer(rs.getInt("id")),
      rs.getString("description"));
}
```

Because there are several places where we need to perform these tasks, building methods to simplify the mapping saves us some errors and time when creating our real methods later.

The next method creates our `PreparedStatement` for the "query-by-example" methods in the DAO interface. This is where we have the most complexity, and it's where the SQL Map implementation starts to look much more attractive. While the other helper methods were simple but tedious, this one is tedious, error prone, and difficult to test—not a good combination to have to write:

```
private PreparedStatement prepareQBEStatement(
    Account account,
    Connection connection,
    PreparedStatement ps,
    String baseSql
) throws SQLException {
  StringBuffer sqlBase = new StringBuffer(baseSql);
  StringBuffer sqlWhere = new StringBuffer("");
  List<Object> params = new ArrayList<Object>();

  String city = account.getCity();
  if (!nullOrEmpty(city)) {
    sqlWhere.append(" city like ?");
    params.add(account.getCity());
  }

  Integer accountId = account.getAccountId();
  if (!nullOrZero(accountId)) {
    if sqlWhere.length() > 0) {
      sqlWhere.append(" and");
    }
    sqlWhere.append(" accountId = ?");
    params.add(account.getAccountId());
  }

  if (sqlWhere.length() > 0) {
    sqlWhere.insert(0, " where");
    sqlBase.append(sqlWhere);
  }

  ps = connection.prepareStatement(sqlBase.toString());
  for (int i = 0; i < params.size(); i++) {
```

```
      ps.setObject(i+1, params.get(i));
    }
    return ps;
  }
```

Now that we have all of the helper methods in place, we can start to build the public interface. The insert method is the most involved, because it requires both a query and an insert:

```
public Integer insert(Account account) {
  Connection connection = this.getConnection();
  Statement statement = null;
  PreparedStatement ps = null;
  ResultSet rs = null;
  Integer key = null;
  if (null != connection) {
    try{
      statement = connection.createStatement();
      rs = statement.executeQuery(sqlGetSequenceId);
      if (rs.next()) {
        key = new Integer(rs.getInt(1));
        account.setAccountId(key);
        if (log.isDebugEnabled()) {
          log.debug("Key for inserted record is " + key);
        }
      }
      ps = connection.prepareStatement(sqlInsert);
      int i = 1;
      ps.setObject(i++, account.getAccountId());
      ps.setObject(i++, account.getUsername());
      ps.setObject(i++, account.getPassword());
      ps.setObject(i++, account.getFirstName());
      ps.setObject(i++, account.getLastName());
      ps.setObject(i++, account.getAddress1());
      ps.setObject(i++, account.getAddress2());
      ps.setObject(i++, account.getCity());
      ps.setObject(i++, account.getState());
      ps.setObject(i++, account.getPostalCode());
      ps.setObject(i++, account.getCountry());
      ps.executeUpdate();
    } catch (SQLException e) {
      log.error("Error inserting data", e);
      throw new DaoException(e);
    } finally {
      closeStatement(ps);
      closeResources(statement, rs);
    }
  }
  return key;
}
```

Here, we get the new `id` for the record to be inserted, set it on the bean that was passed in, and then insert that bean into the database. The code is very simple to follow, just a bit verbose when compared to either the iBATIS or Hibernate versions.

The other methods are equally straightforward, so we will not take up any more space on them.

11.2 Using the DAO pattern with other data sources

The DAO pattern is very similar to the Gateway pattern, which makes it suitable for many other data sources such as LDAP or web services.

If you are not familiar with the Gateway pattern, it is also sometimes referred to as a Wrapper, because that is what it does. It "wraps" an API to make it look like a simple object, as shown in figure 11.1, where the `WebServiceGateway` interface hides the underlying implementation.

If you are thinking that sounds familiar, it should, because that is also the idea behind the DAO pattern, which is just a specialized gateway that also helps you manage transactions, pooling, and other database-specific issues.

11.2.1 Example: using a DAO with LDAP

LDAP is an awesome tool for storing hierarchical data, and is often used by network administrators for tracking users, group memberships, and other similar data. For example, both Novell Directory Services (NDS) and Microsoft's ActiveDirectory are based on LDAP and expose LDAP APIs.

Using the DAO pattern to access a directory using LDAP is a great way to keep the nuances of JNDI programming out of your application code. By creating a

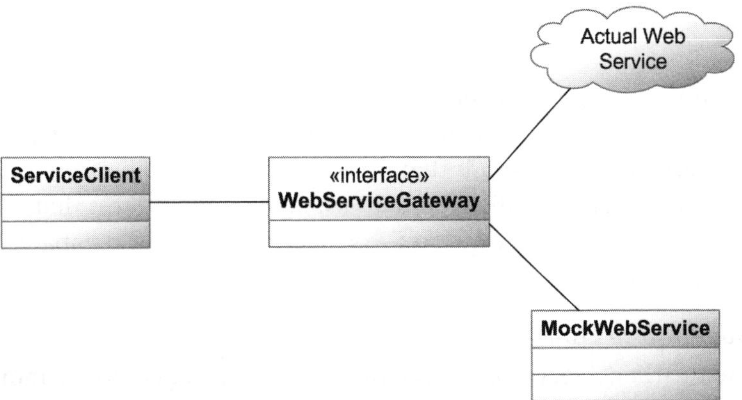

Figure 11.1 The DAO pattern is similar to the Gateway pattern.

small special-purpose set of classes, you can build lightweight, testable JNDI components, and then hook them into your DAO implementation without exposing the data source.

Understanding LDAP terminology

Before launching into a complete example of building an LDAP directory–based DAO implementation, let's review some terminology. LDAP is intentionally vague, because it is intended to be a very flexible general-purpose protocol for accessing a repository of hierarchical data.

The basic building block of an LDAP directory is called an *entry*, which can contain data (called *attributes*), other entries, or both. Every entry has exactly one parent and is uniquely identified by a Distinguished Name (DN), which is unique across the entire directory. The data elements in that entry are defined by one or more object classes that the entry represents.

The data stored in LDAP directory entries are made up of attributes, which are name/value pairs that are virtually identical to Java's `Map` interface. The object class (or classes) of the entry will determine which optional attributes the entry can have, as well as which required attributes it must have.

For example, if we want to create a contact manager that manages normal LDAP entities with a Java application, we might have a bean to represent an entry, and that bean would look like this:

```
public class Contact {
  private String userId;
  private String mail;
  private String description;
  private String firstName;
  private String lastName;
  // Getters and Setters to make properties...
}
```

One approach to storing this object in an LDAP directory would be to simply serialize the Java object into the directory. For our example, we are not going to do that for two reasons. One reason is that we want to be able to use our directory to interoperate with other, potentially non-Java systems. The other is that we want to take advantage of LDAP-based queries—we want to use the database as it was intended to be used.

Mapping from Java to LDAP

As mentioned earlier, every LDAP directory entry represents one or more object classes. These object classes define groups of attributes. Because of the similarity between these attributes and Java's `Map` interface, it would be trivial to create a Map-based version of the DAO that simply used a Map to hide the JNDI attributes structure. In this section however, we will create a DAO that will use the bean from the previous section by mapping it to an LDAP `inetOrgPerson` entry using the mapping in table 11.2.

Table 11.1 JavaBean to LDAP attribute mapping

Bean property	LDAP attribute
userId	uid
mail	mail
description	description
lastName	sn
firstName	givenName

This mapping will be accomplished in our DAO implementation by using methods to create a bean from an `Attributes` object, or an `Attributes` object from a bean. While it would be possible to create a reflection-based mapping mechanism for this, we are going to make our DAO implementation very simple and just hardcode the mapping. Listing 11.5 contains the three methods from our DAO implementation that are responsible for that mapping.

Listing 11.5 Support methods for our LDAP DAO implementation

```
private Attributes getAttributes(Contact contact){
    Attributes returnValue = new BasicAttributes();
    returnValue.put("mail", contact.getMail());
    returnValue.put("uid", contact.getUserId());
    returnValue.put("objectClass", "inetOrgPerson");
    returnValue.put(
      "description", contact.getDescription());
    returnValue.put("sn", contact.getLastName());
    returnValue.put("cn", contact.getUserId());
    returnValue.put("givenName", contact.getFirstName());
    return returnValue;
  }

  private Contact getContact(Attributes attributes) {
    Contact contact = new Contact();
    contact.setDescription(
      getAttributeValue(attributes, "description"));
    contact.setLastName(
      getAttributeValue(attributes, "sn"));
```

```
      contact.setFirstName(
        getAttributeValue(attributes, "givenName"));
      contact.setMail(getAttributeValue(attributes, "mail"));
      contact.setUserId(
        getAttributeValue(attributes, "uid"));
      return contact;
    }

    private String getAttributeValue(
      Attributes attributes, String attrID
    ) {
      Attribute attribute = attributes.get(attrID);
      try {
        return (null==attribute?"":(String)attribute.get());
      } catch (NamingException e) {
        throw new DaoException(e);
      }
    }
```

The `Attributes` interface is part of the JNDI package that comes with Sun's JDK, and is implemented by the `BasicAttributes` class, which is also part of that package. The `Contact` class is our bean that we want to map to our LDAP directory. Finally, the `getAttributeValue()` method is a helper method that simplifies the mapping process by handling null values and turning JNDI-specific exceptions into `DaoExceptions`.

Just as with other DAO implementations, we need to make some decisions about where and how we will get to our database. If you are working with a J2EE container that can provide you with a JNDI context, you might be tempted to use it. If it meets your needs, there is no reason not to. However, there are some trade-offs when doing this. Although this approach will simplify the code, it will make testing more difficult. Depending on your requirements, this may be an acceptable sacrifice.

In this example, we wanted to make things as testable as possible, so we used constructor-based injection to configure the DAO class at runtime. Because the iBATIS DAO does not allow this, we also created a default constructor that uses the two values we wanted as the defaults. In section 11.3, we look at using the Spring framework for our DAO layer, which allows us to do this via configuration files, but for now, let's use the default constructor method.

The second constructor takes two parameters for the two settings I hardcoded into the default constructor. One of those was the determination of the LDAP DN attribute for our contact bean. This attribute is analogous to the primary key of a database table, but is unique through the entire directory, not just in a single segment of it like the primary key for a row in a table. The following method in the DAO implementation creates a unique DN for our contact bean:

```
private String getDn(String userId){
  return MessageFormat.format(this.dnTemplate, userId);
}
```

The second setting we need is for getting the initial directory context. The default constructor for our DAO will use the hardcoded properties to connect to our LDAP directory, but again, the second constructor will allow us to inject custom properties if needed for other purposes. Those properties are used to get the initial directory context:

```
private DirContext getInitialContext() {
  DirContext ctx = null;
  try {
    ctx = new InitialDirContext(env);
  } catch (NamingException e) {
    log.error("Exception getting initial context", e);
    throw new DaoException(e);
  }
  return ctx;
}
```

Now that we have all of the required infrastructure code in place to deal with mapping our bean and connecting to our LDAP directory, we can start to build our DAO implementation.

The first method we will look at is the simplest—we will look up a contact by `userId`. Here is the code to implement that method:

```
public Contact getById(String id) {
  DirContext ctx = getInitialContext();
  Attributes attributes;
  try {
    attributes = ctx.getAttributes(getDn(id));
  } catch (NamingException e) {
    throw new DaoException(e);
  }
  return getContact(attributes);
}
```

Here, we take the directory context, and use it to get the attributes of our contact, based on the DN of the passed-in user's `id` value. Once we have the attributes, we convert them into a contact bean and return it. If an LDAP-specific `NamingException` is thrown, it is re-thrown as `DaoException` instead to make sure that the method signature does not indicate the data source.

The insert operation is called *binding* in LDAP-speak. Our application will never know this, because we are going to wrap that in the DAO, and call it `insert` instead.

```
public Contact insert(Contact contact) {
  try {
    DirContext ctx = getInitialContext();
    ctx.bind(getDn(
      contact.getUserId()),
      null,
      getAttributes(contact));
  } catch (Exception e) {
    log.error("Error adding contact", e);
    throw new DaoException(e);
  }
  return contact;
}
```

Similarly, the update and delete methods use LDAP-specific classes to accomplish their work and re-throw exceptions using the same technique. In JNDI terminology, updating is called *rebinding*, and deleting is called *unbinding*. However, because of our use of the DAO pattern, those terms will never appear in our application—it is completely unaware of the LDAP dependency that we have created in our DAO implementation.

LDAP is not the only strange data source we'll ever have to deal with, and while there is no way to look at them all in one chapter (or even one book!), we will take a look at another that you will most likely have to deal with in the near future: the web service.

11.2.2 Example: using a DAO with a web service

Using a DAO pattern for web services is a great idea. The reason for using a web service with some sort of abstraction layer is to simplify testing the components that use it. For example, if you have a credit card processor service that you want to use or some other distant service that takes time to connect to, time to execute, and time to process results, it can seriously hinder testing if you have to wait for it (possibly several times). In addition, if the service requires a payment per call, or is a public one (like Amazon, Google, or eBay) where the data that is returned may change unexpectedly, it could be prohibitive to use for any purpose other than integration or user acceptance testing because of the cost or variability of the returned data. Adding to those issues is the need to prepare data that may change over time for the tests—instead, you want to have reasonably static (or easily predictable) data requirements around your unit tests.

So let's say you were making a system and wanted to give your users the ability to do Google searches from within your application. The Google API for calling their web service is simple enough to use, but because other search engines are providing similar APIs now, we are going to create a more generic search API that will be used to wrap the Google implementation, and call that API from our application.

First we need to come up with a search interface and structure for returning search results, so let's start with a simple bean and an interface:

```
public class SearchResult {
  private String url;
  private String summary;
  private String title;
  // getters and setters omitted...
}

public interface WebSearchDao {
  List<SearchResult> getSearchResults(String text);
}
```

Our bean has three properties, and our interface has one method that returns a typed list. Here is the implementation of that search API, using the Google API:

```
public class GoogleDaoImpl implements WebSearchDao {
  private String googleKey;

  public GoogleDaoImpl(){
    this("insert-your-key-value-here");
  }

  public GoogleDaoImpl(String key){
    this.googleKey = key;
  }

  public List<SearchResult> getSearchResults(String text){
    List<SearchResult> returnValue = new
                              ArrayList<SearchResult>();
    GoogleSearch s = new GoogleSearch();
    s.setKey(googleKey);
    s.setQueryString(text);
    try {
      GoogleSearchResult gsr = s.doSearch();
      for (int i = 0; i < gsr.getResultElements().length;
           i++){
        GoogleSearchResultElement sre =
                              gsr.getResultElements()[i];
        SearchResult sr = new SearchResult();
        sr.setSummary(sre.getSummary());
        sr.setTitle(sre.getTitle());
        sr.setUrl(sre.getURL());
```

```
            returnValue.add(sr);
          }
          return returnValue;
        } catch (GoogleSearchFault googleSearchFault) {
          throw new DaoException(googleSearchFault);
        }
      }
    }
```

The Google API is very similar to the DAO interface, which is no surprise, but it requires a key to work. This is not a problem in our example, because we just hardcoded the key into our implementation. In a production application, you would want something better than that, perhaps providing a way for you to use a user-specific key instead of a shared key.

This shows another limitation of the iBATIS DAO layer. Because it cannot provide multiple instances of a DAO class and can only use the default constructor, making this DAO work the way we want it to will require that we jump through some extra hoops.

In the next section, we look at how to use the Spring framework to make a more capable DAO layer that allows us to perform some pretty advanced tricks with configuration.

11.3 Using the Spring DAO

There are many different ways that you could use the Spring framework in the data access layer of your application that do not have anything to do with iBATIS. In this section, you'll learn how to use Spring's support for iBATIS to build a data access layer.

11.3.1 Writing the code

The Spring framework supports iBATIS using a template pattern for the data access objects, meaning that you start with an existing Spring class (`SqlMapClientTemplate`) and extend it for your DAO. Using this technique, our `AccountDao` implementation would look like listing 11.6 using Spring.

Listing 11.6 Spring version of our SQL Maps Account DAO

```
public class AccountDaoImplSpring
    extends SqlMapClientTemplate
    implements AccountDao
{
  public Integer insert(Account account) {
    return (Integer) insert("Account.insert", account);
```

```
  }

  public int update(Account account) {
    return update("Account.update", account);
  }

  public int delete(Account account) {
    return delete(account.getAccountId());
  }

  public int delete(Integer accountId) {
    return delete("Account.delete", accountId);
  }

  public List<Account> getAccountListByExample(
                                 Account account) {
    return queryForList("Account.getAccountListByExample",
                        account);
  }

  public List<Map<String, Object>>
                   getMapListByExample(Account account) {
    return queryForList("Account.getMapListByExample",
                        account);
  }

  public List<IdDescription>
         getIdDescriptionListByExample(Account account) {
    return
      queryForList("Account.getIdDescriptionListByExample",
                   account);
  }

  public Account getById(Integer accountId) {
    return (Account) queryForObject("Account.getById",
                                    accountId);
  }

  public Account getById(Account account) {
    return (Account) queryForList("Account.getById",
                                  account);
  }
}
```

The astute reader may notice that this is almost exactly the same as the code we saw in listing 10.11; the only difference is the class that we extend. Everything else in this class is identical. Right now, you might be asking yourself when you would want to use one class or the other. Let's take a look at that next.

11.3.2 Why use Spring instead of iBATIS?

This is a fair question to ask—this is a book about iBATIS, so why are we talking about using something else for the DAO layer? Both Spring and iBATIS have their advantages and disadvantages, and the decision requires that you have an understanding of those pros and cons as well as the needs of your application.

The advantage of the iBATIS DAO layer is that it is a quick and easy solution. If you have the iBATIS SQL Map download, you have the iBATIS DAO framework, too. It is a much simpler framework than Spring if all you need is transaction and connection management. In that case, the iBATIS DAO layer is probably adequate for your application.

The simplicity of the iBATIS DAO is also its biggest disadvantage: once you begin using the DAO pattern, and start taking advantage of the testability that decoupling provides, you will want to use the same approach in different areas of your application.

For example, in a Struts application we will use the same approach with our `Action` class and our business logic class that we use between our business logic class and our DAO class. Instead of the code knowing the implementations it needs, it only knows the interfaces that it needs, and the implementations are plugged in through configuration. This keeps the `Action` classes simple, and makes every layer easier to test.

In addition to being able to manage that separation, Spring can be used to manage your connections and transactions, just like the iBATIS DAO layer does. The big advantage of Spring is that it is not only for DAO classes but for all segments of your application.

11.4 Creating your own DAO layer

Sometimes, neither the iBATIS DAO support nor the Spring DAO support is exactly what you need. In those cases, you need to "roll your own" DAO layer.

Creating a DAO layer from scratch may sound like a daunting task. However, you could be surprised, because it is actually a fairly straightforward pattern to implement. There are essentially three tiers to an effective DAO layer:

1. Separate interface from implementation.
2. Decouple implementation with an externally configured factory.
3. Provide transaction and connection management.

For our purposes, we will look at what is required to accomplish the first two tiers, but for transaction and connection management, you will need to refer to chapter 7, and go from there.

11.4.1 Separating interface from implementation

The reason you want to separate your DAO into an interface and an implementation is twofold. First, you want to be able to replace the implementation if you have to support a different type of data access. Second, separation makes testing much simpler and faster because you can plug in a mock DAO instead of working with the database.

If you use an IDE, you may think that this is going to be the easiest part of the process. With most development environments, you have a refactoring tool to extract an interface from the class. However, that is only a small part of the process.

If you are just getting started with the DAO pattern, it is likely that your interface is exposing classes specific to JDBC, iBATIS, or some other tool for dealing with your database. That is the part of the interface that is more difficult to manage. This creates a problem because it binds more of your application to the data access implementation than just the DAO. Although it is not a huge difficulty, it is not a trivial matter either.

Changing code that uses a result set to use a collection (such as a List of beans) is straightforward, but as with any change, it will require testing, and depending on where the code is located in your application, the process can be challenging. For example, if you have a web application that uses a "Fast Lane Reader" pattern to provide lightweight reporting over large data sets, your JDBC code may interact directly with the view layer. This can be very difficult to test, because anything requiring human interaction takes more time. In addition, it may be difficult to rewrite in a way that performs as well as the original. One solution is to write the code using callbacks to speed up the data access (so, in this example, you may want to consider a `RowHandler` that responds to view requests for data).

Changing applications that directly access the SQL Map API to access a more encapsulated API is a reasonably trivial matter. For example, if you are developing a class that calls `queryForList()` on a `SqlMapClient` object, you simply need to refactor that call into your DAO class, and then return the List object from it so that your data consumer only talks to your DAO.

11.4.2 Decoupling and creating a factory

So, now that we have separated the interface and implementation, we do not want to introduce both of those into our classes that use the DAO, because instead of removing the dependency on the implementation, we have just added a dependency on the interface.

What we mean is that if you have an interface for your DAO and an implementation for it, how do you use the implementation? If you are not using a factory, you are likely doing it this way:

```
AccountDao accountDao = new AccountDaoImpl();
```

See the problem? While we have separated our DAO and its implementation, we are still referring to each of them in a single place. This is not adding much value, unless you pass the DAO all over your application. A better pattern would be to use something like this:

```
AccountDao accountDao =
          (AccountDao)DaoFactory.get(AccountDao.class);
```

In that example, what is the implementation? We neither know nor care, because the `DaoFactory` handles it for us. All we care about is that this `DaoFactory` item returns an object that implements the `AccountDao` interface. We do not care if it uses LDAP, JDBC, or smoke and mirrors to make it happen, as long as it does.

Creating an abstract factory is fun and easy! OK, maybe not fun, but still easy. In this section, we build a simple one, and talk about why you would want to use one for your DAO classes.

So, what does this `DaoFactory` look like under the hood? Surprisingly, it is just a few dozen lines of code, as listing 11.7 shows.

Listing 11.7 A super simple DAO factory

```
public class DaoFactory {
  private static DaoFactory instance = new DaoFactory();
  private final String defaultConfigLocation =
                            "DaoFactory.properties";
  private Properties daoMap;
  private Properties instanceMap;

  private String configLocation = System.getProperty(
      "dao.factory.config",
      defaultConfigLocation
  );

  private DaoFactory(){                ❶ Declares a Private constructor—it's a singleton
    daoMap = new Properties();
    instanceMap = new Properties();
    try {
      daoMap.load(getInputStream(configLocation));
```

```
    } catch (IOException e) {
      throw new RuntimeException(e);
    }
  }

  private InputStream getInputStream(String configLocation)
  {
    return Thread
        .currentThread()
        .getContextClassLoader()
        .getResourceAsStream(configLocation);
  }

  public static DaoFactory getInstance() {     ❷ Declares a simple factory method
    return instance;
  }

  public Object getDao(Class daoInterface){    ❸ Gets a DAO
    if (instanceMap.containsKey(daoInterface)) {
      return instanceMap.get(daoInterface);
    }
    return createDao(daoInterface);
  }

  private synchronized Object createDao(     ❹ Makes sure we only have one DAO per type
    Class daoInterface
  ) {
    Class implementationClass;
    try {
      implementationClass = Class.forName((String)
                              daoMap.get(daoInterface));
      Object implementation =
                          implementationClass.newInstance();
      instanceMap.put(implementationClass, implementation);
    } catch (Exception e) {
      throw new RuntimeException(e);
    }
    return instanceMap.get(daoInterface);
  }
}
```

Clearly, this is not the greatest factory ever written, but it is pretty darn small and efficient. Its public interface consists of only two methods: `getInstance()` and `getDao()`. The private constructor ❶ loads the configuration file, which in this case is just a properties file with name/value pairs for the interface and implementation names. This class is a self-contained singleton, so the `getInstance()` method ❷ just returns the one instance of the class. The `getDao()` method ❸ returns an implementation of an interface. Creation of the DAOs comes later in the `createDao()` method ❹ when they are actually requested.

11.5 Summary

In this chapter, we wrapped up our exploration of the Data Access Object (DAO) pattern, and you learned how to use it with data access tools other than iBATIS `SqlMaps`. You also saw how the DAO pattern could be used as a type of gateway pattern, and how to adapt it to wrap not just typical data sources but also more unusual sources of data, such as an LDAP directory or web service.

We explored some of the limitations of the iBATIS DAO framework in terms of the creation of the DAOs that it provides. You saw how by using the Spring framework it is possible to do almost anything to create and configure your DAO classes.

We also looked briefly at what would be required to build a custom DAO layer, and even put together a very simple starter DAO factory.

At this point, you have seen all that comes with iBATIS. In the next chapter, you will learn how you can extend the framework to do things beyond what is possible through configuration only!

12 Extending iBATIS

This chapter covers

- Custom type handlers
- Cache controllers
- Custom data sources

No framework meets everyone's needs out of the box, which is why it is important that the framework provide extension points where the users can modify the behavior of the framework—in other words, it is essential that the framework be *pluggable.*

Although iBATIS is open source software, and end users could easily modify the code to do whatever they need, it is important to provide a consistent and supportable means of extending the framework. Otherwise, every time a new version of iBATIS was released, the users who had modified their copies of iBATIS would have to merge their changes and recompile the entire framework.

iBATIS provides a number of levels of customization. First, as a general best practice, iBATIS uses interfaces between design layers of the framework. This means that even if there isn't a standard extension supported by the framework, the most an end user would need to do is implement the interface and replace the standard implementation with their own. We'll see an example of this later in this chapter when we discuss customizing the `SqlMapClient` interface.

For areas that are more likely to require customization on a per-application, or per-platform, basis, iBATIS provides a standard pluggable component architecture for features such as type handlers, transaction managers, data sources, and cache controllers.

The next sections examine each of these in detail. Let's first discuss general concepts in plug-in architecture.

12.1 Understanding pluggable component design

A pluggable component design is generally made up of three parts:

- Interface
- Implementation
- Factory

The interface describes the intended functionality and is a contract that all implementations must follow. The interface describes what the feature does.

The implementation is the specific behavior that describes how the feature works. It may have dependencies on third-party frameworks or even large infrastructure, such as an advanced caching system or application server.

The factory is responsible for binding the implementation to the interface based on some configuration. The whole idea is to ensure that the application is not dependent on anything other than the single consistent interface to the framework. The framework would be failing at its job if the application were to still require dependencies on the third-party implementation details.

Figure 12.1 depicts this. The arrows can be read as "depends on," or at least "knows about."

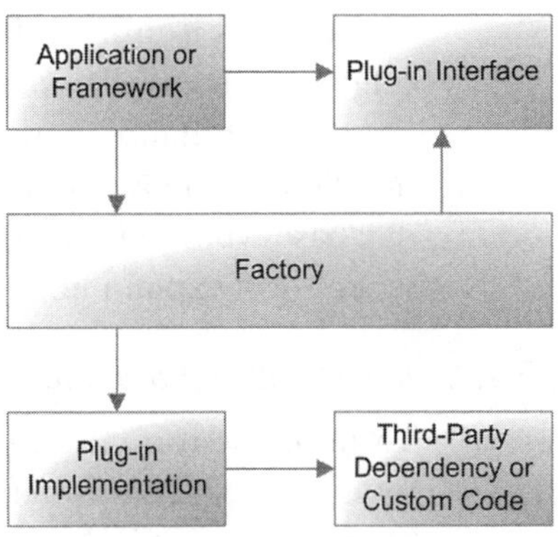

Figure 12.1 Example of a pluggable framework design

As stated earlier, iBATIS supports pluggable component design for a number of its features. But what exactly does that mean? Generally a *plug-in* is an extension to an application or framework that adds new functionality that wasn't there before, or that replaces existing functionality with something different. For the most part, iBATIS extension involves replacing existing functionality.

iBATIS is designed in layers, and it is within each layer that iBATIS may provide a plug-point into which you can inject your own functionality. Table 12.1 describes the iBATIS layers, and summarizes the extensibility at a high level.

Table 12.1 Layered extension summary

Extendible feature	Description
`TypeHandlerCallback`	Implement your own type handling logic to deal with nonstandard databases, drivers, and/or data types.
`CacheController`	Implement your own `CacheController` for your own cache code or to provide support for a third-party caching solution.
`DataSourceFactory`	Supply any standard `JDBC DataSource` implementation.
`TransactionConfig`	Implement a custom transaction manager to work best with your environment.

The next sections describe each of these in more detail, beginning with the most common type of extension: `TypeHandlerCallback`.

12.2 Working with custom type handlers

As much as we'd all like relational database management systems to be standard, unfortunately they just aren't. They all tend to implement their own SQL extensions, as well as their own data types. Although more common data types like binary large objects (BLOBs) and character large objects (CLOBs) are supported by most relational databases, they are usually handled differently by each driver.

Therefore it is difficult for the iBATIS framework to support all databases using a single type handler implementation. To deal with these situations, iBATIS supports custom type handlers that allow you to customize the way that certain types are handled. Using a custom type handler, you can tell iBATIS how to map relational database types to Java types. You can even override the built-in type handlers. This section will explain how.

12.2.1 Implementing a custom type handler

To implement a custom `TypeHandler`, you only need to implement part of the functionality. That functionality is defined in a simple interface called `TypeHandlerCallback`. It is defined in listing 12.1.

Listing 12.1 TypeHandlerCallback

```
public interface TypeHandlerCallback {

  public void setParameter(
    ParameterSetter setter, Object parameter)
      throws SQLException;

  public Object getResult(ResultGetter getter)
      throws SQLException;

  public Object valueOf(String s);

}
```

Let's step through the implementation of a `TypeHandlerCallback`. For the purposes of this example, let's assume we have a database that uses the words "YES" and "NO" to represent boolean values (i.e., true and false, respectively). Table 12.2 shows this example.

Table 12.2 Using YES and NO to represent boolean values

UserID	Username	PasswordHashcode	Enabled
1	asmith	1190B32A35FACBEF	YES
2	brobertson	35FACBEFAF35FAC2	YES
3	cjohnson	AF35FAC21190B32A	NO

Imagine we're mapping this table to a class as the following:

```
public class User {
      private int id;
      private String username;
      private String passwordHashcode;
      private boolean enabled;
      // assume compliant JavaBeans properties
     // (getters/setters) below
}
```

Notice the mismatch between data types here. In the database, the Enabled column is a VARCHAR storing `YES` and `NO` values, whereas our Java class is a boolean type. We can't directly set a value of `YES` or `NO` to a boolean type. Therefore, we need to translate it. It's certainly possible that a JDBC driver could do this for us, but let's assume that is not the case.

The purpose of a `TypeHandlerCallback` is to deal with these situations. So let's write the implementation that would do just that.

12.2.2 Creating a TypeHandlerCallback

As we've seen, the `TypeHandlerCallback` interface is simple. All we need to do is create a class that implements the interface. We'll give the new class a nice, descriptive name, and also include a couple of private constants:

```
public class YesNoTypeHandlerCallback
                implements TypeHandlerCallback {

    private static final String YES = "YES";
    private static final String NO = "NO";

    public void setParameter(
      ParameterSetter setter, Object parameter)
        throws SQLException {
    }

    public Object getResult(ResultGetter getter)
        throws SQLException {
    }

    public Object valueOf(String s) {
    }
}
```

This is just a skeletal implementation of a type handler; in the following sections we'll flesh it out.

Setting parameters

When we send a value to the database, it has to be `YES` or `NO`. In this case, null is not valid. From the Java class, we're going to get a strongly typed boolean value of `true` or `false`. So we need to translate `true` into a `YES` value and `false` into a `NO` value. To do that, we could use a simple method like this:

```
private String booleanToYesNo(Boolean b) {
  if (b == null) {
    throw new IllegalArgumentException (
      "Could not convert null to a boolean value. " +
      "Valid arguments are 'true' and 'false'.");
  } else if (b.booleanValue()) {
    return YES;
  } else {
    return NO;
  }
}
```

We can now use this method to translate parameter values before we set them. Setting a parameter is easy. The `setParameter()` method of the `TypeHandlerCallback` interface takes two parameters. The first, `ParameterSetter`, gives you access to a number of setter methods, each of which works for a different data type. For example, there is a `setString()` method, a `setInt()` method, and a `setDate()` method. There are too many to list here completely, but rest assured that almost any Java data type you're familiar with will probably have an associated set method. In our case, the data type in the database table is a VARCHAR, so we'll use the `setString()` method of the `ParameterSetter`.

The second parameter is the value we're passing to the database that needs to be translated. In our case, we will be receiving the boolean value from the `enabled` property from our `User` class. Here's the code for our `setParameter()` method that uses our convenient `booleanToYesNo()` method that we wrote earlier:

```
public void setParameter(
  ParameterSetter setter, Object parameter
) throws SQLException {
    setter.setString(booleanToYesNo((Boolean) parameter));
}
```

The body of the method simply uses the `ParameterSetter` to set the string value translated by our conversion method. We have to cast the incoming parameter to `Boolean`, as the `TypeHandlerCallback` is an interface that can support any type.

That was simple, was it not? As you'll see in the next section, attaining results is just as easy.

Getting results

When we receive the YES or NO value from the database, we need to translate it into a boolean value of true or false. This is the exact opposite of what we just did to set parameters. So why don't we start the same way? Let's build a method to translate the string type to the boolean type, like this:

```
private Boolean yesNoToBoolean(String s) {
  if (YES.equalsIgnoreCase(s)) {
    return Boolean.TRUE;
  } else if (NO.equalsIgnoreCase(s)) {
    return Boolean.FALSE;
  } else {
    throw new IllegalArgumentException (
        "Could not convert " + s +
        " to a boolean value. " +
        "Valid arguments are 'YES' and 'NO'.");
  }
}
```

We can now use this method to translate the String results from the database into the boolean values we need. We can do this by calling our new translation method from the getResult() method of the TypeHandlerCallback. The getResult() method has only one parameter: ResultGetter. ResultGetter contains methods for retrieving values of different types. In our case, we need to get a String value. Here's the code for the getResult() implementation:

```
public Object getResult(ResultGetter getter)
    throws SQLException {
  return yesNoToBoolean(getter.getString());
}
```

In this case we're calling getString() on the ResultGetter to return the database value as a String. We then pass the returned value to our convenient translation method, which returns the Boolean value that we ultimately want to be set in the enabled property of our User class.

Dealing with nulls: what the heck is this valueOf() method for?

iBATIS has a null value translation feature that allows you to work with nullable columns in the database without requiring a nullable type in the object model. This is especially valuable when you don't have full design control over the object model or the database but you must map the two together. So for example, if you have an int typed property on your Java class, it will not accept a null value. If you must map that property to a nullable column in the database, then you have to use a constant to represent the null value. Sometimes this is called a "magic number," and generally speaking, using it is a bad practice. But sometimes, you don't have any choice—and in some cases it may make perfect sense.

Because iBATIS is configured with XML files, the null value replacement is specified as a String. For example:

```
<result property="enabled" column="Enabled" nullValue="NO"/>
```

For that reason, something has to perform the translation into the real type. iBATIS relies on the `valueOf()` method of the `TypeHandlerCallback` to do the translation. In our case, we'd need to translate the value `NO` into a boolean value of `false`. Luckily, doing this is usually very similar to the translation we've already done to get a result. In fact, in the case of our `YesNoTypeHandlerCallback`, it is exactly the same. So the implementation would look like this:

```
public Object valueOf(String s) {
    return yesNoToBoolean(s);
}
```

That's it! We've completed our custom type handler. Listing 12.2 contains the complete source.

Listing 12.2 A TypeHandler

```
public class YesNoTypeHandlerCallback
    implements TypeHandlerCallback {

  public static final String YES = "YES";    <-- Contains constants for yes and no database values
  public static final String NO = "NO";

  public void setParameter(                  <-- Sets parameters with our type handler
    ParameterSetter setter, Object parameter
  )
      throws SQLException {
    setter.setString(booleanToYesNo((Boolean)parameter));
  }

  public Object getResult(ResultGetter getter)    <-- Gets results with our type handler
      throws SQLException {
    return yesNoToBoolean(getter.getString());
  }

  public Object valueOf(String s) {    <-- Converts string to our type
    return yesNoToBoolean(s);
  }

  private Boolean yesNoToBoolean(String s) {    <-- Converts string to Boolean
    if (YES.equalsIgnoreCase(s)) {
      return Boolean.TRUE;
```

```
      } else if (NO.equalsIgnoreCase(s)) {
        return Boolean.FALSE;
      } else {
        throw new IllegalArgumentException (
            "Could not convert " + s +
            " to a boolean value. " +
            "Valid arguments are 'YES' and 'NO'.");
      }
    }

    private String booleanToYesNo(Boolean b) {    <-- Converts Boolean to string
      if (b == null) {
        throw new IllegalArgumentException (
          "Could not convert null to a boolean value. " +
          "Valid arguments are 'true' and 'false'.");
      } else if (b.booleanValue()) {
        return YES;
      } else {
        return NO;
      }
    }
  }
```

Now that we've written our TypeHandlerCallback, we need to register it to be used. The next section deals with that.

12.2.3 Registering a TypeHandlerCallback for use

To use a TypeHandlerCallback, we need some way to specify where and when it should be used. There are three options:

- Register it globally, in the SqlMapConfig.xml file.
- Register it locally, within a single SqlMap.xml file.
- Register it for a single result or parameter mapping.

To register the TypeHandlerCallback globally, simply add a <typeHandler> element to your SqlMapConfig.xml. Here is the full example of the <typeHandler> element:

```
<typeHandler
    callback="com.domain.package.YesNoTypeHandlerCallback"
    javaType="boolean" jdbcType="VARCHAR" />
```

The <typeHandler> element accepts two or three attributes. The first is the TypeHandlerCallback class itself. Simply specify the fully qualified class name, or if you like, you can also use a type alias to keep your configuration more readable. The second is the `javaType` attribute, which specifies which Java types should be handled by this `TypeHandlerCallback`. Finally, the third attribute, which is optional, allows you to specify the JDBC (i.e., database) type that this `TypeHandlerCallback` should be applied to. So in our case, we're working with a Java type of boolean and a JDBC type of VARCHAR. If we didn't specify the data type, this type handler would be used by default for all boolean types. However, it would not override any type handlers with a more specific definition. Thus the type handler registration that most specifically matches both the Java type and the JDBC type is the one that will be used.

Custom type handlers are by far the most common form of extension in iBATIS. This is mostly due to the wide range of nonstandard features and data types supported by relational database systems. In the remaining sections, we discuss other forms of extension that are rarer but still useful to know about.

12.3 Working with a CacheController

iBATIS includes a number of built-in caching implementations. These have already been discussed in previous chapters, but to refresh your memory, table 12.3 summarizes the various cache implementations.

Table 12.3 Summary of cache implementations

Class	Description
`LruCacheController`	The least recently used (LRU) cache keeps track of cached entries based upon when they were last accessed. The cache entry accessed least recently is removed if needed to make room for newer entries.
`FifoCacheController`	The first-in, first-out (FIFO) cache simply removes the oldest item in the cache to make room for new items.
`MemoryCacheController`	The Memory cache allows the Java memory model and garbage collector to determine when cached entries should be removed.
`OSCacheController`	The OpenSymphony cache is an adapter to a very advanced third-party caching solution called OSCache. OSCache supports various caching models of its own, as well as advanced features such as distributed caching.

iBATIS provides an interface called `CacheController` that allows you to implement your own custom caching solution, or to plug in an existing third-party caching solution. The `CacheController` interface is fairly simple, and looks like this:

```
public interface CacheController {
  public void configure(Properties props);
  public void putObject(CacheModel cacheModel,
                        Object key, Object object);
```

```
  public Object getObject(CacheModel cacheModel,
                          Object key);
  public Object removeObject(CacheModel cacheModel,
                             Object key);
  public void flush(CacheModel cacheModel);
}
```

The next few sections will take you through an example of implementing a cache. This is not meant to teach you how to write an enterprise capable cache controller. We're going to employ a simple caching approach using a Map. A more common case would be to plug in a third-party cache that has advanced features. We do not recommend that you make the following example your caching strategy of choice.

12.3.1 Creating a CacheController

The `CacheController` implementation starts out with configuration. Configuration is achieved by implementing the `configure()` method; this method takes a Java `Properties` instance, which can contain relevant configuration information. For our cache, we don't need any configuration properties, but we will need the map in which to store our objects. Here's a start to implementing our `CacheController`:

```
public class MapCacheController {

  private Map cache = new HashMap();

  public void configure(Properties props) {
    // There is no configuration necessary, and therefore
    // this cache will depend upon external
    // flush policies (e.g. time interval)
}

  // other methods implied …
}
```

OK, now that we have a skeletal cache model, let's build the rest of it.

12.3.2 Putting, getting, and flushing a CacheController

At this point, we can start to think about adding objects to the cache. The iBATIS `CacheModel` manages all of the keys and determines how to distinguish various statement calls and result sets. So to put an object on the cache, all you need to do is pass the key and the object to your cache implementation of choice.

For example, here are the put, get, and remove methods:

```
public void putObject(CacheModel cacheModel, Object key,
                      Object object) {
  cache.put (key, object);
```

```
}

public Object getObject(CacheModel cacheModel,
                        Object key) {
  return cache.get(key);
}

public Object removeObject(CacheModel cacheModel,
                           Object key) {
  return cache.remove(key);
}
```

Notice how each method also provides access to the `CacheModel` instance that is controlling the cache. This allows you to access any properties from the `CacheModel` that you might need. The `key` parameter is an instance of `CacheKey`, a special class within iBATIS that compares sets of parameters passed to a statement. For the most part, you shouldn't have to manipulate it in any way. In the case of `putObject()`, the `object` parameter contains the instance or collection of objects to cache.

The last method that `CacheModel` describes is the `flush()` method. This method simply clears the entire cache.

```
public void flush(CacheModel cacheModel) {
  cache.clear();
}
```

That is, in a nutshell, a complete `CacheController` implementation. Now we need to learn how to use our `CacheController`.

12.3.3 Registering a CacheController for use

Like all other iBATIS configurations, `CacheModels` and `CacheControllers` are configured within the XML configuration files. The easiest way to start using your `CacheModel` is to first declare a type alias for your new class. This will save you some typing later.

```
<typeAlias alias="MapCacheController"
           type="com.domain.package.MapCacheController"/>
```

Now that we've saved ourselves some keystrokes, we can apply the cache controller type to a `<cacheModel>` definition, just like we do with any other cache model type. For example:

```
<cacheModel id="PersonCache" type="MapCacheController" >
    <flushInterval hours="24"/>
    <flushOnExecute statement="updatePerson"/>
```

```
    <flushOnExecute statement="insertPerson"/>
    <flushOnExecute statement="deletePerson"/>
</cacheModel>
```

That completes the custom cache implementation. Remember, though, this was a simple example. You probably want to look into other caching alternatives to plug into iBATIS, as writing your own may cost you more time than writing the rest of your application!

12.4 Configuring an unsupported DataSource

iBATIS includes support for the most common `DataSource` alternatives, including JNDI (application server–managed `DataSource`), Apache DBCP, and a built-in `DataSource` implementation called `SimpleDataSource`. You also have the option of adding support for additional `DataSource` implementations.

To configure a new `DataSource` implementation, you need to provide iBATIS with a factory that will supply the framework with an instance of the `DataSource`. This factory class must implement the `DataSourceFactory` interface, which looks like this:

```
public interface DataSourceFactory {

  public void initialize(Map map);
  public DataSource getDataSource();

}
```

The `DataSourceFactory` has only two methods: one to initialize the `DataSource`, and another to access the `DataSource`. The `initialize()` method provides a Map instance which contains configuration information, such as the JDBC driver name, database URL, username, and password.

The `getDataSource()` method simply needs to return the configured `DataSource`. This is a simple interface, and the implementation only gets as complex as the `DataSource` implementation you plug into it. The following is an example taken from the iBATIS source code. This is the `DataSourceFactory` for the `SimpleDataSource` implementation. As you can see, it truly is "simple."

```
public class SimpleDataSourceFactory
  implements DataSourceFactory {

  private DataSource dataSource;

  public void initialize(Map map) {
```

```
        dataSource = new SimpleDataSource(map);
    }

    public DataSource getDataSource() {
        return dataSource;
    }
}
```

As we've said before, more complex `DataSource` implementations might take a lot more work, but we hope that never becomes an issue you need to worry over.

The final topic we will cover in extending iBATIS is customizing your transaction management.

12.5 Customizing transaction management

iBATIS offers a number of transaction options, as you've read in earlier chapters. However, there is always room for customization with today's wide range of application servers and custom approaches to transaction management. From the outside, transactions seem simple, offering only a few functions: start, commit, roll back, and end. But on the inside, transactions are very complex and are one of the behaviors of application servers that tend to deviate from the standard. For that reason, iBATIS allows you to customize your own transaction management system. If you've had any experience in the area, that statement probably sent shivers down your spine—and so it should. Implementing a transaction manager correctly is a terribly difficult thing to do. For that reason, we won't even bother tackling a true implementation here. Instead, we'll discuss the interfaces in detail, which will help you gain a head start should you ever be tasked with implementing them. If you do want an example, iBATIS comes with three implementations: JDBC, JTA, and EXTERNAL. Table 12.4 summarizes these, in case you missed them in previous chapters.

Table 12.4 Built-in transaction manager configurations

Implementation	Description
`JdbcTransactionConfig`	Uses the transaction facilities provided by the JDBC Connection API
`JtaTransactionConfig`	Starts a global transaction, or joins an existing global transaction
`ExternalTransactionConfig`	"No-op" implementation of commit and rollback, thus leaving commit and rollback to some external transaction manager

In most cases, one of the options in table 12.4 should work for you. However, if your application server or transaction manager is nonstandard (or buggy), iBATIS provides interfaces for you to build your own transaction management adapter: `TransactionConfig` and `Transaction`. You will generally need to implement both to have a complete implementation, unless your situation allows you to reuse one of the `Transaction` classes from one of the other implementations.

12.5.1 Understanding the TransactionConfig interface

The `TransactionConfig` interface is a factory of sorts, but is mostly responsible for configuring the transaction facilities for the implementation. The interface is as follows:

```
public interface TransactionConfig {

  public void initialize(Properties props)
      throws SQLException, TransactionException;

  public Transaction newTransaction(int
                                    transactionIsolation)
      throws SQLException, TransactionException;

  public int getMaximumConcurrentTransactions();

  public void setMaximumConcurrentTransactions(int max);

  public DataSource getDataSource();

  public void setDataSource(DataSource ds);

}
```

The first method is `initialize()`. As we've seen with other parts of the framework that can be extended, this method is used to configure the transaction facilities. It takes a `Properties` instance as its only parameter, which can contain any number of configuration options. For example, the JTA implementation requires a `User-Transaction` instance that is retrieved from a JNDI tree. So one of the properties passed to the JTA implementation is the JNDI path to the `UserTransaction` it needs.

Next is the `newTransaction()` method. This is a factory method for creating new instances of transactions. It takes an `int` parameter (unfortunately; it should be a type-safe enumeration) that describes the transaction isolation level within which the transaction should behave. Available transaction isolation levels are defined on the JDBC `Connection` class as constants as follows:

- TRANSACTION_READ_UNCOMMITTED
- TRANSACTION_READ_COMMITTED
- TRANSACTION_REPEATABLE_READ
- TRANSACTION_SERIALIZABLE
- TRANSACTION_NONE

Each of these is documented in the JDBC `Connection` API, and you can learn more in chapter 7. The important thing to note here is that if your transaction manager implementation does not support one or more of these, you should be sure to throw an exception to let the developer know. Otherwise, there could be unexpected consequences that are difficult for your users to debug.

The next pair of methods are `getDataSource()` and `setDataSource()`. These methods describe a `JavaBeans` property for the `DataSource` associated with this `TransactionConfig` instance. Usually you won't have to do anything special with the `DataSource`, but it is provided here so that you can decorate it with additional behavior if you need to. Many transaction manager implementations wrap the `DataSource` and the `Connection` objects it provides, to add transaction related functionality to each of them.

The final pair of methods makes up another `JavaBeans` property that allows the framework to configure a maximum number of concurrent transactions supported. Your implementation may or may not be configurable, but it is important to ensure that you throw an appropriate exception if the number set is too high for your system to handle.

12.5.2 Understanding the Transaction interface

Recall the factory method called `newTransaction()` on the `TransactionConfig` class discussed in the previous section. The return value of that method is a `Transaction` instance. The `Transaction` interface describes the behavior necessary to support transactions within the iBATIS framework. It's a pretty typical set of functionality, which will be familiar to anyone who has worked with transactions before. The `Transaction` interface looks like this:

```
public interface Transaction {

    public void commit() throws SQLException,
                                TransactionException;

    public void rollback() throws SQLException,
                                  TransactionException;
```

```
    public void close() throws SQLException,
                               TransactionException;

    public Connection getConnection()
        throws SQLException, TransactionException;

}
```

There's really nothing special about this particular interface. If you have any experience with transactions at all, it will look familiar. The `commit()` method is, as expected, the means of making permanent all of the changes involved in the unit of work. The `rollback()` method, on the other hand, is meant to undo all of the changes that have occurred in the unit of work, or at least since the last commit. The `close()` method is responsible for releasing any, and all, resources that may have been allocated or reserved for the transaction.

The last method, `getConnection()`, is the one that you may not have expected. By design, iBATIS is a high-level framework around the JDBC API. Loosely speaking, the connection is the transaction in JDBC. At the very least, transactions are managed, controlled, and understood at the JDBC connection level. For that reason, most transaction implementations are bound to a `Connection` instance. This is useful, because iBATIS needs access to the connection currently associated to the transaction.

12.6 Summary

In this chapter we've explored various ways of extending iBATIS. Standard extensions are important, even for open source software, to avoid uncontrolled customization of the framework in potentially undesirable and unmaintainable ways. iBATIS supports a number of different extensions, including `TypeHandlerCallback`, `CacheController`, `DataSourceFactory`, and `TransactionConfig`.

`TypeHandlerCallback` is the most common type of extension, since it deals with the common problem of proprietary data types. `TypeHandlerCallback` is simple to implement; it requires only a few methods to be implemented that allow for customization of the mapping between Java types and JDBC types. In a nutshell, `TypeHandlerCallback` becomes responsible for setting parameters on statements, getting results from the result set, and translating null value replacements for mapping nullable database types to non-nullable Java types.

`CacheControllers` provide a simple means of integrating third-party caching solutions into iBATIS. Of course, you could also write your own, but writing a decent cache is amazingly difficult. The `CacheController` interface includes methods for configuring the implementation, putting items in the cache, retrieving items from the cache, and removing or flushing items from the cache.

A `DataSourceFactory` is responsible for configuring and providing access to a standard JDBC `DataSource` implementation. You'll likely be configuring some third-party `DataSources`, unless you have a really compelling reason to write your own, which we suggest avoiding if possible. The `DataSourceFactory` has only two methods: one configures the `DataSource`, and the other provides access to the `DataSource`.

The `TransactionConfig` and `Transaction` interfaces are the most complex to implement and the least common as well. Situations that require a custom `TransactionConfig` should be rare, but if you absolutely need to, iBATIS allows you to write your own.

These are the standard, supported extension points in iBATIS. Wherever possible, iBATIS uses interfaces by design to allow you to replace existing functionality. We couldn't explore all of the possibilities in this chapter, or even in this book, but if you look through the code, most layers of the design offer a decent separation of interface and implementation. In most cases the design will be similar to that presented here.

Part 4

iBATIS recipes

By now you should have a good handle on the basic and advanced features of iBATIS, as well as a complete understanding of how and when to use it. This fourth and final section of the book wraps up with a discussion of the best practices, and then demonstrates them in a full sample application. If a picture is worth a thousand words, then a sample application is worth a few thousand lines of code. We hope you enjoy it.

13 iBATIS best practices

This chapter covers

- Unit testing
- Configuration management
- Naming
- Data structures

iBATIS is all about best practices—it is largely the reason iBATIS was created. For starters, iBATIS helps you maintain separation of concerns between your application and the persistence layer. It also helps you avoid mixing Java and SQL and ending up with a mess of twisted code. iBATIS lets you separate the design of your object-oriented domain model from your relational data model. This chapter discusses a number of best practices that will help you get the most out of iBATIS.

13.1 Unit testing with iBATIS

Unit testing has become a very important part of modern software development methodologies. Even if you don't subscribe to the benefits of extreme programming or other agile methods, unit testing should be a cornerstone practice in your software development life cycle.

Conceptually, the persistence tier is separated into three layers, and iBATIS makes it easy to unit-test those layers, as illustrated in figure 13.1.

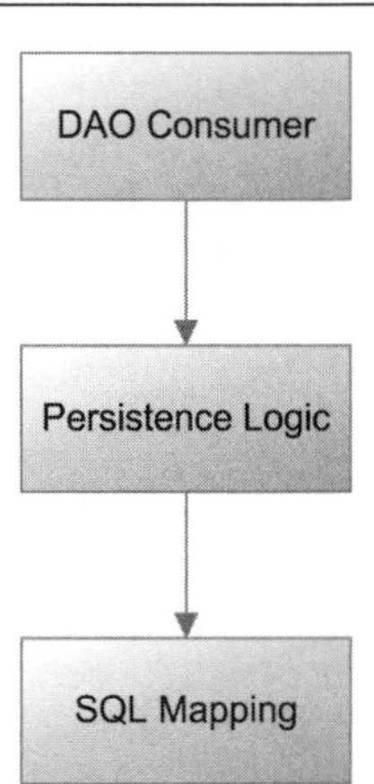

Figure 13.1 These are the typical layers immediately involved with persistence (nonpersistence-related layers are not shown in this diagram).

iBATIS facilitates testing these layers in at least three ways:

- Testing the mapping layer itself, including the mappings, SQL statements, and the domain objects they're mapped to
- Testing the DAO layer, which allows you to test any persistence specific logic that may be in your DAO
- Testing within the DAO consumer layer

13.1.1 Unit-testing the mapping layer

This is generally the lowest level of unit testing that will take place in most applications. The process involves testing the SQL statements and the domain objects they're mapped to as well. This means that we'll need a database instance to test against.

The test database instance

The test database instance might be a true instance of a database that you're actually using, such as Oracle or Microsoft SQL Server. If your environment is friendly to unit testing, then this is a simple option to get up and running. Using real databases might be necessary if you're planning to take advantage of nonstandard database features such as stored procedures. Stored procedures and other non-portable database design choices make it difficult to unit-test the database in any way other than against a real instance of the database.

The disadvantage of using a real database instance is that your unit tests can only run when connected to the network. Alternatively, you could use a local instance of one of these databases, which means your unit tests would require additional local environment setup before they could run. Either way, you'll also be faced with having to rebuild the test data and possibly even the schema between test suites or even between each unit test. Doing so can be an extremely slow process even on large enterprise-class database servers. Another problem is that with a centralized database, multiple developers running the unit tests at the same time may cause a collision. Therefore, you will have to isolate each developer with a separate schema. As you can see, the general problem with this approach is that the unit tests are dependent on a fairly large piece of infrastructure, which is not ideal to most experienced test-driven developers.

Luckily for Java developers, there is at least one fantastic in-memory database that makes unit testing of relatively standard database designs quite easy. HSQLDB is an in-memory database written entirely in Java. It doesn't require any files on disk or network connectivity to work. Furthermore, it is capable of reproducing most database designs from typical databases such as Oracle and Microsoft SQL Server. Even if it can't re-create an entire database due to design complications (such as stored procedures), it should be able to reproduce most of it. HSQLDB allows you to rebuild a database, including the schema and test data, very quickly. The suite of unit tests for iBATIS itself uses HSQLDB and rebuilds the schema and test data between each individual test. We've personally witnessed test suites of nearly 1,000 database-dependent tests that run in under 30 seconds using HSQLDB.

For more information about HSQLDB, visit http://hsqldb.sourceforge.net/. Microsoft .NET developers will be happy to know that there are initiatives to port HSQLDB as well as to create other in-memory database alternatives.

Database scripts

Now that we have the database instance, what do we do about the schema and the test data? You probably have scripts to create the database schema and to create the test data. Ideally, you have checked the scripts into your version control system (such as CVS or Subversion). These scripts should be treated as any other code in your application. Even if you are not in control of your database, you should expect regular updates from the people who are. Your application source code and database scripts should always be in sync, and your unit tests are there to ensure that they are. Each time you run your unit-test suite, you should also run these scripts to create the database schema. Using this approach, it should be easy to commit a new set of database-creation scripts to your version control system, and then run your unit tests to see if any changes caused problems for your application. This is the ideal situation. If you are using an in-memory database such as HSQLDB to run your tests, there might be an additional step to convert the schemas. Consider automating this conversion as well to avoid the potential for human error and speed up your integration time.

The iBATIS configuration file (i.e., SqlMapConfig.xml)

For the purposes of unit testing, you might want to use a separate iBATIS configuration file. The configuration file controls your data source and transaction manager configuration, which will likely vary greatly between the testing and production environments. For example, in production you might be in a managed environment such as a J2EE application server. In such an environment, a managed `DataSource` instance is probably retrieved from JNDI. You may also be leveraging global transactions in production. However, in your test environment your application will probably not be running in a server; you'll have a simple `DataSource` configured and will be using local transactions. The easiest way to configure the test and production configurations independently is to have a different iBATIS configuration file that references all of the same SQL mapping files as the production one.

An iBATIS SqlMapClient unit test

Now that all of our prerequisites are ready, including a database instance, automated database build scripts, and a configuration file for testing, we're ready to create a unit test. Listing 13.1 shows an example of using JUnit to create a simple unit test.

Listing 13.1 Example of a SqlMapClient unit test

```
public class PersonMapTest extends TestCase {

  private SqlMapClient sqlMapClient;

  public void setup () {                              ❶ Setting up unit test and test data
    sqlMapClient = SqlMapClientBuilder.
      build("maps/TestSqlMapConfig.xml");
    runSqlScript("scripts/drop-person-schema.sql");
    runSqlScript("scripts/create-person-schema.sql");
    runSqlScript("scripts/create-person-test-data.sql");
  }
```

```
    public void testShouldGetPersonWithIdOfOne() {    ❷ Testing retrieval of single
      Person person = (Person) sqlMapClient.             person by primary key value
        queryForObject("getPerson", new Integer(1));
      assertNotNull("Expected to find a person.", person);
      assertEquals("Expected person ID to be 1.",
        new Integer(1), person.getId());
    }
  }
```

The example in listing 13.1 uses the JUnit unit-testing framework for Java. (You can find out more about JUnit at www.junit.org. Similar tools are available for the .NET Framework, including NUnit, which you can find at www.nunit.org.) In our setup method ❶, we drop and re-create our database tables and then repopulate them. Rebuilding everything for each test ensures test isolation, but this approach may be too slow to use on an RDBMS like Oracle or SQL Server. In cases where that is an issue, consider an in-memory database like HSQLDB. In our actual test case ❷, we fetch a record, map it into a bean, and assert that the values in the bean are the values that we expected to be there.

That's all there is to testing our mapping layer. The next layer we need to test is the DAO layer, assuming your application has one.

13.1.2 Unit-testing data access objects

The data access object layer is an abstraction layer, so by their very nature DAOs should be easy to test. DAOs make testing consumers of the DAO layer easier as well. In this section, we'll discuss testing a DAO itself. DAOs are generally separated into an interface and an implementation. Because we're testing the DAO directly, the interface does not play a role. We'll work directly with the DAO implementation for the purposes of testing. This might sound contrary to how the DAO pattern is supposed to work, but that's the great thing about unit testing… it lets us get bad habits out of our system!

If possible, testing at the DAO level should not involve the database or underlying infrastructure. The DAO layer is an interface to the persistence implementation, but in testing a DAO we're more interested in testing what is inside the DAO itself, not what is beyond it.

The complexity of testing a DAO depends solely on the DAO implementation. For example, testing a JDBC DAO can be quite difficult. You'll need a good mocking framework to replace all of the typical JDBC components such as `Connection`, `ResultSet`, and `PreparedStatement`. Even then, it's a lot of work managing such a complicated API with mock objects. It's somewhat easier to mock the iBATIS `SqlMapClient` interface. Let's try that now.

Unit-testing a DAO with mock objects

Mock objects are objects that stand in place of true implementations for the purpose of unit testing. Mocks don't generally have very much functionality; they satisfy a single case to allow the unit test to focus on some other area without having to worry about additional complexity. We'll use mocks in this example to demonstrate an approach to testing the DAO layer.

In our example, we'll use a simple DAO. We'll leave out the iBATIS DAO framework so that we don't have to worry about transactions and such. The purpose of this example is to demonstrate testing the DAO layer regardless of which DAO framework you use, if any at all.

First, let's consider the DAO we want to test. Listing 13.2 shows a `SqlMapPersonDao` implementation that calls a SQL map similar to the example in section 13.1.1.

Listing 13.2 A simple DAO to test

```
public class SqlMapPersonDao implements PersonDao {

  private SqlMapClient sqlMapClient;

  public SqlMapPersonDao(SqlMapClient sqlMapClient) {
    this.sqlMapClient = sqlMapClient;
  }

  public Person getPerson (int id) {
    try {
      return (Person)
        sqlMapClient.queryForObject("getPerson", id);
    } catch (SQLException e) {
      throw new DaoRuntimeException(
        "Error getting person. Cause: " + e, e);
    }
  }
}
```

Notice how we inject the `SqlMapClient` into the constructor of the DAO in listing 13.2. This provides an easy way to unit-test this DAO, because we can mock the `SqlMapClient` interface. Obviously this is a simple example, and we're not testing very much at all, but every test counts. Listing 13.3 shows the unit test that will mock the `SqlMapClient` and test the `getPerson()` method.

Listing 13.3 A unit test for the PersonDao with a mock SqlMapClient

```
public void testShouldGetPersonFromDaoWithIDofOne() {
  final Integer PERSON_ID = new Integer(1);

  Mock mock = new Mock(SqlMapClient.class);
  mock.expects(once())
      .method("queryForObject")
      .with(eq("getPerson"),eq(PERSON_ID))
      .will(returnValue(new Person (PERSON_ID)));

  PersonDao daoSqlMap =
    new SqlMapPersonDao((SqlMapClient) mock.proxy());
  Person person = daoSqlMap.getPerson(PERSON_ID);

  assertNotNull("Expected non-null person instance.",
    person);
  assertEquals("Expected ID to be " + PERSON_ID,
    PERSON_ID, person.getId());
}
```

The example in listing 13.3 uses the JUnit as well as the JMock object-mocking framework for Java. As you can see in the bolded section, mocking the `SqlMapClient` interface with JMock allows us to test the behavior of the DAO without worrying about the actual `SqlMapClient`, including the SQL, the XML, and the database that comes along with it. JMock is a handy tool that you can learn more about at www.jmock.org. As you might have already guessed, there is also a mocking framework for .NET called NMock, which you can find at http://nmock.org.

13.1.3 Unit-testing DAO consumer layers

The other layers of your application that use the DAO layer are called *consumers*. The DAO pattern can help you test the functionality of those consumers without depending on the full functionality of your persistence layer. A good DAO implementation has an interface that describes the available functionality. The key to testing the consumer layer lies in having that interface. Consider the interface in listing 13.4; you may recognize the `getPerson()` method from the previous section.

Listing 13.4 Simple DAO interface

```
public interface PersonDao extends Dao {
  Person getPerson(Integer id);
}
```

The interface in listing 13.4 is all we need to begin testing the consumers of our DAO layer. We don't even need a completed implementation. Using JMock, we can easily mock the expected behavior for the `getPerson()` method. Consider the service that makes use of the `PersonDao` interface (listing 13.5).

Listing 13.5 A service that makes use of PersonDao

```
public class PersonService {

  private PersonDao personDao;

  public PersonService(PersonDao personDao) {
    this.personDao = personDao;
  }

  public Person getValidatedPerson(Integer personId) {

    Person person = personDao.getPerson(personId);

    validateAgainstPublicSystems(person);
    validateAgainstPrivateSystems(person);
    validateAgainstInternalSystems(person);

    return person;
  }

}
```

The target of our unit tests is not the DAO—it's the `getValidatedPerson()` method logic, such as the various validations it performs. Each of the validations may be a private method, and for argument's sake, let's just agree that we're only testing the private interface here.

Testing this logic without a database will be easy, thanks to that `PersonDao` interface that we saw earlier. All we need to do is mock the `PersonDao`, pass it to the constructor of our service, and call the `getValidatedPerson()` method. Listing 13.6 shows the unit test that does exactly that.

Listing 13.6 Using a mock instead of the real DAO to avoid hitting the database

```
public void testShouldRetrieveAValidatedPerson (){
    final Integer PERSON_ID = new Integer(1);

    Mock mock = new Mock(PersonDao.class);
    mock.expects(once())
        .method("getPerson")
```

```
        .with(eq(PERSON_ID))
        .will(returnValue(new Person(PERSON_ID)));

    PersonService service =
      new PersonService((PersonDao)mock.proxy());
    service.isPersonalInformationValid(
            new Person(new Integer(1)), new Integer(1));

    assertNotNull("Expected non-null person instance.",
      person);
    assertEquals("Expected ID to be " + PERSON_ID,
      PERSON_ID, person.getId());
    assertTrue("Expected valid person.",
      person.isValid());
}
```

Again we're making use of both JUnit and JMock. As you can see in listing 13.6, the testing approach is consistent at each layer of the application. This is a good thing, as it makes for simple, focused unit tests that are easy to maintain.

That's as far as we'll go with unit testing for iBATIS. There are a number of great resources that discuss unit testing in general. Try a Google search for "unit testing." You'll find plenty to help you to improve your unit-testing skills and perhaps discover even better ways than those described here.

13.2 Managing iBATIS configuration files

By now it's pretty clear that iBATIS uses XML files for configuration and statement mapping. These XML files can become unwieldy very quickly. This section discusses some best practices for organizing your SQL mapping files.

13.2.1 Keep it on the classpath

Location transparency is one of the most important aspects of application maintainability. It simplifies testing and deployment of your application. Part of location transparency is keeping your application free of static file locations such as `/usr/local/myapp/config/` or `C:\myapp\`. Although iBATIS will allow you to use specific file locations, you are better off using the classpath. The Java classpath is helpful when you want to keep your application free of any specific file paths. You can think of the classpath as a mini file system that your application can refer to internally through the use of a classloader. A classloader is able to read resources from the classpath, including classes and other files. Let's take a look at an example. Imagine the following file structure on your classpath:

```
/org
  /example
    /myapp
      /domain
      /persistence
      /presentation
      /service
```

Given this structure, we can refer to the persistence package using the fully qualified classpath of `org/example/myapp/persistence`. A good place to put our maps might be in `org/example/myapp/persistence/sqlmaps`, which would look like this in the structure:

```
/org
  /example
    /myapp
      /domain
      /persistence
        /sqlmaps
            SqlMapConfig.xml
            Person.xml
            Department.xml
      /presentation
      /service
```

Alternatively, if you want a more shallow structure for configuration files, you could put the mapping files in a common configuration package. For example, we could use `config/sqlmaps`, which would look like this:

```
/config
  /sqlmaps
    SqlMapConfig.xml
    Person.xml
    Department.xml
/org
  /example
  /myapp
    /domain
    /persistence
    /presentation
    /service
```

With your mapping files on the classpath, iBATIS makes it easy to load these files using the included `Resources` utility class. This class contains methods like `getResourceAsReader()`, which is compatible with `SqlMapBuilder`. So given the previous classpath, we could load `SqlMapConfig.xml` as follows:

```
Reader reader = Resources
  .getResourceAsReader("config/maps/SqlMapConfig.xml");
```

If you're in an environment where you find it necessary to keep the configuration of database resources in a centralized location, such as a fixed file path, then you should still keep the mapping files on the classpath. That is, use a hybrid approach where SqlMapConfig.xml is at the fixed file location but the mapping files are still on the classpath. For example, consider the following structure:

```
C:\common\config\
  /sqlmaps
    SqlMapConfig.xml

  /config
    /sqlmaps
      Person.xml
      Department.xml
  /org
    /example
      /myapp
        /domain
        /persistence
        /presentation
        /service
```

Even though SqlMapConfig.xml is at a fixed location, internally it can still refer to the XML mapping files on the classpath. This keeps most of your resources where you want them, and reduces the chance of having inappropriate mapping files deployed with your application.

13.2.2 Keep your files together

Keep your mapping files together; avoid spreading them out through your classpath. Don't attempt to organize them beside the classes that they work with or into separate packages. Doing so will complicate your configuration and make it difficult to get an idea of what mapping files are available. The internal structure inside the mapping files themselves makes further categorization is unnecessary. Use smart filenames and keep the XML files in a single directory by themselves. Try to avoid keeping classes in the same directory (i.e., package), and of course don't mix them with other XML files!

This approach makes it easier to navigate your mapping files and the project in general. It makes no difference to the iBATIS framework where you put your files, but it will make a difference to your fellow developers.

13.2.3 Organize mostly by return type

The most common question with regard to mapping file organization is what to organize them by. Should you organize them by database table? How about by class? Perhaps organize them by the type of statement?

The answer depends on your environment. Although there is no "right" answer, don't get too fancy about it. iBATIS is very flexible, and you can always move the statements around later.

As a starting point, it's best to organize your maps by the type that the statements return and the types they take as a parameter. This generally creates a nice organization of maps that you can navigate based on what you're looking for. So for example, in a `Person.xml` mapping file, you should expect to find mapped statements that return `Person` objects (or collections of `Person` objects), as well as statements that take a `Person` object as a parameter (like `insertPerson` or `updatePerson`).

13.3 Naming conventions

There can be a lot of things to name in iBATIS: statements, result maps, parameter maps, SQL maps, and XML files all need names. Therefore, it's a good idea to have some sort of convention. We'll discuss one convention here, but feel free to use your own. As long as you're consistent within your application, you won't have any trouble.

13.3.1 Naming statements

Statements should generally follow the same naming convention as methods in the language in which you're programming. That is, in a Java application, use statement names like `loadPerson` or `getPerson`. In C#, use statement names like `SavePerson` or `UpdatePerson`. Using this convention will help you maintain consistency, but it also will help with method-binding features and code-generation tools.

13.3.2 Naming parameter maps

Most of the time parameter maps will not have to be named, because inline parameter maps are much more common than explicitly defined ones. Due to the nature of SQL statements, parameter maps have limited reusability. You generally can't use the same one for both an `INSERT` statement and an `UPDATE` statement. For this reason, if you do use an explicitly defined parameter map, we recommend adding the suffix `Param` to the name of the statement that uses it. For example:

```
<select id="getPerson" parameterMap="getPersonParam" ... >
```

13.3.3 Naming result maps

Result maps are bound to a single class type and the reusability of result maps is quite high. For this reason, we recommend naming result maps using the type they are bound against; also, append `Result` to the name. For example:

```
<resultMap id="PersonResult" type="com.domain.Person">
```

13.3.4 XML files

There are two kinds of XML files in iBATIS. The first is the master configuration file and the others are the SQL mapping files.

The master configuration file

The master configuration file can be called whatever you like; however, we recommend calling it `SqlMapConfig.xml`. If you have multiple configuration files for different parts of the application, then prefix the configuration filename with the name of the application module. So if your application has a web client and a GUI client with different configurations, you might use `WebSqlMapConfig.xml` and `GuiSqlMapConfig.xml`. You may also have multiple environments in which you deploy, such as production and test environments. In this case, prefix the filename with the type of environment as well. Continuing with the previous example, you might have `ProductionWebSqlMapConfig.xml` and `TestWebSqlMapConfig.xml`. These names are descriptive, and the consistency creates opportunities to automate builds to different environments.

The SQL mapping files

How you name the SQL mapping files will depend a lot on how you've organized your mapped statements. Earlier in this book we recommended that you organize your mapped statements into separate XML files based on their return types and parameters. If you've done that, naming the file after the return types and parameters will also work. For example, if one mapping XML file contains SQL statements involving the `Person` class, then naming the mapping file `Person.xml` would be appropriate. Most applications will do fine with this naming approach. There are other considerations, though.

Some applications may require multiple implementations of the same statement to match different databases. For the most part, SQL can be written in a portable way. For example, the original JPetStore application that was written with iBATIS was compatible with 11 different databases. However, sometimes there are features of the database that are not portable but that are ideal for the solution being implemented. In cases like this, it becomes acceptable and even important to name your mapping files so that they include the database for which they were specifically written. For instance, if we had an Oracle-specific file for `Person`, we'd name it `OraclePerson.xml`. Another approach is to use a separate directory for each database, named after the database. Don't go crazy with these approaches. Only specifically name the files or directories that you have to, and make sure there's enough Oracle-specific matter in the mapping file to make the name appropriate. If there's only a single statement that is Oracle dependent, then you might be better off naming the one statement to include the word `Oracle`.

13.4 Beans, maps, or XML?

iBATIS supports many types for parameter and result mappings. You have a choice of JavaBeans, Maps (such as HashMap), XML, and of course primitive types. Which should you choose to map your statements to? Our default position is always JavaBeans.

13.4.1 JavaBeans

JavaBeans provide the highest performance, the greatest amount of flexibility, and type safety. JavaBeans are fast because they use simple, low-level method calls for property mappings. JavaBeans won't degrade performance as you add more properties, and they are more memory efficient than the alternatives. A more important consideration is that JavaBeans are type safe. This type safety allows iBATIS to determine the appropriate type of value that should be returned from the database and binds it tightly. There is not the guesswork that you experience with maps or XML. You also have more flexibility with JavaBeans because you are able to customize your getters and setters to fine-tune your data.

13.4.2 Maps

iBATIS supports maps for two purposes. First, iBATIS uses maps as the mechanism for sending multiple complex parameters to mapped statements. Second, maps are supported because sometimes a table in a database represents just that—a set of keyed values.

However, maps make horrible domain models, and therefore you should not use maps to represent your business objects. This is not an iBATIS-specific recommendation; you shouldn't use maps to model your domain regardless of your persistence layer. Maps are slow, they are not type-safe, they use up more memory than JavaBeans, and they can become unpredictable and difficult to maintain. Use maps judiciously.

13.4.3 XML

iBATIS supports XML directly to and from the database, either as a Document Object Model (DOM) or simply as a String. There is somewhat limited value in doing so; however, it can be useful in simpler applications that just need to convert data into a portable and parsable format quickly.

However, like maps, XML should not be your first choice for a domain model. XML is the slowest, least type-safe, and most memory-demanding type of all. It is the closest thing to the end state of your data (i.e., often HTML), but that advantage comes at the price of being difficult to manipulate and hard to maintain over time. As with maps, use XML judiciously.

13.4.4 Primitives

Primitives are supported directly by iBATIS as parameters and results. There is no issue with using a primitive in either way. Primitives are fast and type-safe. Obviously you're somewhat limited with how complex your data can be; however, if you have a simple requirement to count the rows for a given query, a primitive integer is the way to go. Feel free to use primitives as long as they can satisfy the requirement.

13.5 Summary

Using iBATIS is not hard, but as with any framework, you can always improve the results if you follow the recommended best practices.

In this chapter we discussed how to ensure that the persistence layer of your application is appropriately tested. Using two popular unit-testing frameworks, JUnit and JMock, we are able to test three separate layers of our application in a simple and consistent way. We discussed appropriate ways to set up a test database to ensure that your tests don't require a network connection or a complex piece of infrastructure such as a relational database management system.

We also discussed the best way to manage your XML files. Location transparency is the key to simple deployment and ensures easy testing and future maintainability. Location transparency can be achieved in Java applications by keeping all of the SQL map files in the classpath. Because in some cases you can't keep all of them in the classpath, we discussed an approach to separating the configuration so that it can be kept in a centralized location while keeping all of the other mapping files on the classpath where you want them.

Next, we discussed how to name all of the different iBATIS objects. Naming is as important as organization to ensure that your maps are easy to read and follow. Keeping statement names consistent with method names makes for a familiar paradigm, as mapped statements are not unlike methods. Parameter map names, if used at all, are based on statement names because they have limited reusability. However, result maps are reusable and are therefore named after the type that they map.

Choosing which type to map was the focus of the final topic of the chapter. Should you use JavaBeans, maps, or XML in your domain model? The answer is clear. You should use JavaBeans for your business object model. Maps and XML suffer from similar disadvantages, including poor performance and lack of type safety, and both can be a maintenance nightmare in the future.

14 Putting it all together

This chapter covers

- Choosing tools
- Setting up your project
- Wiring components together

iBATIS is not an island unto itself—it is meant to be part of a whole. iBATIS can be used in conjunction with any application that accesses a SQL database. Given that there are a lot of different applications that may access a SQL database, we'll focus on one popular type. Web applications are well known and usually access a SQL database somewhere behind the scenes. To put iBATIS into a useful context, we will walk through the creation of a shopping cart application. We tried to come up with something original, so we decided to make it a game store rather than a pet store. Let's move ahead with putting this application together.

14.1 Design concept

It's always good to begin writing an application with some sense of direction. A good overview of what we want an application to accomplish is important. Another term for this is *requirements*. Shopping carts are an easy concept to delineate requirements for because they have been done many times. Tiresome as it may be, we will do the same thing for this round. (Hey, at least it's not a pet store!)

We are going to keep the design of this shopping cart simple and focus our efforts on the design of four major parts: the account, the catalog, the cart, and the order. We'll forgo any management portions to the application, as those add significant time and complexity to the requirements while adding little to the bottom line of this book. With the group of application components defined, let's now provide some details on each of their requirements.

14.1.1 Account

The *account* will house information relevant to a user. An account will contain personal address information and preferences. The user should be able to create and edit an account. The account will also handle security for customer logins.

14.1.2 Catalog

The *catalog* will house a significant number of the pieces we need to code. The *category*, *product*, and *item* will be utilized here. The category, product, and item will be only one level deep and will contain products. A product will then contain items. Items are variations of the product. For example, a category named *Action* would contain a game/product like Doom. The game/product would then contain items like PC, PlayStation, XBox, and similar variations.

14.1.3 Cart

The *cart* will be used to maintain a user's product selections. The cart should tally up the current items that are in the cart in preparation for the order.

14.1.4 Order

The *order* portion of the application will be used for checkout. Once the customer has made all of their item selections and wants to purchase the items, they will select checkout from the cart. The cart will take them through a process of confirmation, payment, billing, shipping, and final confirmation. Once the order is completed, it will be viewable by the user in their order history.

14.2 Choosing technologies

Now that we have derived some perspective on our requirements, we need to make some decisions about what technologies we will use to meet the required functionality. Since this is a web application, we will look at options for different layers. The standard web application can be broken into a few pieces:

- The presentation layer, the portion of the application that is web specific
- The service layer, where most of our business rules will exist
- The persistence layer, where we will deal with elements specific to database access

14.2.1 Presentation

For the presentation layer we have several options. Some of the top frameworks are Struts, JSF, Spring, and WebWork. All of these frameworks have their evangelists and are known to perform well in their own right. Out of all of these we choose to use Struts. Struts is stable and predictable, continues to be progressive, and is very much alive for both new and existing applications. From this point on we will assume that you have a moderate understanding of the Struts framework. If you don't, then *Struts in Action* by Ted N. Husted, Cedric Dumoulin, George Franciscus, and David Winterfeldt (Manning, 2002) is an excellent resource.

14.2.2 Service

The service layer will be pretty straightforward. Since this is a book about iBATIS, we will utilize the iBATIS DAO within the service classes. The iBATIS DAO will be used to retrieve and store the data access object instances as instance variables on the service classes. This will allow us to hide the DAO implementation from the service classes. The iBATIS DAO will also be used for transaction demarcation so that we can aggregate fine-grained calls against the persistence layer.

14.2.3 Persistence

We're sure it won't surprise you that we plan to use iBATIS `SQLMaps` in the persistence layer. iBATIS `SQLMaps` will fulfill the responsibility of managing SQL, persistence caches and executing calls against the database. We'll avoid going into too much detail about this since this is a book on the very subject.

14.3 Tweaking Struts: the BeanAction

Recently, web application frameworks have experienced a bit of a transformation. Features like state management, bean-based presentation classes, enhanced GUI components, and sophisticated event models have been introduced to make development easier. Even in the midst of these next-generation frameworks, Struts continues to enjoy a strong presence. In assessing the best approach for the JGameStore application, we wanted to use Struts while keeping a forward relevance to the new-generation frameworks. With this in mind, we decided to use an approach that we have dubbed the `BeanAction`. The `BeanAction` allows developers of standard Struts applications to easily grasp how iBATIS fits into a standard Struts application. At the same time, developers who use next-generation frameworks like JSF, Wicket, and Tapestry will understand the semantics of the `BeanAction` approach. In the end, we are not trying to make Struts different; we are simply making our application relevant to a wider audience.

The `BeanAction` successfully flattens the responsibilities of the `Action` and `ActionForm` into one class. It also abstracts you away from direct access to the web-specific components like session and request. This type of architecture is reminiscent of WebWork and JSF. This flattening is accomplished through a few key components: the `BeanAction` that extends the Struts `Action` class, the `BaseBean`, and the `ActionContext`. These components are important to understanding how the `BeanAction` works, and are illustrated in figure 14.1.

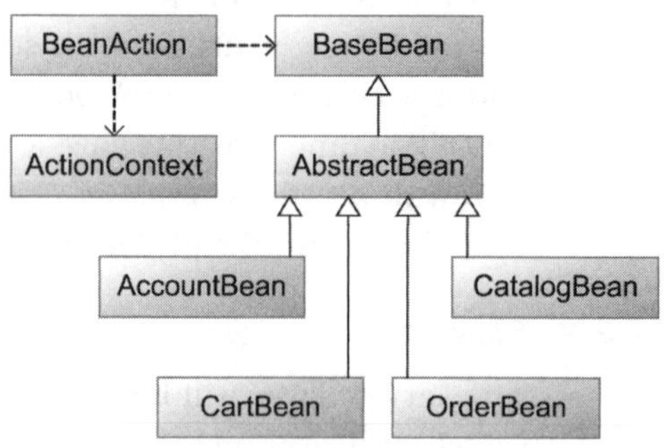

Figure 14.1 UML diagram of the BeanAction architecture

14.3.1 BeanBase

It's important to understand the purpose of the BaseBean before we look into the ActionContext and the BeanAction. The BaseBean extends ValidatorActionForm to allow for standard Struts validation to occur. Instead of extending an ActionForm directly, you extend the BaseBean. The BaseBean contains your normal properties, as an ActionForm normally would. Thus, it is populated as Struts would populate the ActionForm because it *is* an ActionForm. The only difference is that your extended BaseBean would also contain behavior methods that follow the simplified signature of public String methodName().

14.3.2 BeanAction

The next piece of this puzzle that we should introduce is the BeanAction. The BeanAction has a couple of responsibilities. First, the BeanAction populates the ActionContext. Next, it routes behavior calls to your extended BaseBean and translates the returned behavior method's String into an ActionForward for Struts. This is how the BaseBean is able to stay clear of Struts-specific components in the behavior signatures. The BeanAction class looks in two different places to determine which behavior method to call on the extended BaseBean. First, it checks to see if the action mapping has a specified parameter that explicitly states the method to call. If the parameter specifies *, then a method is not called and the success action forward is used. If the action mapping parameter attribute is not specified or is empty, then the ActionBean looks at the path and uses the filename minus the extension for the method call. So, if you used a standard .do mapping and had a path that ended with /myMethod.do, the myMethod behavior method would be called on your extended BaseBean.

14.3.3 ActionContext

Finally, the ActionContext is used to abstract from specific web semantics. It provides you access to the request, parameters, cookies, session, and application all through a Map interface. This gives you the option of reducing direct dependencies on the web layer. Most of the ActionContext successfully isolates you from Struts and even the Servlet API. However, the ActionContext still provides direct access to the HttpServletRequest and the HttpServletResponse for those times when you need access to it.

There are several advantages to this approach. First of all, we don't need to spend time and code casting ActionForm objects to their extended types. This is avoided because the Action is the ActionForm. All you need to do is access the properties directly on the bean object that extends BaseBean. Second, the behavior methods that are called are reduced in their complexity. Normally, you would need to have a signature that receives an `HttpServletRequest`, an `HttpServletResponse`, an `ActionForm`, and an `ActionMapping`. The `Action` execute method also requires that you return an `ActionForward`. The `BeanAction` reduces all this by simply requiring an empty signature with a String as a return value. Third, it is far easier to unit-test a simple bean than it is to unit-test an `ActionForm` and an `Action`. Testing Struts `Action` classes is thoroughly possible with the use of `MockObjects` and or `Struts-TestCase`. However, it is quite a bit easier to test a simple bean. Finally, since the `BeanAction` architecture works seamlessly with existing Struts applications, it allows you to migrate your application architecture to a modern approach without destroying all of your previous hard work.

14.4 Laying the foundation

Now let's set up our development environment. We won't concentrate on specific tools to use for the development of an iBATIS-enabled application, but we'd like to take some time to provide a basic structure that has been useful for us. Organizing your source tree is an important part of writing good, clean, and simple code. If you'd like, you can use the source in the iBATIS JGameStore application to follow along with the rest of this chapter. We won't be able to cover all of the requirements we specified previously. However, if you examine the iBATIS JGameStore application's source, you will be able to examine the code we did not cover and understand what is going on.

Let's start by creating a base folder called jgamestore. This will be your project folder and will contain your source tree. You can set this folder up in your favorite IDE and name the project jgamestore, or you can simply do this manually from the OS. Below the project folder create several folders: src, test, web, build, devlib, and lib:

```
/jgamestore
  /src
  /test
  /web
  /build
  /devlib
  /lib
```

Let's take a close look at each of these folders.

14.4.1 src

The name *src* is short for source. The src folder will hold all Java source code and any property or XML files that must exist on the classpath. These files will be used in the distributed application. This folder should not contain any test code, such as unit tests.

All source will be contained within the org.apache.ibatis.jgamestore base package. Each package beneath the base package categorizes components of the application.

The subpackages will be as follows:

- *domain*—This package will contain DTO/POJO classes that are the transient objects in the application. These objects will be passed among and used by each of the other layers of the application.
- *persistence*—This is where our data access interfaces and implementations will reside along with the `SQLMap` XML files. The data access implementations will use the iBATIS `SQLMaps` API.
- *presentation*—This package will contain our presentation beans. These classes will contain properties and behaviors that are relevant to different screens in the web application.
- *service*—This package will contain the business logic. These coarse-grained classes will be used to group together fine-grained calls to the persistence layer.

14.4.2 test

The test directory will hold the entire unit-testing code. The package structure will be identical to that of the src directory. Each of the packages will contain unit tests that test the classes located in the sister packages of the `src` directory. There are various reasons for this and most have to do with maintaining secure and testable code.

14.4.3 web

The web folder will contain all web-related artifacts such as JSP, images, Struts config files, and similar files.

The web folder structure is as follows:

- *JSP directories*—The account, cart, catalog, common, and order directories all contain JSPs for the relevant portion of the application. Their directory names are pretty self-explanatory as to what the contained JSPs represent.
- *css*—This directory contains the Cascading Style Sheets (CSS). If you are not familiar with CSS, you can find many resources on them using a quick web search.

- *images*—This directory will contain all images relevant to the site.
- *WEB-INF*—This directory contains configuration files relevant to Servlet spec configuration files and Struts configuration files.

14.4.4 build

The build directory will hold the Ant scripts along with helper shell scripts and Windows BAT scripts to easily run the build.

14.4.5 devlib

The devlib directory will contain JAR files that are necessary for compilation but will not be distributed in the WAR.

Libraries required for development (devlib) include the following:

- `ant.jar`
- `ant-junit.jar`
- `ant-launcher.jar`
- `cgilib-nodep-2.1.3.jar`
- `emma_ant.jar`
- `emma.jar`
- `jmock-1.0.1.jar`
- `jmock-cglib-1.0.1.jar`
- `junit.jar`
- `servlet.jar`

14.4.6 lib

The lib directory will contain all JARs that are required for compilation and are distributed with the WAR.

Libraries required for runtime and distribution (lib) include the following:

- `antlr.jar`
- `beanaction.jar`
- `commons-beanutils.jar`
- `commons-digester.jar`
- `commons-fileupload.jar`
- `commons-logging.jar`
- `commons-validator.jar`
- `hsqldb.jar`
- `ibatis-common-2.jar`
- `ibatis-dao-2.jar`

- ibatis-sqlmap-2.jar
- jakarta-oro.jar
- struts.jar

With this basic source tree structure in place, let's move on to coding our working application. Since the catalog portion of the application is the first one that a customer views, let's concentrate our efforts there.

14.5 Configuring the web.xml

Setting up web.xml is pretty straightforward. We will set up our Struts ActionServlet and some simple security to prevent direct access to the JSP pages (see listing 14.1).

Listing 14.1 ActionServlet configuration in web.xml

```
<servlet>
  <servlet-name>action</servlet-name>
<servlet-class>
   org.apache.struts.action.ActionServlet</servlet-class>
  <init-param>
    <param-name>config</param-name>
    <param-value>/WEB-INF/struts-config.xml</param-value>
  </init-param>
  <init-param>
    <param-name>debug</param-name>
    <param-value>2</param-value>
  </init-param>
  <init-param>
    <param-name>detail</param-name>
    <param-value>2</param-value>
  </init-param>
  <load-on-startup>2</load-on-startup>
</servlet>

<servlet-mapping>
  <servlet-name>action</servlet-name>
  <url-pattern>*.shtml</url-pattern>
</servlet-mapping>
```

When setting up the ActionServlet to process requests, we do so with the <servlet> tag. The settings for the ActionServlet are plain-vanilla Struts—nothing fancy. The ActionServlet specified in the <servlet-class> tag is the standard ActionServlet. We provide a standard struts-config.xml location, a debug level of 2, a detail level of 2, and a load-on-startup setting of 2.

Notice the <servlet-mapping> tag. Because we like to feel as if we are clever, we decided to depart from the standard .do extension to map requests to the ActionServlet. Instead of the standard .do, we have gone with an .shtml. The only reason for this is to jokingly make it look as if we are using an old technology. Who knows—perhaps it will also deter a few people from trying to hack the site (not likely).

When using Struts, it is important to prevent direct access to JSP pages. All JSP pages that are used by JGameStore are placed under the pages directory. Since all the JSP pages are under a directory, we can simply prevent direct access to that directory (listing 14.2). This ensures that access to the JSP pages goes through the Struts ActionServlet.

Listing 14.2 security configuration in web.xml

```
<security-constraint>
  <web-resource-collection>
    <web-resource-name>
      Restrict access to JSP pages
    </web-resource-name>
    <url-pattern>/pages/*</url-pattern>
  </web-resource-collection>
  <auth-constraint>
    <description>
      With no roles defined, no access granted
    </description>
  </auth-constraint>
</security-constraint>
```

Having set up our web.xml, we can focus on creating the specific classes and configurations for the Struts presentation layer. We'll go into some detail on taking advantage of Struts' BeanAction approach.

14.6 Setting up the presentation

Because the catalog is the portion of the application that is used first by shopping cart visitors, let's focus our efforts next on setting up the presentation portion that supports it.

14.6.1 The first step

When a visitor arrives in JGameStore, they are greeted with an initial page. It is an important rule in web applications that when using Struts you *always* forward requests through the Struts controller (`ActionServlet`). To get people into that initial page by passing through the Struts framework, we must create a simple `index.jsp` with a forward, define the URL we are forwarding to in the `struts-config.xml` file, define the tile in the `tiles-defs.xml` file, and create the initial JSP page our visitors will be arriving at.

In order for the JSP forward to work, we first need to set up the initial page (figure 14.2) for our visitors.

This page will be located in the `web/catalog/` directory of our source tree and will be named `Main.jsp`. Since the catalog is the first thing a visitor will view, we'll place our main page in the catalog directory.

In addition, we will need to drop a definition for the page in the `tiles-defs.xml` file (listing 14.3). Tiles make it easier to create common templates and reuse them, thus avoiding the redundant JSP includes. To learn more about tiles, check out *Struts in Action*.

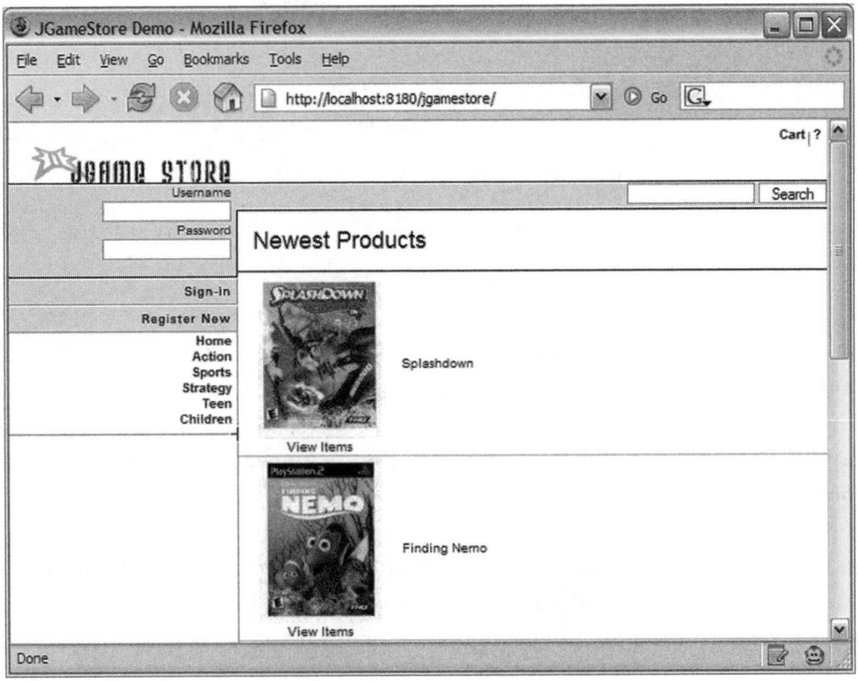

Figure 14.2 The Main.jsp page is the first page a visitor will view.

Listing 14.3 Tiles definition config

```
<tiles-definitions>
...
  <definition name="layout.main" path="/pages/main.jsp" >
      <put name="header"
           value="/pages/common/header.jsp" />
      <put name="footer"
           value="/pages/common/footer.jsp" />
      <put name="left"
           value="/pages/common/left-blank.jsp" />
  </definition>

  <definition name="layout.catalog"
              extends="layout.main" >
      <put name="header"
           value="/pages/common/header.jsp" />
      <put name="footer"
           value="/pages/common/footer.jsp" />
      <put name="left"
           value="/pages/common/left.jsp" />
  </definition>

  <definition name="index.tiles"
              extends="layout.catalog" >
      <put name="body"
           value="/pages/catalog/Main.jsp" />
  </definition>
...
<tiles-definitions>
```

In tiles-defs.xml there needs to be a layout.main and a layout.catalog definition before we can define index.tiles. The index.tiles definition extends the layout.catalog definition, which further extends the layout.main definition. layout.main defines the base template JSP located at web/pages/main.jsp in the source tree.

Once we have our main page set up, we need to define a forward to it so that our index.jsp forward works. Note that we defined the parameter attribute as index in our action mapping configuration. As a result, the index() method (listing 14.4) will be called on the catalogBean before being forwarded to /catalog/Main.jsp.

Listing 14.4 Struts config action mapping

```
<action-mappings>
  <action path="/index"
          type="org.apache.struts.beanaction.BeanAction"
```

```
          name="catalogBean" parameter="index"
          validate="false">
    <forward name="success" path="index.tiles"/>
  </action>
</action-mappings>
```

In the JGameStore application, the `index()` method of the `CatalogBean` makes a call to the `CatalogService` to populate a List of the newest products from each category. Since we provide a better example of this bit later, we won't explain it here. At this point, we'll just accept that the `index()` method returns a success String and is forwarded to the first page in the cart (see listing 14.5).

Listing 14.5 index() method of catalogBean

```
public String index() {
  ...
  return SUCCESS;
}
```

Next, we can use our `index.jsp` to successfully forward to the main page through the Struts controller. There is nothing to the `index.jsp` except a forward. Be sure to specify the `.shtml` extension on your forward URL so that your servlet container will route the request through the Struts controller (see listing 14.6).

Listing 14.6 JSP forward

```
<jsp:forward page="/index.shtml"/>
```

Next, you'll learn how to set up a presentation bean and create a behavior method that can be called.

14.6.2 Utilizing a presentation bean

When visitors arrive at the cart, they select a category they wish to examine. Our next step is to capture the category and display a listing of products on a subsequent page. To achieve this, we need to create the following:

- A tiles definition in our `tiles-defs.xml`
- Our `Category` domain object (see listing 14.7)
- Our `Product` domain object (see listing 14.8)

- Our presentation bean with properties and behaviors to capture visitor input (see listing 14.9)
- A JSP page that lists products of a category (see listing 14.10)

Then we'll add an action mapping to our Struts configuration.

Since what we are about to code involves the use of the category, let's go ahead and create this object in the org.apache.ibatis.jgamestore.domain package as `Category.java`. The `Category` domain object (listing 14.7) is a simple object that consists only of a `categoryId`, a name, a description, and an image. Since our category is never more than one level deep, we won't need to concern ourselves with any parent categories.

Listing 14.7 Category domain object

```
...
public class Category implements Serializable {

  private String categoryId;
  private String name;
  private String description;
  private String image;


  // simple setters and getters
...
```

The code we are writing will also involve the use of the `Product` domain object (listing 14.8). The product objects will be loaded in a list for display on the JSP page. This means that the product will not be accessed directly by any Java code at this point. Regardless, it will be smart to code it for the sake of thoroughness. Let's add it to the org.apache.ibatis.jgamestore.domain package as `Product.java`. The `Product` object will consist of a `productId`, `categoryId`, name, description, and image. `Product` is not much different from the `Category` domain object except that the `Product` domain object contains an associated `categoryId`.

Listing 14.8 Product domain object

```
...
public class Product implements Serializable {

  private String productId;
  private String categoryId;
  private String name;
```

```
    private String description;
    private String image;

    // simple setters and getters
  ...
```

Now that we have our domain classes set up, let's tackle the presentation bean. Looking at the `CatalogBean` presentation class (listing 14.9) will provide our first glimpse at how the `BeanAction` functions in the real world. We need to create the `CatalogBean` with a `viewCategory` behavior. The behavior method will use the `BeanAction` style behavior signature of `public String <behaviorName> ()`. The `viewCategory` behavior is quite simple. Its job is to retrieve a list of products that are related to the selected category, fully populate the `Category` object, and then forward to a view. In the body of our `viewCategory` method, the `productList` and the `categoryList` are populated by making calls to the `CatalogService` class. We will get into the service class later. For now, suffice it to say we'll assume that the service class will return our objects appropriately.

Listing 14.9 CatalogBean presentation class with properties and viewCategory Behavior

```
...
private String categoryId;
private Category category;
...
private PaginatedList productList;
...
public String viewCategory() {
  if (categoryId != null) {
    productList =
     catalogService.getProductListByCategory(categoryId);
    category = catalogService.getCategory(categoryId);
  }
  return SUCCESS;
}
...
// category setter/getter
...
// productList setter/getter
...
```

To get the `CatalogBean` to compile, we'll create a simple `CatalogService` interface in the org.apache.ibatis.jgamestore.service package. We'll add two necessary methods—`public List getProductListByCategory(Integer categoryId)` and `public`

Category getCategory(Integer categoryId)—to the interface. Then, we can continue coding without worrying about the implementation.

When the viewCategory method completes, it uses a public static String called SUCCESS as the return value. The value of the SUCCESS variable is success. The returned String is used to provide the BeanAction with the name of the action forward to call. This results in our JSP display (see listing 14.10).

Listing 14.10 Product listing - /catalog/Category.jsp

```
...
<c:set var="category"
       value="${catalogBean.category}"/>    ❶
<c:set var="productList"
       value="${catalogBean.productList}"/>

<table width="100%">
<tr>
 <td colspan="2" class="PageHeader" align="left">
  <c:out value="${category.name}"/>
 </td>
</tr>
<tr>
 <td colspan="2" align="left">
  <html:link page="/index.shtml" styleClass="BackLink">
   Return to Main Page
  </html:link>
 </td>
</tr>

<c:forEach var="product" items="${productList}">    ❷
 <tr>
  <td width="128" align="center"
      style="border-bottom: 1px solid #ccc">
   <html:link paramId="productId"    ❸
              paramName="product"
              paramProperty="productId"
              page="/viewProduct.shtml">
    <c:out value="${product.image}"
           escapeXml="false"/>
   </html:link>
   <html:link paramId="productId"    ❸
              paramName="product"
              paramProperty="productId"
              page="/viewProduct.shtml">
    View Items
   </html:link>
  </td>
  <td align="left"
      style="border-bottom: 1px solid #ccc">
```

❶ **Sets Category object and productList to page scope**

❷ **Iterates over productList**

❸ **Renders links and display text**

```
<html:link styleClass="ZLink"    <-- 3 Renders links and display text
           paramId="productId"
           paramName="product"
           paramProperty="productId"
           page="/viewProduct.shtml">
   <c:out value="${product.name}"/>
  </html:link>
 </td>
</tr>
</c:forEach>
...
```

The <c:set> tags ❶ are initially used to expose our Category object and productList to the page scope. Once these objects are exposed to the page, they are available for the other tags that need them. The list of products and the category will be used by the JSTL core tags ❷ and the Struts <html> tags ❸ to accomplish the display of these objects. The <c:out> tag is used to display the name property of our Category object. The <c:forEach> tag is used to iterate over the list of products and expose each product in the list to its body, <html:link> is then able to use the exposed product and create a link to the page that views the product. Within the body of the <html:link> tag we use the <c:out> tag to render the value of the product name.

The Struts tags use a common nomenclature for working with objects. The name attribute is the key that points to the object which is exposed in a scope. For example, suppose you expose an object to the page using the name category. category is what the name attribute should refer to. A corresponding attribute to the name attribute is the property attribute, which gives the tag access to a particular property of the named object.

In contrast, the JSTL tags have an EL (Expression Language) that is more robust than the name and property attributes of the Struts tags. The EL is used to expose objects in a scope to a particular JSTL attribute. We will not discuss EL in detail here, but if you want to learn more we recommend Shawn Bayern's *JSTL in Action* (Manning, 2002).

After coding all of the necessary components, we can now add an action mapping to our struts-config.xml (see listing 14.11) so that our application can use those components. We first specify our CatalogBean as a form bean by assigning the name catalogBean and providing a type of our fully qualified class name for the CatalogBean. We now have a form bean that our action mapping can take advantage of.

Listing 14.11 Action mapping for /viewCategory

```
<form-bean
  name="catalogBean"
  type=
"org.apache.ibatis.jgamestore.presentation.CatalogBean"/>
...
<action
  path="/viewCategory"
  type="org.apache.struts.beanaction.BeanAction"
  name="catalogBean" scope="session" validate="false">
  <forward name="success" path="/catalog/Category.jsp"/>
</action>
```

For the final touch, let's configure the action mapping, as shown in listing 14.11. The mapping requires us to specify a path—in this case, `/viewCategory`. We then use the `type` attribute to identify the fully qualified class name of the `Action` class that will be used to process the request. In this example, our type is `BeanAction`. `BeanAction` will relay the request to a behavior method located on the form bean that the action mapping uses. This is determined based on the form bean name used in the `name` attribute of the action mapping. Here we will use the `catalogBean` that we configured earlier. We then use the `scope` attribute to specify that the form remain in a session scope. We set the `validate` attribute to false because there is no input to validate.

Lastly, the `<forward>` tag, which rests in the body of the action mapping, is used to determine which page will be forwarded to. The `name` attribute maps to the value returned by the behavior method of the presentation bean. In our case, we will always receive a return value of `success` and thus forward to `/catalog/Category.jsp`.

Next let's try our hand at the service layer.

14.7 Writing your service

The service layer will consist of just two pieces: the service interface and the implementation. The service class is meant to be a coarse-grained class that pulls together more fine-grained data access calls. This may sound quite simple, but the contents of a service class can pose some difficulties. Since it is important to keep our service classes clean of any database-specific information, we need to take extra measures to ensure proper abstraction.

Because the service layer needs to call the data access layer and handle transaction demarcation, it would be easy to simply retrieve a database connection and manage the transaction demarcation with the database connection. But if we did this, we'd introduce a JDBC-specific semantic into our service layer. This means that the service layer would now be aware of the data-store implementation we are using. As soon as our service layer becomes aware of the type of data store we are using, we compromise its purpose.

As you learned in chapter 10, iBATIS provides a small framework called iBATIS DAO that will be of use to us here. iBATIS DAO will fill a couple of important responsibilities. First, it will be our *data access object* factory. Second, we will use the iBATIS DAO for transaction demarcation, thus reducing the dependency our service layer has on the underlying data access technology. In this section, we continue with our previous example and you'll learn how to set up our service layer using iBATIS DAO.

14.7.1 Configuring dao.xml

Unlike with our presentation layer, we will start our exploration of the service layer by first configuring the iBATIS DAO framework. This makes it easier for us to understand the components involved in the service layer. The iBATIS DAO framework allows us to manage the necessary abstraction through configuration, so it is appropriate to start here.

The first component to configure in the iBATIS DAO is the transaction manager (see listing 14.12). The transaction manager is used to handle transaction demarcation over calls to the data access layer. In our example, we will use a transaction manager type of SQLMAP; this is the type that integrates with the iBATIS `SQLMap` framework. Even though it may be difficult to distinguish iBATIS DAO from iBATIS `SQLMap`, they are indeed different frameworks. The SQLMAP transaction manager is a nice and easy route to go. Unless you are using the iBATIS DAO framework in conjunction with another persistence layer, SQLMAP is the best transaction manager to use for most occasions. The only property that needs to be specified for the SQLMAP transaction manager is `SqlMapConfigResource`, which is specified using the `<property>` tag in the body of the `<transactionManager>` tag. The value of the `SqlMapConfigResources` property simply points to the `sql-map-config` file that will contain all the necessary connection configuration information. Whenever calls are made to start, commit, and end transactions, they will transparently make the necessary calls against the hidden connection object specified in the `SQLMap` configuration file.

Listing 14.12 transactionManager configuration in dao.xml

```
<transactionManager type="SQLMAP">
  <property name="SqlMapConfigResource"
   value=
"org/apache/ibatis/jgamestore/persistence/sqlmapdao/sql/sql -map-
  config.xml"/>
</transactionManager>
```

The next step involved in configuring `dao.xml` is mapping the interface to the implementation (see listing 14.13). This is quite easy to do—it only requires that the `<dao>` tag provide a value to the `interface` attribute that corresponds with a fully qualified interface name. The implementation will then be a fully qualified class name implementation of that interface. If the configured implementation class does not utilize the specified interface, iBATIS DAO will be sure to let you know at runtime.

Listing 14.13 DAO configuration in dao.xml

```
<dao
interface=
  "org.apache.ibatis.jgamestore.persistence.iface.ProductDao"
implementation=
  "org.apache.ibatis.jgamestore.persistence.sqlmapdao.ProductSqlMapDao"/>
```

14.7.2 Transaction demarcation

When using the SQLMAP type with the iBATIS DAO framework, you have implicit and explicit transaction management. By default, if you do not specify a transaction explicitly, it will be started automatically for you. There are ways to avoid this; you can read about that in chapters 4 and 10.

Implicit transaction management with the SQLMAP type is simple—all we need to do is call the method on our data access object (see listing 14.14). The transaction management is performed automatically for us. In the case of a select, we don't need the transaction, but it doesn't hurt to have it.

Listing 14.14 Example of implicit transaction management

```
public PaginatedList getProductListByCategory(
  String categoryId
) {
```

```
    return productDao.getProductListByCategory(categoryId);
  }
```

Explicit transaction management (see listing 14.15) is a bit more involved. It is only needed when we are making more than one call to the data access objects. Within a `try` block, we would first call `daoManager.startTransaction()`; we would then perform our calls to one or more data access objects. When we have completed our calls to the data access layer, we would commit the transaction by calling `daoManager.commitTransaction()`. If the call(s) were to fail for any reason, we would have a `daoManager.endTransaction()` located in the `finally` block. This would roll back our transaction and prevent any damage to our data store. For the simple select we are performing, there is no need for this level of transaction management. However, you could do it either way if you prefer.

Listing 14.15 Example of explicit transaction management

```
public PaginatedList getProductListByCategory(
  String categoryId
) {
  PaginatedList retVal = null;
  try {
    // Get the next id within a separate transaction
    daoManager.startTransaction();
    retVal = productDao
      .getProductListByCategory(categoryId);
    daoManager.commitTransaction();
  } finally {
    daoManager.endTransaction();
  }
  return retVal;
}
```

Now that we have made it through the service layer in our simple view category example, let's finish this up by assembling the remaining pieces in the DAO layer.

14.8 Writing the DAO

The data access layer is where the Java code touches the database. The iBATIS `SQLMap` framework is used here to make handling SQL easier. A data access layer that uses iBATIS `SQLMaps` can be broken out into three basics pieces: the `SQLMap` configuration file, the associated `SQLMap` SQL files, and the data access objects.

Let's see how to apply them in our view category example in order to retrieve our product list.

14.8.1 SQLMap configuration

We will use `sql-map-config.xml` to specify database properties, set up the transaction manager, and tie together all of the `SQLmap` files (see listing 14.16). The `<properties>` tag will point to a `database.properties` file that contains key/value pairs that are used to substitute the items written as `${…}`. We should make sure that our `database.properties` file contains the appropriate driver, URL, username, and password for the chosen database.

Listing 14.16 SQLMAP transaction manager configuration

```
<sqlMapConfig>
<properties resource="properties/database.properties"/>
<transactionManager type="JDBC">
  <dataSource type="SIMPLE">
    <property value="${driver}" name="JDBC.Driver"/>
    <property value="${url}" name="JDBC.ConnectionURL"/>
    <property value="${username}" name="JDBC.Username"/>
    <property value="${password}" name="JDBC.Password"/>
  </dataSource>
</transactionManager>

<sqlMap resource= ~CCC
"org/apache/ibatis/jgamestore/persistence/sqlmapdao/sql/Product.xml"/>
</sqlMapConfig>
```

Next, we'll move on to configuring our transaction manager. For our purposes, we will use the easiest transaction manager type of JDBC. The JDBC type specifies that the `SQLMap` will use the standard `Connection` object commit and rollback methods. Since we are handling the transaction demarcation on the service layer, this configuration is more important. However, this transaction manager configuration is required in order for the transaction manager configured with iBATIS DAO to work correctly.

The data source inside the `transactionManager` defines the JDBC data source that the transaction manager will use to retrieve connections. We specify a type of SIMPLE because we will have iBATIS handling the data source connection pool. The `<property>` tag is then used to specify the driver, connection URL, username, and password. Each `<property>` tag uses the `${…}` notation and retrieves values from the `database.properties` file.

The final element to set up is the `<sqlMap>` tag. This tag specifies the location of the `SQLMap` configuration files. Whenever iBATIS is accessed for the first time, the configured `SQLMaps` and their contents will be loaded into memory so that the SQL contents can be executed when needed.

14.8.2 SQLMap

We'll need to create a `SQLMap` file to house our SQL call for the category product list. Within this file, which we'll name `Product.xml`, we will need to define a `typeAlias` for the `Product` object, a cache model to cache results, and a select statement to house our select SQL (see listing 14.17).

Listing 14.17 SQLMap Product.xml SQL file

```
<sqlMap namespace="Product">

  <typeAlias
   alias="product"
   type="org.apache.ibatis.jgamestore.domain.Product"/>

  <cacheModel id="productCache" type="LRU">
    <flushInterval hours="24"/>
    <property name="size" value="100"/>
  </cacheModel>
…
  <select
    id="getProductListByCategory" resultClass="product"
    parameterClass="string" cacheModel="productCache">
    SELECT
      PRODUCTID,
      NAME,
      DESCRIPTION,
      IMAGE,
      CATEGORYID
    FROM PRODUCT
    WHERE CATEGORYID = #value#
  </select>
…
</sqlMap>
```

The `typeAlias` will define an alias to the fully qualified class name of the `Product` domain object. Here, we'll specify the alias `product`. This saves us time typing the fully qualified class name every time we refer to the `Product` domain object.

Our cache model is going to be quite simple. We'll configure its type as LRU and name it `productCache`. Since the LRU has the potential to last a long time, we will make sure it doesn't hang around longer than the 24 hours indicated by the `<flushInterval>` tag. This will help to keep things relatively fresh in our application. Setting the size of our LRU will allow one hundred different results to be stored in the `productCache` cache model. If we receive high traffic on our site, we are sure to retain good performance with at least a daily mandatory flush.

Next comes our select statement. We provide the `id` of the select with something that represents what the SQL actually does. Don't be afraid of verbosity; verbosity clarifies the purpose of the SQL that is contained in the body of the select. In this case we provide an `id` of `getProductListByCategory`. There is no mistaking that the SQL contained within will return a list based on the category provided.

Taking advantage of the `typeAlias` that we defined, we will specify the select statement's `resultClass` as product. Note that even though we are retrieving a list by running this select in our data access object, we do not specify a List as our return result. The reason is that this same select could be used to return a single `Product` object. This may seem absurd since we named it `getProductListByCategory`, but there are situations where a select will be multipurpose and return a single object or a list of objects.

The `parameterClass` for this select will use an alias of `string` (defined by default). As you have probably guessed, this alias represents the String object. A `parameterClass` attribute may also use a user-defined alias.

The final attribute that we take advantage of on our select is `cacheModel`, which references our previously defined `productCache` cache model. Specifying `cacheModel` ensures that all category product lists that are queried will be cached. This provides us with speedy performance and fewer unnecessary hits on the database.

The next step is to fill the body of the select tag with our SQL. Our select statement will retrieve a result set of records from the `Product` table and map them into a list of product objects as specified by our select tag configuration. All of the fields will map smoothly to properties in the `Product` object because the column names correspond with the property names.

Once we have finished configuring our `sql-map-config.xml`, our alias, our `cacheModel`, and our select, we are ready to use the iBATIS API in Java code. We will take advantage of the `SQLMap` by writing an implementation to our `ProductDao` interface.

14.8.3 Interface and implementation

It's a good practice to code against an interface when working between layers of an application. In this case we are working between the service layer and the data access layer. The service layer should always interact with the DAO interface and be free of any DAO implementations. This case is no different, as you can see here:

```
public interface ProductDao {
  PaginatedList getProductListByCategory(
    String categoryId);
...
}
```

We have a `ProductDao` interface that will be used by the `CatalogService` class. Since `CatalogService` interacts with the `ProductDao` interface, it doesn't care about the actual implementation. On our `ProductDao`, we need to define a `getProductListByCategory` method that `CatalogService` is able to take advantage of. The return type is `PaginatedList` and the method signature consists of a `categoryId` of type String:

```
public class ProductSqlMapDao
extends BaseSqlMapDao
implements ProductDao {
...
  public ProductSqlMapDao(DaoManager daoManager) {
    super(daoManager);
  }
...
  public PaginatedList getProductListByCategory(
    String categoryId
  ) {
    return queryForPaginatedList(
      "Product.getProductListByCategory",
      categoryId, PAGE_SIZE);
  }
...
}
```

The implementation of the `ProductDao` will be the `ProductSqlMapDao`, which is located in the org.apache.ibatis.jgamestore.persistence.sqlmapdao package. `ProductSqlMapDao` extends `BaseSqlMapDao`, and in turn `BaseSqlMapDao` extends `SqlMapDaoTemplate`. `SqlMapDaoTemplate` is a base iBATIS `SQLMap` class; this class contains methods that are used to call the SQL that is defined in the `SQLMap` XML files. We will use the `queryForPaginatedList` method in the body of the `getProductListByCategory` method implementation on the `ProductSqlMapDao` class. When we call `queryForPaginatedList` we pass in the namespace and the statement name we want to call (i.e., `Product.getProductListByCategory`), the `categoryId` that we are querying against, and the page size that we want the returned list to represent.

14.9 Summary

That's it! We have now put together all the components of a simple application. We walked through the presentation, service, and data access layers. Each layer has its own set of classes and frameworks to explore. We examined Struts, `BeanAction`, iBATIS DAO, and iBATIS `SQLMaps`, but there remains plenty more to experiment with. We didn't touch on updates, inserts, deletes, and searches that require Dynamic SQL. Much of this is covered in the JGameStore sample application. It would be beneficial to take the understanding that you gained here and explore the whole of JGameStore.

appendix: iBATIS.NET Quick Start

Early in this book we stated that iBATIS is a portable concept. It wasn't long after the release of iBATIS 2.0 that a new group of team members ported iBATIS to the .NET platform. This appendix will give you a quick overview of iBATIS for the .NET platform.

A.1 Comparing iBATIS and iBATIS.NET

It's common in open source projects to have half-hearted ports to other platforms that often fizzle out shortly after their inception. Not so with iBATIS.NET.

The iBATIS.NET team has been diligently keeping iBATIS.NET up to date with the Java version, as well as improving the core feature set. iBATIS.NET is under the same project umbrella as iBATIS for Java; we are the same team. This is a significant advantage, because we are in constant communication and the developers for each platform learn from each other every day. There are a lot of advantages to both the Java and .NET platforms that we have been using to help encourage innovation between the two.

Why should Java developers care about iBATIS.NET?

The fact is, .NET is here to stay. We are in a heterogeneous environment, and we always have been. If you're a professional software developer who intends to stay in the field for any length of time, you will need to expand your horizons beyond Java. That's not to say that Java is going anywhere, but neither is .NET. If you're an independent consultant, .NET is probably 50 percent of your market. Ignoring this market is not good for business. If you're a full-time employee in a large organization, then chances are .NET will find its way into your environment in one form or another. .NET is a valid platform that has its place in the enterprise.

The value to you as a Java developer learning iBATIS is that you can apply all of the same principles to the persistence layer in .NET as you do in Java. There's no difference, and there's no reason to be different. .NET has a lot of neat features like `DataSets`, which make a compelling argument for quick-and-dirty software development, but for real enterprise applications, you're always better off with a domain model. As you've learned by reading this book, the ability to map domain models to databases in the enterprise is an advantage of using iBATIS.

Why should .NET developers care about iBATIS.NET?

Many .NET developers are new to open source. .NET is a commercial product, and therefore many of the recommended third-party solutions are commercial, closed source products. One might say that open source freeware is not within the culture of the .NET community. That is about to change, if it hasn't already.

Free open source solutions are becoming more popular in the .NET community. This is partially due to the increase in open source build and test tools that have been lacking in commercial software for a long time. Projects like Mono, SharpDevelop, NAnt, NUnit, NHibernate, and CruiseControl.NET have been making a significant impact on the traditional .NET developer, who may have only been exposed to Microsoft tools. The .NET community has seen the value of open source software. Even Microsoft has invested in open source with the release of www.CodePlex.com. Welcome to .NET open source mania!

What are the major differences?

The talented iBATIS.NET developers have done a great job of keeping iBATIS consistent. There are a few minor differences that have mostly to do with design philosophies that differ between the Java and .NET platforms. Obviously things like naming conventions for classes, interfaces, and methods were honored for the .NET platform. In addition, the XML structure differs somewhat, but we'll discuss that more in a moment.

What are the similarities?

iBATIS.NET holds all of the same principles and values as the Java version. Simplicity is the goal, while maintaining a great deal of flexibility to ensure that iBATIS.NET will work for as many applications as possible. iBATIS.NET has few dependencies and makes few assumptions about your application architecture. This means that many of the same benefits and considerations apply to iBATIS.NET as we discussed for iBATIS for Java earlier in this book.

The remainder of this appendix will describe the basic usage of the iBATIS.NET Data Mapper framework. iBATIS.NET also has a DAO framework called IbatisNet.DataAccess. However, we do not explore the full feature set of iBATIS.NET, including the DAO framework, in great detail in this book.

A.2 Working with iBATIS.NET

If you have any experience with iBATIS, you'll become comfortable with iBATIS.NET very quickly. This section explores the key points you need to understand in order to use iBATS.NET. We start with a look at the dependencies (DLLs) and configuration of iBATIS.NET. We then draw on your existing iBATIS knowledge and demonstrate the usage of various SQL mapping files.

DLLs and dependencies

Luckily, having read the rest of this book, there is little else you need to know. Because we're working with .NET now, there are of course no JAR files. Instead, iBATIS.NET Data Mapper is deployed as DLL files that you need to include as references in your assembly. Like its Java sibling, the .NET version has very few dependencies. In fact, only three DLLs are required; see table A.1.

Table A.1 iBATIS.NET has dependencies only on these three assemblies.

Filename	Purpose
`IbatisNet.Common.dll`	The common utilities of the iBATIS.NET framework. Generally these common classes are shared between the iBATIS Data Mapper and Data Access frameworks.
`IbatisNet.DataMapper.dll`	The core classes for the iBATIS.NET data Mapper. Contained within are the classes that you will most often use to interact with iBATIS.NET.
`Castle.DynamicProxy.dll`	One of only two third-party dependencies, Castle Dynamic Proxy provides functionality to support dynamic extension of classes and implementation of interfaces at runtime. iBATIS uses such proxies for lazy loading as well as automatic transaction management in some cases.

The XML configuration file

iBATIS.NET has an XML configuration file, just as iBATIS for Java does. The structure of the file is a bit different, but it's similar enough that you can no doubt understand it. All of the configuration files are validated by XSD schemas. If you install the XSD for these files in Visual Studio, you will gain the benefit of having IntelliSense support. This will make coding these files a lot easier. See the Visual Studio documentation for information on installing XSD files. Listing A.1 shows a sample iBATIS.NET configuration file for a simple application.

Listing A.1 SqlMap.config XML configuration file

```
<?xml version="1.0" encoding="utf-8"?>
<sqlMapConfig
  xmlns="http://ibatis.apache.org/dataMapper"
  xmlns:xsi="http://www.w3.org/2001/XMLSchema-instance">

    <providers resource="providers.config"/>

    <!-- Database connection information -->
    <database>
        <provider name="sqlServer2.0"/>
```

```
        <dataSource name="Northwind"
➥ connectionString="server=localhost,1403;database=Northwind;
➥ user id=sa;password=sa;connection reset=false;connection
➥ lifetime=5;min pool size=1; max pool size=50"/>
    </database>

      <sqlMaps>
            <sqlMap resource="Employee.xml"/>
      </sqlMaps>

  </sqlMapConfig>
```

If you're familiar with iBATIS for Java, then the configuration file in listing A.1 should look somewhat familiar. It begins with a declaration of providers, which are included configurations for various database drivers. The ADO.NET database driver model requires a bit more initial setup than JDBC does. That configuration is contained within the `providers.config` file, which is included with the iBATIS.NET distribution. Notice that the database connectivity configuration is quite different. It goes without saying that iBATIS.NET makes use of ADO.NET, whereas Java uses JDBC. Each of these low-level APIs uses different driver models and different connection strings—hence the difference in the structure of this part of the XML. However, the configuration file maintains its simplicity. Usually, you need only specify the provider, a data source name, and a connection string.

The provider tells iBATIS which kind of database you are connecting to. Providers are pluggable components of iBATIS.NET, and there is one for each database type supported. However, you might want to look in `providers.config` and disable or remove any providers that you don't have drivers for; otherwise, you'll get an error if you try to run the application without them.

The database name and connection string set up a database connection using the credentials and other information that you provide (e.g., username and password). If you're used to Java, this is not unlike a typical JDBC connection URL.

The last part of the configuration file is the `<sqlMaps>` stanza, which lists all of the SQL mapping files that contain the SQL statements, result maps, and other iBATIS elements. In this example, we have only one mapping file, which is called `Employee.xml`.

As you've probably noticed, these examples all make use of the Northwind database included with Microsoft SQL Server and Microsoft Access. This database is popular for sample code such as that listed throughout this appendix.

The configuration API

The configuration file in listing A.1 is used to configure an instance of `SqlMapper`, the class that you'll be using to work with your mapped statements. The `SqlMapper` instance is created by a factory class called `DomSqlMapBuilder`, which reads through the XML configuration file to build the `SqlMapper`. The following is an example of what this configuration looks like:

```
ISqlMapper sqlMap =
new DomSqlMapBuilder().Configure("SqlMap.config");
```

This single line of code (split in this example) is all you need.

We now have a configured `ISqlMapper` instance that we can use to call the statements in `Employee.xml`. The next section takes a look at what's inside `Employee.xml`.

SQL mapping files

Like the configuration file in listing A.1, the SQL mapping files are also a bit different, but they are similar enough to make any iBATIS user comfortable. iBATIS.NET supports all of the same types of statements, including stored procedures. Here is a simple query statement from `Employee.xml`:

```
<select id="SelectEmployee" parameterClass="int"
        resultClass="Employee">
select
        EmployeeID as ID,
        FirstName,
        LastName
      from
        Employees
      where
        EmployeeID = #value#
</select>
```

The select statement takes an integer as a parameter, and returns an `Employee` object populated with some of the data from the Employees table from the Northwind database. As you might recognize, this particular statement is making use of automapping. That is, no result map is specified. Instead, columns are mapped to class properties by their names. Notice how `EmployeeID` is aliased to `ID`, as that is the name of the property in the `Employee` class. We could have defined an explicit result map, which would have changed the listing as follows:

```
<resultMap id="EmployeeResult" class="Employee">
     <result property="ID" column="EmployeeId"/>
      <result property="FirstName" column="FirstName"/>
      <result property="LastName" column="LastName "/>
</resultMap>
```

```
<select id="SelectEmployee" parameterClass="int"
        resultMap="EmployeeResult">
select *
      from
        Employees
      where
        EmployeeID = #value#
</select>
```

Notice how we were able to simplify the SQL statement, but at the cost of an additional XML element called `<resultMap>`. This is a trade-off that you'll make often, but as with the Java version, sometimes the `<resultMap>` is necessary because it provides added functionality to your results processing.

Now that we've mapped the statement, we can call it from C# as follows:

```
Employee emp =
          sqlMap.QueryForObject<Employee>("SelectEmployee", 1);

// You can get a sense of the result by writing out to the
// console… which should return "1: Nancy Davolio"
Console.WriteLine(emp.ID + ": " + emp.FirstName + " " +
                  emp.LastName);
```

Nonquery statements are no different in iBATIS.NET. The following examples show how we define an insert statement.

First, take a look at this code:

```
<insert id="InsertEmployee" parameterClass="Employee">
      insert into Employees
        ( FirstName, LastName )
      values
        ( #FirstName#, #LastName# )
      <selectKey resultClass="int" property="ID" >
            select @@IDENTITY
      </selectKey>
</insert>
```

For the most part, this is just a simple insert statement. However, notice the bolded section of the statement. The embedded `<selectKey>` stanza should be familiar to any iBATIS user: it is the mechanism used to acquire the values of generated primary key columns.

When we call this statement from C#, the generated key is returned from the `Insert()` method, and it is also set as the value of the `ID` property of the `Employee` instance passed to the `Insert()` method. Let's take a look at the example C# code to make this clearer:

```
Employee employee = new Employee();
employee.FirstName = "Clinton";
employee.LastName = "Begin";
Object id = sqlMap.Insert("InsertEmployee", employee);
```

The Northwind database uses an IDENTITY column for the `EmployeeId` primary key of the Employees table. Therefore we don't pass the value of the primary key into the insert statement. However, the employee instance ID property will be updated with the generated primary key value. The generated key is also returned from the `Insert()` method.

As with iBATIS for Java, once you've seen a couple of statements, the rest become fairly obvious. Updates and deletes are implemented much like inserts, but with their own `<update>` and `<delete>` elements, respectively.

A.3 Where to go for more information

As you've seen, there is not a lot of difference between iBATIS for Java and iBATIS.NET. They are distinguished primarily by features that are relevant to each language, but they maintain a consistent feel. There is much more to learn about iBATIS.NET, though, and resources are available on the Web for you. Visit http://ibatis.apache.org, where you'll find the iBATIS.NET user guide as well as the NPetShop sample application.

index

Symbols

A

B

D

N

Q

R

S

T

MORE JAVA TITLES FROM MANNING

Java Persistence with Hibernate
Revised Edition of Hibernate in Action
by Christian Bauer
and Gavin King
ISBN: 1-932394-88-5
880 pages
$59.99
November 2006

iText in Action: Creating and Manipulating PDF
by Bruno Lowagie
ISBN: 1-932394-79-6
688 pages
$49.99
December 2006

For ordering information on these and other Manning titles, please visit www.manning.com

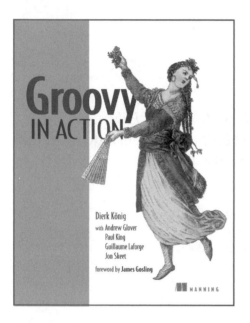

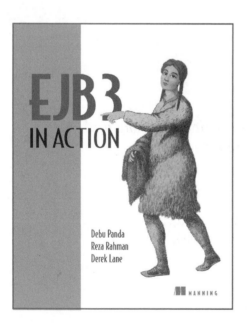

MORE JAVA TITLES FROM MANNING

Ajax in Practice
by David Crane, Jord Sonneveld,
and Bear Bibeault
ISBN: 1-932394-99-0
450 pages
$44.99
April 2007

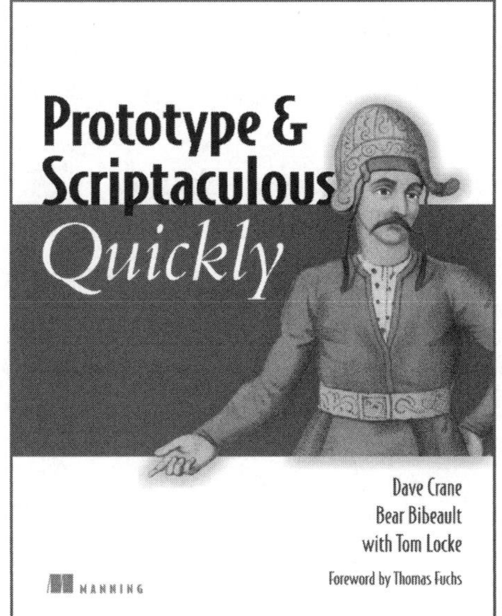

Prototype and Scriptaculous Quickly
by David Crane and Bear Bibeault
with Tom Locke
Foreword by Thomas Fuchs
ISBN: 1-933988-03-7
350 pages
$44.99
March 2007

For ordering information on these and other Manning titles, please visit www.manning.com

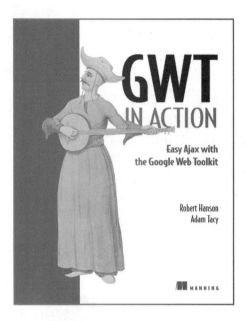

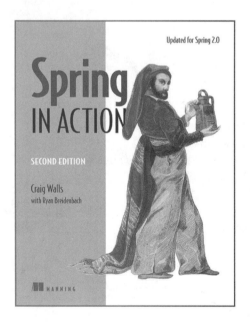